A SHORT HISTORY OF THE MIDDLE AGES

SECOND EDITION

VOLUME I: FROM *c*.300 TO *c*.1150

BARBARA H. ROSENWEIN

broadview press

National Library of Canada Cataloguing in Publication
Rosenwein, Barbara H.
A short history of the Middle Ages / Barbara H. Rosenwein. — 2nd ed.
Includes bibliographical references and index.
Contents: v. 1. From c. 300 to c. 1150 – v. 2. From c. 900 to c. 1500.
ISBN 1-55111-667-7 (v. 1). ISBN 1-55111-668-5 (v. 2)
1. Middle Ages—History. 2. Europe—History—476-1492. I. Title.
D117.R67 2004 940.1 C2004-901640-7

Broadview Press Ltd. is an independent, international publishing house, incorporated in 1985. Broadview believes in shared ownership, both with its employees and with the general public; since the year 2000 Broadview shares have traded publicly on the Toronto Venture Exchange under the symbol BDP.

We welcome comments and suggestions regarding any aspect of our publications—please feel free to contact us at the addresses below or at broadview@broadviewpress.com
www.broadviewpress.com

North America:

PO Box 1243, Peterborough,
Ontario, Canada K9J 7H5

3576 California Road, Orchard Park,
NY, USA 14127

Tel: (705) 743-8990;
Fax: (705) 743-8353
E-mail: customerservice@
broadviewpress.com

UK, Ireland, and continental Europe:

NBN Plymbridge
Estover Road
Plymouth PL6 7PY UK

Tel: 44 (0) 1752 202301;
Fax: 44 (0) 1752 202331
Fax Order Line: 44 (0) 1752 202333
Customer Service:
cservs@nbnplymbridge.com
Orders: orders@nbnplymbridge.com

Australia and New Zealand:

UNIREPS,
University of New South Wales
Sydney, NSW, 2052

Tel: 61 2 9664 0999;
Fax: 61 2 9664 5420
E-mail: info.press@unsw.edu.au

Text design and composition by George Kirkpatrick

PRINTED IN CANADA

To the memory of my father, Norman Herstein (May 27, 1921–May 25, 2002).

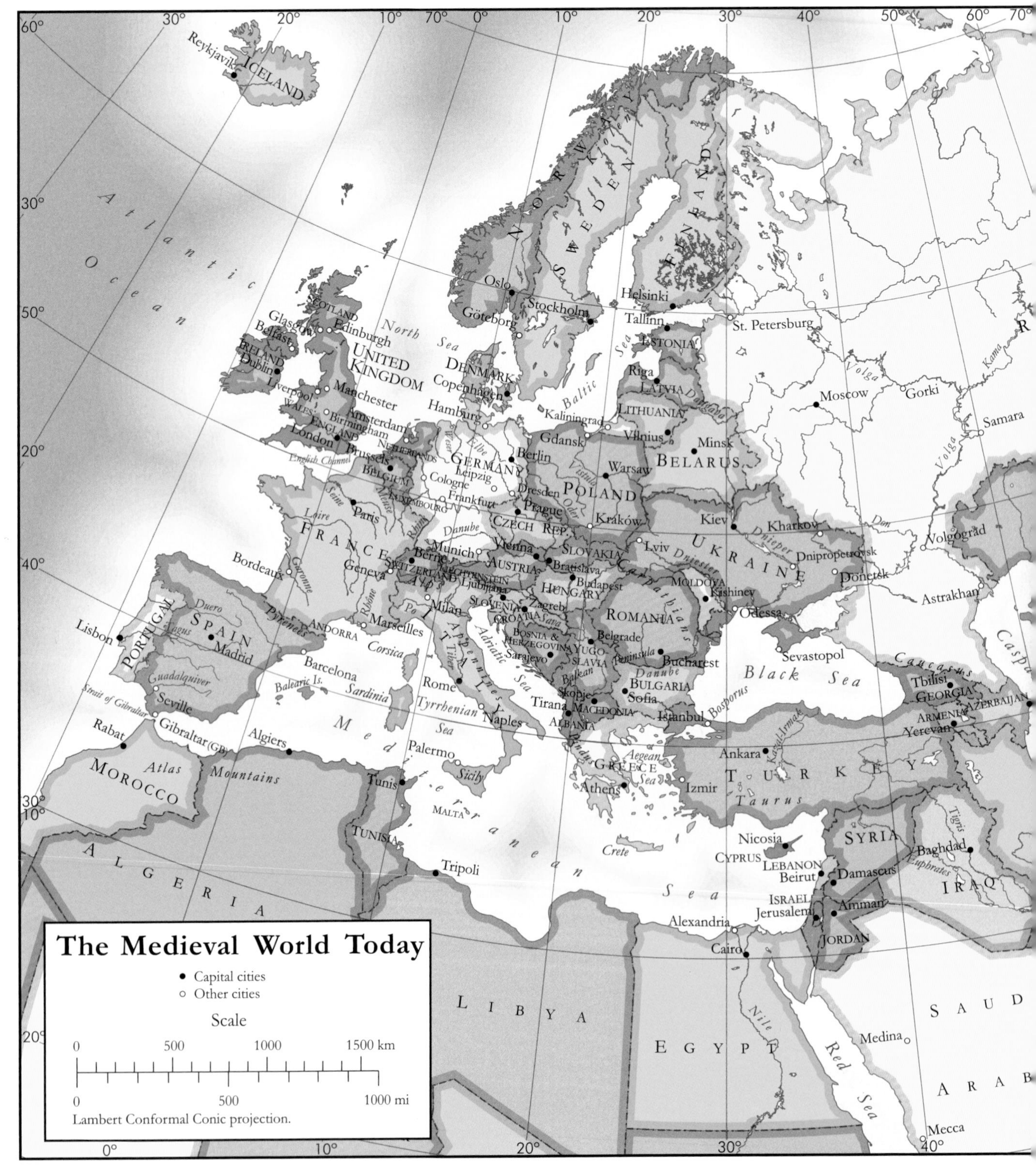

The Medieval World Today
Capital cities
Other cities
Scale
0
500
1000
1500 km
0
500
1000 mi
Lambert Conformal Conic projection.
Atlantic Ocean
North Sea
Baltic Sea
English Channel
Mediterranean Sea
Black Sea
Adriatic Sea
Tyrrhenian Sea
Aegean Sea
Red Sea
ICELAND
Reykjavik
NORWAY
SWEDEN
FINLAND
ESTONIA
LATVIA
LITHUANIA
BELARUS
UKRAINE
MOLDOVA
ROMANIA
BULGARIA
POLAND
GERMANY
DENMARK
NETHERLANDS
BELGIUM
LUXEMBOURG
FRANCE
SWITZERLAND
LIECHTENSTEIN
AUSTRIA
CZECH REP.
SLOVAKIA
HUNGARY
SLOVENIA
CROATIA
BOSNIA & HERZEGOVINA
YUGOSLAVIA
MACEDONIA
ALBANIA
GREECE
ITALY
SPAIN
PORTUGAL
ANDORRA
UNITED KINGDOM
SCOTLAND
WALES
ENGLAND
IRELAND
MOROCCO
ALGERIA
TUNISIA
LIBYA
EGYPT
MALTA
CYPRUS
TURKEY
SYRIA
LEBANON
ISRAEL
JORDAN
IRAQ
GEORGIA
ARMENIA
AZERBAIJAN
SAUDI ARABIA
Oslo
Stockholm
Göteborg
Helsinki
Tallinn
St. Petersburg
Riga
Moscow
Gorki
Samara
Kaliningrad
Vilnius
Minsk
Copenhagen
Hamburg
Gdansk
Berlin
Warsaw
Leipzig
Dresden
Cologne
Frankfurt
Prague
Kraków
Lviv
Kiev
Kharkov
Dnipropetrovsk
Donetsk
Volgograd
Astrakhan
Kishinev
Odessa
Sevastopol
Munich
Vienna
Bratislava
Budapest
Berne
Geneva
Ljubljana
Zagreb
Belgrade
Sarajevo
Bucharest
Sofia
Skopje
Tirana
Istanbul
Ankara
Izmir
Athens
Glasgow
Edinburgh
Belfast
Dublin
Liverpool
Manchester
Birmingham
London
Amsterdam
Brussels
Paris
Bordeaux
Marseilles
Milan
Rome
Naples
Palermo
Tunis
Tripoli
Algiers
Rabat
Gibraltar (GB)
Seville
Lisbon
Madrid
Barcelona
Nicosia
Beirut
Damascus
Baghdad
Tbilisi
Yerevan
Amman
Jerusalem
Alexandria
Cairo
Medina
Mecca
Corsica
Sardinia
Sicily
Crete
Balearic Is.
Strait of Gibraltar
Bosporus
Atlas Mountains
Pyrenees
Alps
Apennines
Carpathians
Balkan Peninsula
Caucasus
Taurus
Pindus
Danube
Rhine
Rhône
Seine
Loire
Garonne
Meuse
Elbe
Weser
Oder
Vistula
Po
Tiber
Sava
Duero
Tagus
Guadalquivir
Daugava
Dniester
Dnieper
Don
Volga
Kama
Kızıl Irmak
Tigris
Euphrates
Nile

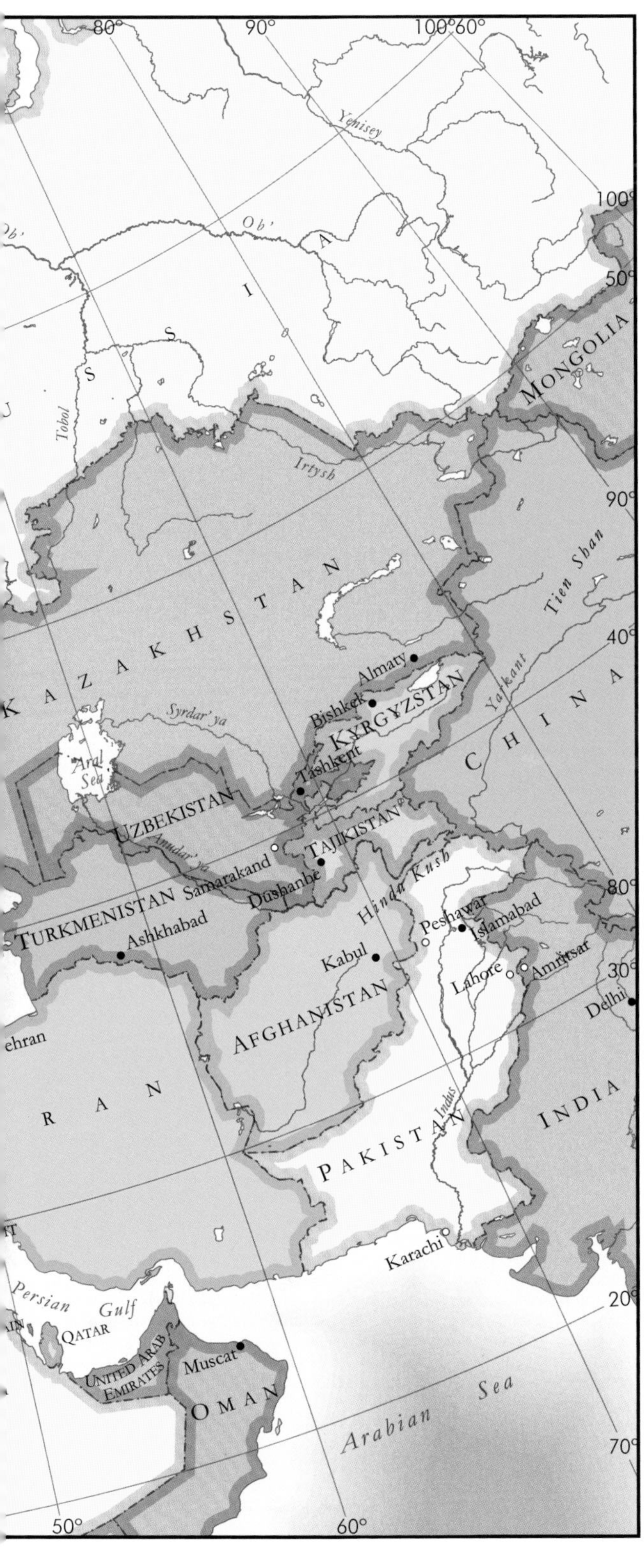

THE UNION of the Roman empire was dissolved; its genius was humbled in the dust; and armies of unknown barbarians, issuing from the frozen regions of the North, had established their victorious reign over the fairest provinces of Europe and Africa.

Edward Gibbon,
The Decline and Fall of the Roman Empire

IT MAY very well happen that what seems for one group a period of decline may seem to another the birth of a new advance.

Edward Hallett Carr,
What is History?

CONTENTS

MAPS

PLATES

GENEALOGIES

FIGURES

LISTS

ABBREVIATIONS, CONVENTIONS, WEBSITES

ABBREVIATIONS

c.	circa. Used in dates to mean that they are approximate.
cent.	century
d.	date of death
emp.	emperor
fl.	flourished. This is given when even approximate birth and death dates are unknown.
pl.	plural. The plural form of a noun.
r.	rule. Indicates the dates of rule.
sing.	singular. The singular form of a noun.

DATE CONVENTIONS

All dates are C.E./A.D. unless otherwise noted (the two systems are interchangeable). The dates of popes are not preceded by *r.* because they took their papal names upon accession to office, and the dates after those names apply only to their papacies.

WEBSITES

www.georgetown.edu/labyrinth/labyrinth-home.html = The Labyrinth: resources for medieval studies sponsored by Georgetown University.

www.fordham.edu/halsall/sbook.html = The International Medieval Sourcebook, which contains important sets of primary sources for the medieval period.

www.broadviewpress.com/shorthistory = The website for this book, which has searchable Genealogies, Key Events, Lists, and Maps.

PREFACE TO VOLUME ONE

At the beginning of the first volume of his long and learned trilogy, *Suicide in the Middle Ages*, Alexander Murray remarks amiably, "Unconventionally long, the book remains, to the author's certain knowledge, 'a mere introduction.'" Well, if *that* is just an introduction (and it undoubtedly is), then what is *this* book?

It is meant to be an easy pass through a dense thicket. It has been written so that you, the reader, may know enough about the first half of the Middle Ages to move on, after reading it, to meatier fare connected to that period: to "secondary sources" (so called not because they are "second best" but because they are present-day interpretations of the past) and to "primary sources," the texts, pictures, artefacts, and other bits and pieces of their lives and thought that medieval people left behind.

There are five chapters in this book, taking you from the end of the Roman empire to what many historians call the Renaissance of the Twelfth Century. If you are in college, your course will last between ten to fifteen weeks. This means that you will probably read a chapter every other week or so and have plenty of time for supplementary material. If you are not a student, you may nevertheless wish to interleave your reading with some of the materials cited in the footnotes here (all primary sources) or in the bibliographies (which list relevant secondary sources). This book has lots of maps, genealogies, lists, and plates to help you figure out the context of the other things that you will need or want to study. The index is a handy way to look up names (which are followed by dates where possible), events, and places. Some technical words are explained in a glossary. The lists of Key Events at the end of each chapter are meant to help you review the material. A web site at Broadview Press allows for map searches and other useful study aids.

Volume One of *A Short History* covers not just Europe but also the Byzantine and Islamic worlds. Furthermore, "Europe" is not limited to France, England, and Germany, so often the focus of books like this. I have tried to write not only political history but also social, economic, and cultural history. There is, however, a conscious emphasis on political history, deriving from my twofold conviction that (1) politics tells us a good deal about the uses and distribution of power, always important if we wish to consider general conditions of life; and (2) politics, with its decisive events, provides a nice, clear grid for everything else. The book is organized chronologically because I am persuaded that everything in a period—intellectual life, religious feelings and aspirations, even methods of rulership—is interconnected.

While preparing this revised text I have incurred many debts that I wish to acknowledge. I thank Giles Constable, Adam Kosto, Graham Loud, and Michael Morony for pointing out errors and suggesting changes to the first edition. Monique Bourin, Samuel Leturcq, Rosamond Mack, R.I. Moore, and Anders Winroth generously contributed their expertise to particular sections. Thomas Head shared some of his photographs. Maureen Miller was, as always, a wonderful resource and sounding-board. I am indebted to my students in History 310; I wish to thank Jamie McGowan, Eric Nethercott, Susie Newman, and Suzette Vela for their thoughtful suggestions. Paul Heersink prepared new maps with his customary professionalism; George Kirkpatrick worked his own magic with the design. Finally I am grateful to the people at Broadview Press—especially Barbara Conolly, Don Le Pan, and Mical Moser (an invaluable advisor)—for their help and support.

ONE

PRELUDE: THE ROMAN WORLD TRANSFORMED (*c*.300–*c*.600)

IN THE THIRD CENTURY, the Roman empire wrapped around the Mediterranean Sea like a scarf. (See Map 1.1.) Thinner on the North African coast, it bulked large as it enveloped what is today Spain, England, Wales, France, and Belgium, then evened out along the southern coast of the Danube river, following that river eastward, taking in most of what is today the Balkans and Greece, crossing the Hellespont and engulfing in its sweep the territory of present-day Turkey, much of Syria, and all of modern Lebanon, Israel, and Egypt. All the regions but Italy comprised what the Romans called the "provinces."

This was the Roman empire whose "decline and fall" was famously proclaimed by the eighteenth-century historian Edward Gibbon. But in fact his verdict was misplaced. The empire was never livelier than at its reputed end. It is true that the old elites of the cities, especially of Rome itself, largely regretted the changes taking place around them *c*.250–350. They were witnessing the end of their political, military, religious, economic, and cultural leadership, which was passing to the provinces. But for the provincials (the Romans living outside of Italy) this was in many ways a heady period, a long-postponed coming of age. They did not regret the division of the Roman empire into two parts under the Emperor Diocletian (*r*.284–305); the partition was tacit recognition of the importance of the provinces. Some did, however, regret losing their place in the sun (as happened *c*.400–500) to people still farther afield, whom they called "barbarians." In turn, the barbarians were glad to be the heirs of the Roman empire even as they contributed to its transformation (*c*.450–600).

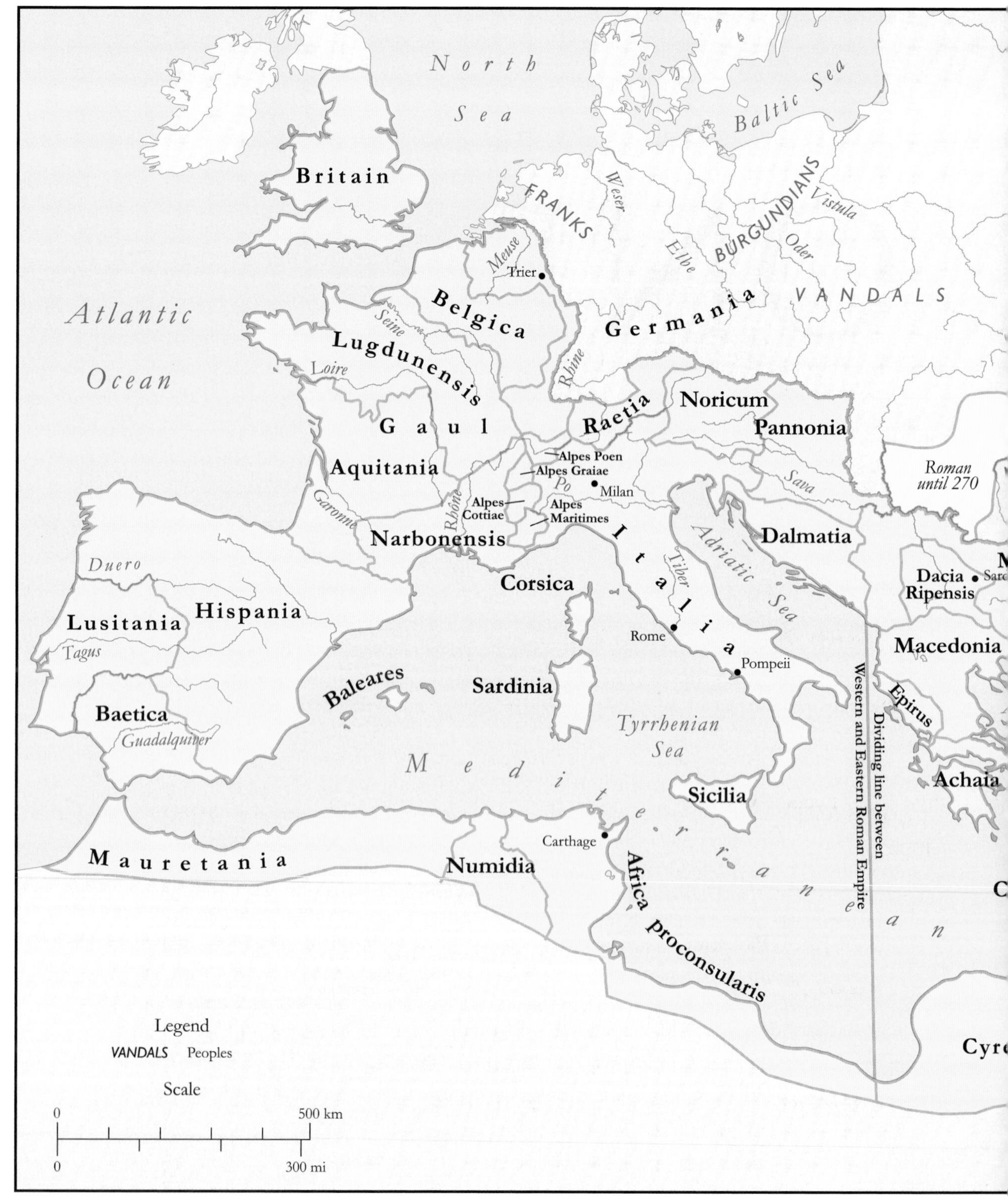

North Sea
Baltic Sea
Atlantic Ocean
Britain
FRANKS
Weser
BURGUNDIANS
Vistula
Oder
Elbe
Meuse
Trier
VANDALS
Belgica
Germania
Seine
Lugdunensis
Loire
Rhine
Raetia
Noricum
Pannonia
Gaul
Aquitania
Alpes Poen
Alpes Graiae
Po
Milan
Roman until 270
Sava
Garonne
Rhône
Alpes Cottiae
Alpes Maritimes
Narbonensis
Italia
Adriatic Sea
Dalmatia
Duero
Tiber
Corsica
Dacia Ripensis
Lusitania
Hispania
Rome
Macedonia
Tagus
Pompeii
Epirus
Baleares
Sardinia
Baetica
Guadalquiver
Tyrrhenian Sea
Mediterranean
Achaia
Sicilia
Carthage
Mauretania
Numidia
Africa proconsularis
Dividing line between Western and Eastern Roman Empire
Legend
VANDALS Peoples
Scale
0
500 km
0
300 mi

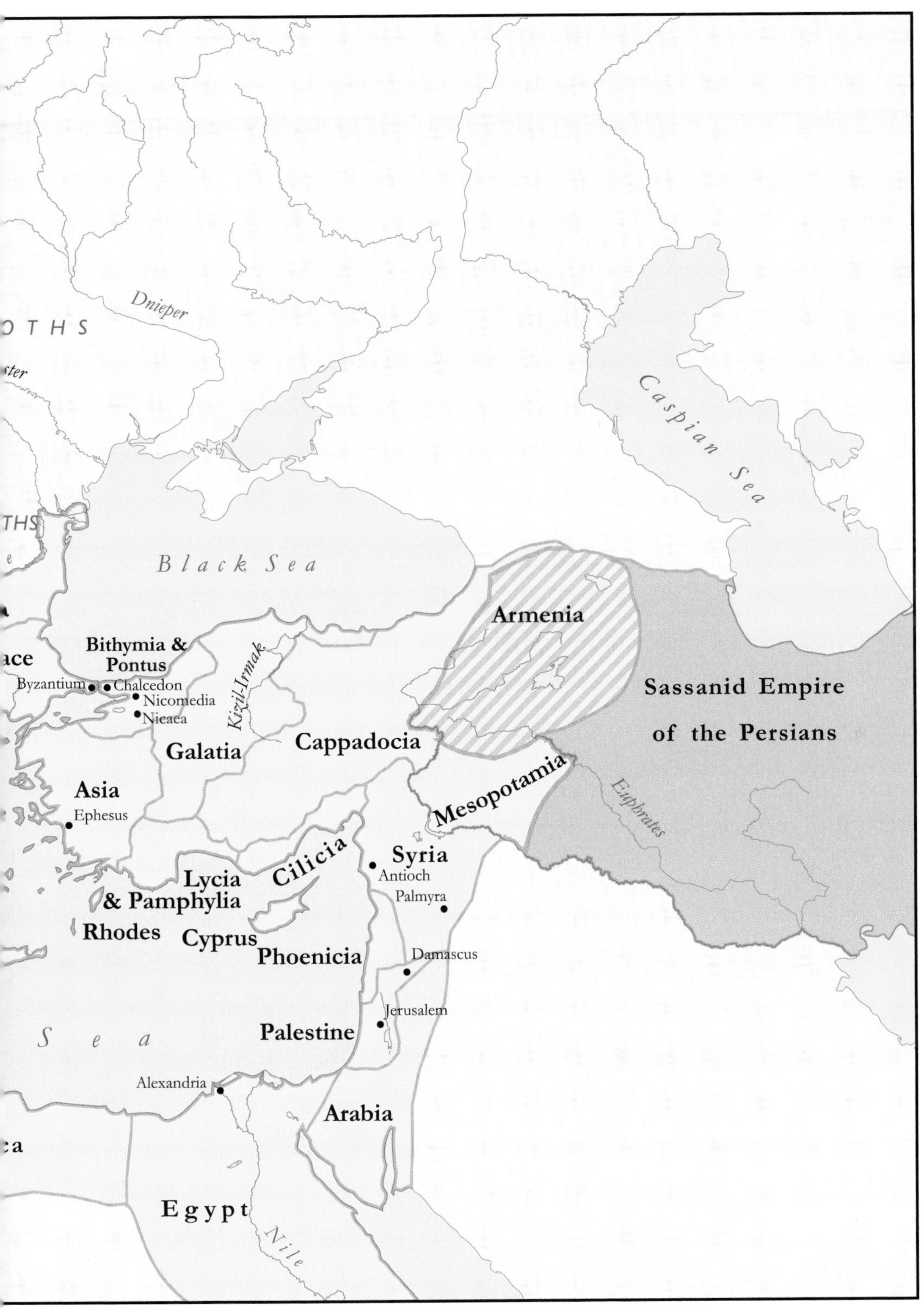

Map 1.1: The Roman Empire in the Third Century

THE PROVINCIALIZATION OF THE EMPIRE (*c.*250-*c.*350)

The Roman empire was too large to be ruled by one man in one place except in peacetime. This became clear during the "crisis of the third century," when two different groups from two different directions came pounding on the borders of the empire. From the north, beyond the Rhine and Danube rivers, came people the Romans called "barbarians"; from the east, the Persians. To contend with these attacks, the Roman government responded with wide-ranging reforms that brought new prominence to the provinces.

Above all, the government expanded the army. It set up new crack mobile forces as well as reinforcing the standing army. Soldier-workers threw up new fortifications, cities hedged themselves with walls, farms gained lookout towers and fences. It was not easy to find enough recruits to man this newly expanded defensive system. Before the crisis, the legions had been largely self-perpetuating. Their soldiers, drawn mainly from local provincial families, had settled permanently along the borders and raised the sons who would make up the next generation of recruits. Now, however, this supply was dwindling: the birthrate was declining, and around 257 an epidemic, perhaps of smallpox, ravaged the population further. Recruits would have to come from farther away, in Germania (beyond the northern borders of the empire) and elsewhere. In fact, long before this time, Germanic warriors had been regular members of Roman army units; they had done their stints and gone home. But in the third century the Roman government regularized the process. They settled Germanic and other barbarian groups within the empire, giving them land in return for military service.

The term "crisis of the third century" refers not only to the wars that the empire had to fight on its borders but also to a political succession crisis that saw more than twenty men claim, then lose (with their lives), the title of emperor between the years 235 and 284. (See list on p.212: Late Roman Emperors; but this names only the most important emperors!) Most of these men were the creatures of the army, chosen to rule by their troops. Often competing emperors wielded authority in different regions at the same time. They had little interest in the city of Rome, which, in any case, was too far from any of the fields of war to serve as military headquarters. For this reason Emperor Valerian (*r.*253-259) shifted the imperial residence and mint from Rome to Milan. Soon other favored imperial places—Trier, Sardica, Nicomedia, and, eventually, Constantinople—joined Milan in overshadowing Rome. The new army and the new imperial seats belonged to the provinces.

The primacy of the provinces was further enhanced by the need to feed and supply the army. To meet its demand for ready money, the Roman government debased the currency, increasing the proportion of base metals to silver. While helpful in the short term, this policy produced severe inflation. Strapped for cash, the state increased taxes and used its power to requisition goods and services. To clothe the troops it confiscated uniforms; to arm them it set up weapons factories staffed by artisans who were bound to produce a regular quota for the state. Food for the army had to be produced and delivered; here too the state depended on the labor of growers, bakers, and haulers. New taxes assessed on both land and individual "heads" were collected. The wealth and labor of the empire moved inexorably towards the provinces, to the hot spots where armies were clashing.

The whole empire, organized for war, became militarized. In about the middle of the third century, the senatorial aristocracy—the old Roman elite—was forbidden to lead the army; tougher men from the ranks were promoted to command positions instead. It was no wonder that those men also became the emperors. They brought new provincial tastes and sensibilities to the very heart of the empire, as we shall see.

Diocletian, a provincial from Dalmatia (today Croatia), brought the crisis under control, and Constantine (*r.*306-337), from Moesia (today Yugoslavia), brought it to an end. For administrative purposes, Diocletian divided the empire into two parts. Although the two emperors who ruled the halves were supposed to confer on all matters, the reform was a harbinger of things to come, when the Greek-speaking East and Latin-speaking West would go their separate ways. Meanwhile, the wars over imperial succession ceased with the establishment of Constantine's dynasty, and political stability put an end to the border wars.

A New Religion

The empire of Constantine was the Roman empire restored. Yet nothing could have been more different from the old Roman empire. It was the beginning of what historians call "Late Antiquity," a period transformed by the culture and religion of the provinces.

The province of Palestine—to the Romans of Italy a most dismal backwater—had been in fact a hotbed of creative religious and social ideas around the beginning of what we now call the first millennium. Chafing under Roman domination, experimenting with new notions of morality and new ethical life-styles, the Jews of Palestine gave birth to religious groups of breathtaking originality. One coalesced around Jesus. After his death, under the impetus of the Jew-turned-Christian Paul (*d.c.*65), a new and radical brand of monotheism under Jesus' name was actively preached to Gentiles (non-Jews) not only in Palestine but beyond. Its core belief was that men and women were saved—redeemed and accorded eternal life in heaven—by their faith in Jesus.

At first Christianity was of nearly perfect indifference to elite Romans, who were devoted to the gods who had served them so well over years of conquest and prosperity. Nor did it attract many of the lower classes, who were still firmly rooted in old local religious traditions. The Romans had never insisted that the provincials whom they conquered give up their beliefs; they simply added official Roman gods into local pantheons. For most people, both rich and poor, the rich texture of religious life at the local level was both comfortable and satisfying. In dreams they encountered their personal gods, who served them as guardians and friends. At home they found their household gods, evoking family ancestors. Outside, on the street, they visited temples and monuments to local gods, reminders of home-town pride. Here and there could be seen monuments to the "divine emperor," put up by rich town benefactors. Everyone engaged in the festivals of the public cults, whose ceremonies gave rhythm to the year. Paganism was thus at one and the same time personal, familial, local, and imperial.

But Christianity had its attractions too. It was, in the first place, persuasive to Romans and other city-dwellers of the middle class, who could never hope to

Map 1.2: Christian Churches Founded Before the Great Persecution of Diocletian (A.D. 304)

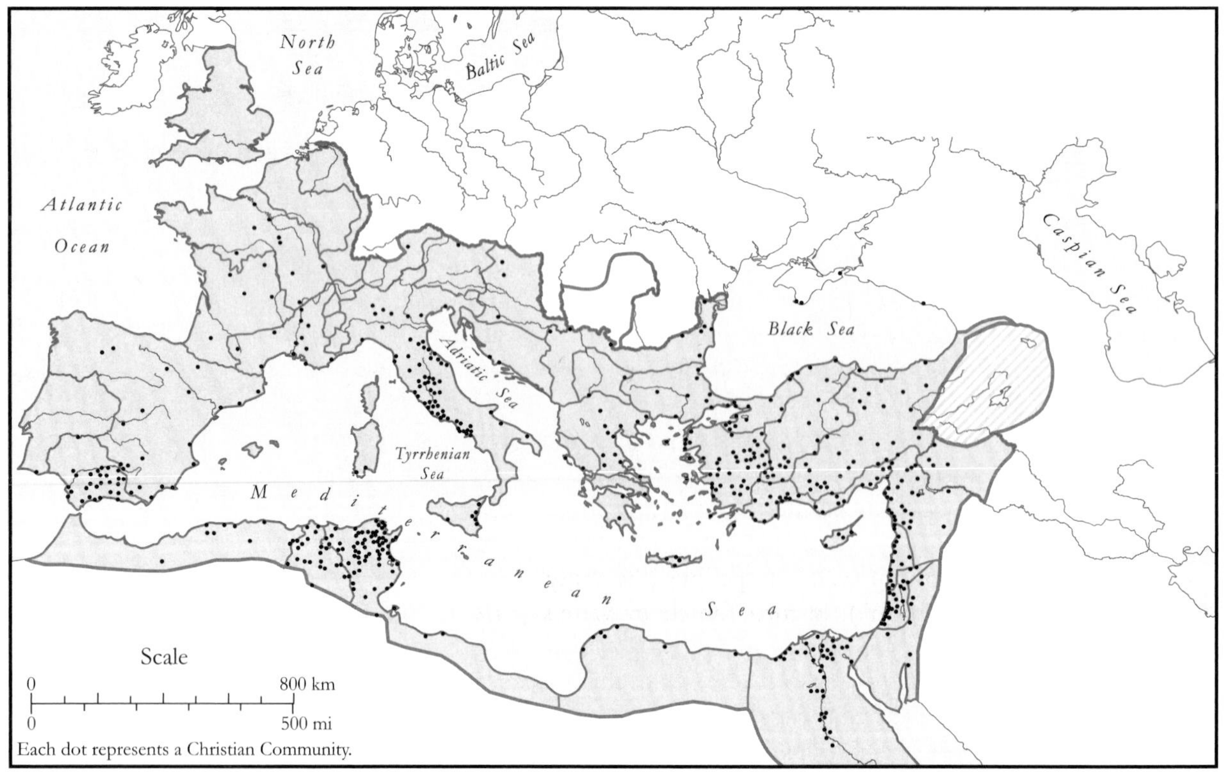

become part of the educated upper crust. Christianity substituted "the elect" for the elite. Education, long and expensive, was the ticket into Roman high society. Christians had their own solid, less expensive knowledge. It was the key to an even "higher" society. Saint Perpetua (*d.*203), imprisoned, awaiting martyrdom, debated her father with the assurance of a Socrates:

> "Father, do you see this vase here...?" "Yes, I do," said he. And I told him: "Could it be called by any other name than what it is?" And he said: "No." "Well, so too I cannot be called anything other than what I am, a Christian."[1]

Christianity attracted as well those provincials who had never been given the chance to feel truly Roman. (Citizenship was not granted to all provincials until 212.) The new religion was confident, hopeful, and universal. As the empire settled into an era of peaceful complacency in the second century, its hinterlands opened to the influence of the center, and vice versa. Men and women whose horizons in earlier times would have stretched no farther than their village now took to the roads as traders—or confronted a new cosmopolitanism right at their doorsteps. Uprooted from old traditions, they found comfort in small assemblies—churches—where they were welcomed as equals and where God was the same, no matter what region the members of the church hailed from.

The Romans persecuted Christians—after besting her father in debate, Perpetua went off joyfully to her martyrdom—but at first only locally, sporadically, and above all in times of crisis. At such moments the Romans feared that the gods were venting their wrath on the empire because Christians would not carry out the proper sacrifices. True, the Jews also refused to honor the Roman gods, but the Romans could usually tolerate—just barely—Jewish practices as part of their particular cultural identity. Christians, however, among whom numbered even Romans, claimed God not only for themselves but for all. Major official government persecutions of Christians began in the 250s, with the third-century crisis.

Meanwhile the Christian community organized itself. By 304, on the eve of the last great persecution, when perhaps only 10 per cent of the population was Christian, numerous churches dotted the imperial landscape. (See Map 1.2.) Each church was two-tiered: at the bottom were the people (the "laity"), at the top the clergy (from *kleros*, or "Lord's portion"). In turn, the clergy were supervised by the bishop, assisted by his "presbyters" (the priests who served with the bishops), deacons, and lesser servitors. Some bishops—those of Alexandria, Antioch, Carthage, Jerusalem, and Rome (whose bishop was later called the "pope"),—were more important than others. No religion was better prepared for official recognition.

This it received in 313, in the so-called Edict of Milan. Emperor Constantine, attributing his imperial triumph to the God of the Christians, declared toleration for all religions. In fact, he converted to Christianity and favored it: he built and endowed church buildings, made sure that property was restored to churches which had been stripped during the persecutions, and gave priests special privileges. Under him, the ancient Greek city of Byzantium became a new Christian city, residence of emperors, and named for the emperor himself: Constantinople. The bishop of Constantinople became a patriarch, a "superbishop," equal to the bishops of Antioch and Alexandria although not as important as the pope. In one of the crowning measures of his career, Constantine called and then presided over the first ecumenical (universal) church council, the Council of Nicaea, in 325. There the assembled bishops hammered out some of the canon law and doctrines of the Christian church.

With Constantine's conversion and his privileging of Christianity, it was simply a matter of time before most people considered it both good and expedient to convert. Though after Constantine's time several emperors espoused "heretical"—unacceptable—forms of Christianity, and one (Julian, the "Apostate") professed paganism, the die had been cast. In 391 Emperor Theodosius (*r.*379-395) declared Christianity the official religion of the Roman empire. All the old public cults were outlawed, and pagan temples were smashed. Soon, at Carthage in 401, Saint Augustine (354-430), bishop of Hippo, and the most influential of the Church Fathers, was telling his congregation that "all superstition of pagans and heathens should be annihilated"; he may well have inspired the massacre of sixty people in a nearby city.[2] In this way—via law, coercion, and conviction—a fragile religion hailing from one of the most backward of the provinces triumphed everywhere in the Roman world.

But with triumph came competition and even strife. Who would control and direct this new religion with its all-powerful God? Who would determine what was holy? Who would know when the old gods, now reclassified as demons, might claim to be gods again? Vigilance was necessary. After Constantine, after the persecutions, Christians fought with each other over doctrine and over the location of the holy.

Doctrine

The men we call the "Church Fathers" were the victors in battles over doctrine. Already in Constantine's day, Saint Athanasius (*c.*295-373)—then secretary to the bishop of Alexandria, later bishop there himself—led the challenge against the beliefs of the Christians next door. He called them "Arians," rather than Christians, after the priest Arius (250-336), another Alexandrian and a competing focus of local loyalties. Athanasius promoted his views at the Council of Nicaea and won. It is because of this that he is the orthodox catholic "Father" and Arius the "heretic." For both

Athanasius and Arius, God was triune, that is, three persons in one: the Father, the Son, and the Holy Spirit. Their debate was about the nature of these persons. For the Arians, the Father was pure Godhead while the Son was created ("begotten"), flesh but not quite flesh, and thus neither purely human nor purely divine. To Athanasius and the assembled bishops at Nicaea, this was heresy—the wrong "choice" (the root meaning of the Greek term *hairesis*)—and a damnable faith. The Council of Nicaea wrote the party line: the Father and Son were co-eternal and equal in divinity. Arius was condemned and banished. His doctrine, however, persisted. It was the brand of Christianity that Wulfilas ("little Wolf")(*c.*311-383) preached to the Goths along the Danube, for example, when he and his followers translated the Bible into Gothic.

Arianism was only the tip of the iceberg. Indeed, the period 350-450 might be called the "era of competing doctrines." As church councils met—especially Ephesus (431) and Chalcedon (451)—to shave ever more closely the contours of right doctrine, dissent multiplied. Monophysites (a later, convenient term for those who opposed the rulings of Chalcedon) held that the "flesh" that God had assumed as Christ was nevertheless divine. Eventually this view, which tended to assimilate human flesh to Christ's and thus divinize humankind, became the doctrine of the Armenian, Coptic (Egyptian), and Ethiopian Christian churches. On the other hand, Pelagius (from Britain, *d.* after 418) was interested less in the nature of Christ than in that of humanity: for him conversion bleached out sins, and thereafter people could follow God by their own will. Entirely opposite to Pelagius was Saint Augustine, for whom human beings were capable of nothing good without God's grace working through them: "Come, Lord, act upon us and rouse us up and call us back! Fire us, clutch us, let your sweet fragrance grow upon us!"[3]

These debates were carried on everywhere, and with passion. Gregory of Nyssa reported that at Constantinople,

> if one asks anyone for change, he will discuss with you whether the Son is begotten or unbegotten. If you ask about the quality of bread you will receive the answer, "the Father is greater, the Son is less." If you suggest a bath is desirable, you will be told "there was nothing before the Son was created."[4]

Like commenting on sports figures today, this was more than small-talk: it identified people's loyalties. It also brought God down to earth. God had debased himself to take on human flesh. It was critical to know how he had done so and what that meant for the rest of humanity.

For these huge questions, Saint Augustine wrote most of the definitive answers, though they were certainly modified and reworked over the centuries. In the *City of*

God, a huge and sprawling work, he defined two cities: the earthly one in which our feet are planted, in which we are born, learn to read, marry, get old, and die; and the heavenly one, on which our eyes, heart, and mind are fixed. The first, the "City of Man," is impermanent, subject to fire, war, famine, and sickness; the second, the "City of God," is the opposite. Only there is true, eternal happiness. Yet the first, however imperfect, is where the institutions of society—local churches, schools, governments—make possible the attainment of the second. Thus, in Augustine's hands, the old traditions of the ancient world were reused and reoriented for a new Christian society.

The Sources of God's Grace

The City of Man was fortunate. There God had instituted his church. Christ had said to Peter, the foremost of his apostles (his "messengers"):

> Thou art Peter [*Petros*, or "rock" in Greek]; and upon this rock I will build my church, and the gates of hell shall not prevail against it. And I will give to thee the keys of the kingdom of heaven. And whatsoever thou shalt bind upon earth, it shall be bound also in heaven; and whatsoever thou shalt loose on earth, it shall be loosed also in heaven. (Matt. 16.18-19)

Although variously interpreted (above all by the popes at Rome, who took it to mean that the popes were the successors of Saint Peter, the first bishop of Rome), no one doubted that this declaration confirmed that the all-important powers of binding (imposing penance on) and loosing (forgiving) sinners were in the hands of Christ's earthly heirs, the priests and bishops. In the Mass, the central liturgy of the earthly church, the bread and wine on the altar became the body and blood of Christ, the "Eucharist." Through the Mass the faithful were joined to one another; to the souls of the dead, who were remembered in the liturgy; and to Christ himself.

The Eucharist was one potent source of God's grace. There were others. Above all, there were certain people so beloved by God, so infused with his grace, that they were both models of virtue and powerful wonder-workers. These were the saints. In the early church, the saints had largely been the martyrs, but martyrdom ended with Constantine. The new saints of the fourth and fifth centuries were "athletes" of God: like Saint Symeon Stylites (396-459), they climbed tall pillars and stood there for decades; or, like Saint Anthony (250-356), they entered tombs to fight, heroically and successfully, with the demons (whose reality was as little questioned as the existence of germs is today). These were neither flights of fancy nor the deeds of madmen. They were considered socially responsible acts by the surrounding community.

Purged of sin by their ascetic rigors—giving up their possessions, fasting, praying, not sleeping, not engaging in sex—and fearless in the face of the demons, holy men and women were intercessors with God on behalf of their neighbors and those who sought them out from afar. Saint Athanasius told the story of Saint Anthony: after years of solitude and asceticism the saint emerged

> as out of a shrine, as one initiated into sacred mysteries and filled with the spirit of God.... He was not embarrassed when he saw the crowd, nor was he elated at seeing so many there to receive him. No, he had himself completely under control—a man guided by reason and stable in his character. Through him the Lord cured many of those present who were afflicted with bodily ills, and freed others from impure spirits. He also gave Anthony charm in speaking; and so he comforted many in sorrow, and others who were quarreling he made friends.[5]

Healer of illnesses and of disputes, Anthony brought spiritual, physical, and civic peace. This was power indeed.

But who would control it? Bishop Athanasius of Alexandria laid claim to Anthony's legacy by writing about it. Yet writing was only one way to appropriate and harness the power of the saints (and also of making sure that demons were not craftily standing in for them). When holy men and women died, their power lived on in their relics (whatever they left behind: their bones, hair, clothes, sometimes even the dust from their tombs). In the fourth century, pious people knew this very well. They wanted access to these "special dead." Rich and influential Romans got their own holy monopolies by simply moving saintly bones home with them:

> [Pompeiana] obtained the body [of the martyr Maximilianus] from the magistrate and, after placing it in her own chamber, later brought it to Carthage. There she buried it at the foot of a hill near the governor's palace next to the body of [Saint] Cyprian. Thirteen days later [Pompeiana] herself passed away and was buried in the same spot.[6]

With enough ladies like Pompeiana, the saints were likely to be appropriated by the rich laity, buried on private estates, made the focal points of family burials. What place would the churches, the clergy, and the wider community have in this privatized system? Churchmen like Saint Ambrose (339-397), bishop of Milan, did not need to think twice. He had the newly discovered relics of Saints Gervasius and Protasius moved from their original resting place into his newly built cathedral and buried under the altar, the focus of communal worship. He allied himself, his successors, and the whole Christian community of Milan with the power of those saints. No single rich patron could thereafter control them. Ambrose set the pattern for other churchmen; henceforth bishops were in charge of the disposition of relics. (For an example of a reliquary, the container in which relics were generally placed, see Plate 6.1 on p.216-17 of volume 2 or go on-line to the website for this book.)

Art from the Provinces to the Center

Just as Christianity came from the periphery to transform the center, so too did provincial artistic traditions. Classical Roman art, nicely exemplified by the wall paintings of Pompeii (Plate 1.1 and Plate 1.2), was characterized by light and shadow, a sense of atmosphere—of earth, sky, air, light—and a feeling of movement, even in the midst of calm. Figures—sometimes lithe, sometimes stocky, always "plastic," suggesting volume and real weight on the ground—interacted, touching one another or talking, and caring little or nothing about the viewer. In Plate 1.1 the craggy mountains are the focus. A shepherd, painted with sketchy lines, pushes a goat toward a shrine, perhaps to sacrifice the animal. On the left, another goat frolics. Shadowy shepherds and goats appear in the distance. The scene is tranquil yet suggests both the grandeur of nature and the solemnity of the occasion. Plate 1.2 pictures a moment well known to Romans from their myths. A nude man—thus clearly an athlete—stands in quiet triumph while people kiss his hands and feet. Any Roman would know, from the "iconography"—the symbolic meaning of the elements—that the man is Theseus and that he has just slain the Minotaur (dying in the doorway on the left), who had demanded a tribute of Athenian youths each year in return for peace. The artist has chosen to depict the very instant that Theseus emerges from the Minotaur's lair, the intended victims crowding around him to express their gratitude. Even though the story is illustrated for the viewers' pleasure, the figures act as if no one is looking at them. They are self-absorbed, glimpsed as if through a window onto their private world.

The relief of Trajan's Column (Plate 1.3) shows that even in the medium of sculpture, classical artists were concerned with atmosphere and movement, figures turning and interacting with one another, and space created by "perspective," where some elements seem to recede while others come to the fore.

But even in the classical period there were other artistic conventions and traditions in the Roman empire. For many years these provincial artistic traditions had been tamped down by the juggernaut of Roman political and cultural hegemony. But in the third century, with the new importance of the provinces, these regional traditions re-emerged. As provincial military men became the new heroes and emperors, artistic

Plate 1.1: Landscape from Pompeii (*c.*79). The Roman artist of this painting created the illusion of space, air, and light directly on the flat surface of a wall (probably of a house).

Following pages:

Plate 1.2: Theseus the Minotaur Slayer, Pompeii (*c.*79). Theseus, hero of a Greek myth, and here portrayed both triumphant and adored, adorned the wall of a private house at Pompeii.

Plate 1.3: Trajan's Column (113). This is a small segment of a towering column built over Emperor Trajan's tomb in his forum at Rome. The entire tower is covered with sculpted reliefs narrating—in a continuous spiral—two of the emperor's military campaigns.

Plate 1.2

Plate 1.3

Plate 1.4: Head from Palmyra (1st half of 1st cent.). Compare this fragment of a woman's head with the head of Theseus in **Plate 1.2** to see the very different notions of the human body and of beauty that co-existed in the Roman empire.

tastes changed as well. The center—Rome, Italy, Constantinople—now borrowed its artistic styles from the periphery.

To understand some of the old regional traditions, consider the sculpted head of a woman from Palmyra, Syria (Plate 1.4), a large stone coffer for holding the bones of the dead from Jerusalem (Plate 1.5), and a tombstone from the region of Carthage—Tunis, Tunisia today—(Plate 1.6). All of these were made in either the first or second century C.E., under the shadow of Roman imperial rule. Yet they are little like Roman works of art. Above all, the artists who made these pieces valued decorative elements. The Jerusalem coffer plays with formal and solemn patterns of light and shadow. The tombstone flattens its figures, varying them by cutting lines for folds, hands, and eyes. Any sense of movement here comes from the incised patterns, certainly not from the rigidly frontal figures. Although the head from Palmyra is more classical, it too is created by an artist in love with decoration. The lady's hair is a series of rings and lines; her pupils are spirals.

There may be something to the idea that such works of art were "inferior" to Roman—but not much. The artists who made them had their own values and were not much interested in classical notions of beauty. The Palmyra head is clearly the work of a sculptor who wanted to show the opposite of human interaction. His lady takes part in no familiar mythological story for viewers to enjoy. She has been

Plate 1.5: Decorated Coffer from Jerusalem (1st cent.?).
The human figure was of no interest to the carver of this stone chest, whose formal floral and architectural motives seemed more appropriate for its sober contents: the bones of the dead.

125345

"abstracted" from any natural context. Her very head, eyebrows, and eyes are "abstract"—simplified until they have become shapes. All of this emphasizes her otherworldliness. Here is a woman who is deeply contemplative. Her eyes, the most prominent feature of her face, gaze outward beyond the viewer, transcending the here and now.

The same emphasis on transcendence explains the horizontal zones of the limestone tombstone. It may seem absurd to compare this piece with the Pompeian painting of mountains and shepherd (Plate 1.1). Yet it is crucial to realize that the subjects are largely the same: people and animals, in the context of a sacrifice. It is the approach that is different. On the provincial tombstone, the stress is on hierarchical order. In the center of the top zone is a god. In the middle zones are people busying themselves with proper religious ceremonies. At the bottom, the lowest rung, are three people praying. The proper order of the cosmos, not the natural order, is the focus. This tombstone is no window onto a private world; rather it teaches and preaches to those who look at it.

The extraordinary development of the fourth century was the center's appropriation of these artistic styles of the provinces. The trend is graphically illustrated by a

Plate 1.6 (facing page): Tombstone from near Carthage (2nd cent.?). The stiff, frontal figures on this relief show a delight in order, hierarchy, and decoration.

Plate 1.7: Base of the Hippodrome Obelisk (*c.*390). Nothing illustrates changing imperial artistic tastes so well as this carving, placed right in the middle of the most imperial part of Constantinople. It was inspired more by the style of **Plate 1.6** than by the older imperial style of **Plate 1.3**.

marble base made at Constantinople *c.*390 to support a gigantic ancient obelisk, transported at great cost from Egypt and set up with considerable difficulty at the Hippodrome, the great sports arena. The four-sided base depicts the games and races that took place in the stadium. The side shown in Plate 1.7 is decisively divided into two tiers: at the top is the imperial family and other dignitaries, formal, frontal, staring straight ahead. Directly in the center is the imperial group, higher than all others. Beneath, in the lower tier, are bearded, hairy-coated barbarians, bringing humble offerings to those on high. The two levels are divided by a decorative frame, a rough indication of the "sky boxes" inhabited by the emperor and his retinue. The folds of the drapery are graceful but stylized. The hair-do's are caps. The ensemble is meant to preach eternal truths: the highness of imperial power and its transcendence of time and place.

This style of art was not Christian in origin, but it was certainly adopted by Christians at the time. It was suited to a religion that saw only fleeting value in the City of Man, that sought to transcend the world, and that had a message to preach. We shall see the influence of this style throughout the Middle Ages. Nevertheless, at the end of the fourth and the beginning of the fifth century, around the same time that the emperor was ordering the Hippodrome base, other, more classical artistic styles were making a brief comeback. Sometimes called the "renaissance of the late fourth and early fifth century," this was the first of many recurring infusions of the classicizing spirit in medieval art. On a small ivory container made in the early fifth century (Plate 1.8), a young man with a book sits like a philosopher, gesturing with his free hand, teaching old and young alike. He moves and turns; his body has weight; his garment stretches exuberantly over knee and ankle. There is a sense of depth and interaction. The carving recalls Trajan's column. But it is Christian art: the teacher is Christ, and the container is a pyx, used to hold the wafers of the Eucharist.

Plate 1.8 (facing page): Ivory Pyx (5th cent.). The lively gestures of these figures and their high relief are reminiscent of the older style of Trajan's column (**Plate 1.3**), but the subject matter is entirely new: Christ teaching the elders.

THE BARBARIANS

The ivory pyx may have been carved just as the Visigoths were sacking Rome (410). The sack was a stunning blow. Like a married couple in a bitter divorce, both Romans and Goths had once wooed one another; they then became mutually and comfortably dependent; eventually they fell into betrayal and strife. Nor was the Visigothic experience unique. The Franks, too, had been recruited into the Roman army, some of their members settling peacefully within the imperial borders. The Burgundian experience was similar.

The Romans called all these peoples "barbarians." They called some of them

"Germani" —Germans—because they materialized from beyond the Rhine, in Germania. Historians today tend to differentiate these peoples linguistically: "Germanic peoples" are those who spoke Germanic languages. Whatever name we use (they certainly had no collective name for themselves), these peoples were long used to a settled existence. Archaeologists have found in northern Europe evidence of small hamlets built and continuously inhabited for centuries by Germanic groups before they entered the empire. At Wijster, one of their settlements near the North Sea, for example, about fifty or sixty families lived in a well-planned community, with hedged streets and carefully aligned houses. Elsewhere, smaller hamlets were the rule. Whether due to their contacts with the Romans or because of indigenous practices, Germanic society was not egalitarian: we can see the evidence of social inequalities in the different sorts of houses that archaeologists have uncovered: long wooden houses for the well-off, sunken cottages for lesser folk. Supporting themselves by herding and farming, Germanic traders bartered with Roman provincials along the empire's border.

There was no biological distinction between "Germanic" traders and "Roman" ones, nor was there any biological distinction between different Germanic tribesmen and -women. However, there were ethnic differences—differences created by preferences and customs surrounding food, language, clothing, hairstyle, customs, behaviors, and all the other elements that go into a sense of identity. But these ethnicities were in constant flux as tribes came together and broke apart.

The "ethnogenesis" of the Goths, for example—the ethnicities that came into being and changed over time—made them not one people but many. If it is true that a people called the "Goths" (Gutones) can be found in the first century C.E. in what is today northwestern Poland, that does not mean that they much resembled those "Goths" who, in the third century, organized and dominated a confederation of steppe peoples and forest dwellers of mixed origins north of the Black Sea (today Ukraine). The second set of Goths was a splinter of the first; by the time it got to the Black Sea, it had joined with many other groups. In short, the Goths were multiethnic.

Taking advantage—and soon becoming a part—of the crisis of the third century, the Black Sea Goths invaded and plundered the nearby provinces of the Roman empire. The Romans first responded with annual payments to buy peace, but then stopped, preferring confrontation. Around 250, Gothic and other raiders and pirates plundered in the Balkans and Anatolia (today Turkey). It took many years of bitter fighting for Roman armies, reinforced by Gothic and other mercenaries, to stop these raids. Afterwards, once again transformed, the Goths emerged as two different groups: eastern (later, Ostrogoths), again north of the Black Sea, and western (later, Visigoths), in what is today Romania. By the mid-330s the Visigoths were allies of the empire and fighting in their armies. Some rose to the position of army leaders.

By the end of the fourth century, many Roman army units were made up of whole tribes—Goths or Franks, for example—fighting as "federates" for the Roman government under their own chiefs.

This was the marriage. It fell apart under the pressure of the Huns, a nomadic people from the semi-arid, grass-covered plains (the "steppeland") of west-central Asia, who invaded the Black Sea region in 376, attacking and destroying its settlements like lightning and moving into Romania. The Visigoths, joined by other refugees driven from their settlements by the Huns, petitioned Emperor Valens (*r.*364–378) to be allowed into the Empire. He agreed; we have seen that barbarians had long been settled within the borders as army recruits. But in this case the numbers were unprecedented: tens of thousands, perhaps even up to 200,000. The Romans were overwhelmed, unprepared, and resentful. About two centuries later a humanitarian crisis was recalled by the Gothic historian Jordanes:

Map 1.3: The Former Western Empire, *c.*500

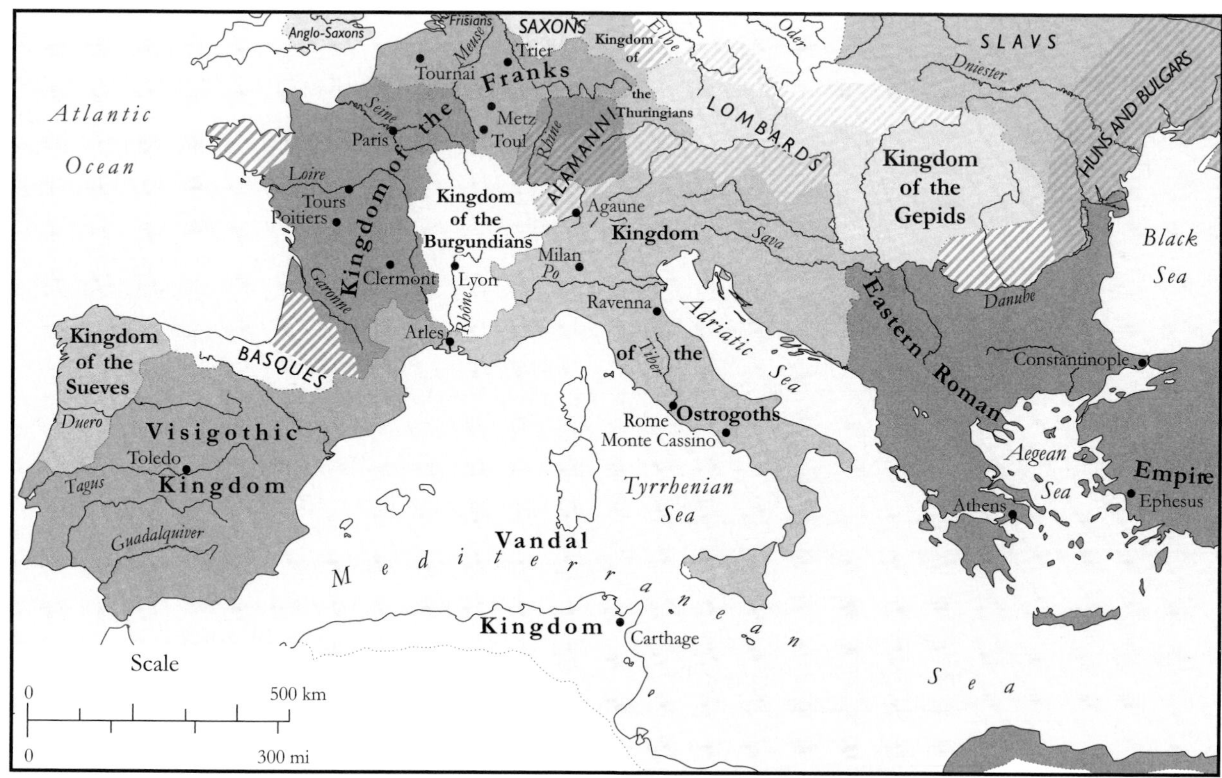

> [The Goths] crossed the Danube and settled Dacia Ripensis, Moesia and Thrace by permission of the Emperor. Soon famine and want came upon them, as often happens to a people not yet well settled in a country. Their princes ... began to lament the plight of their army and begged Lupicinus and Maximus, the Roman commanders, to open a market. But to what will not the "cursed lust for gold" compel men to assent? The generals, swayed by avarice, sold them at a high price not only the flesh of sheep and oxen, but even the carcasses of dogs and unclean animals, so that a slave would be bartered for a loaf of bread or ten pounds of meat. When their goods and chattels failed, the greedy trader demanded their sons in return for the necessities of life. And the parents consented even to this.[7]

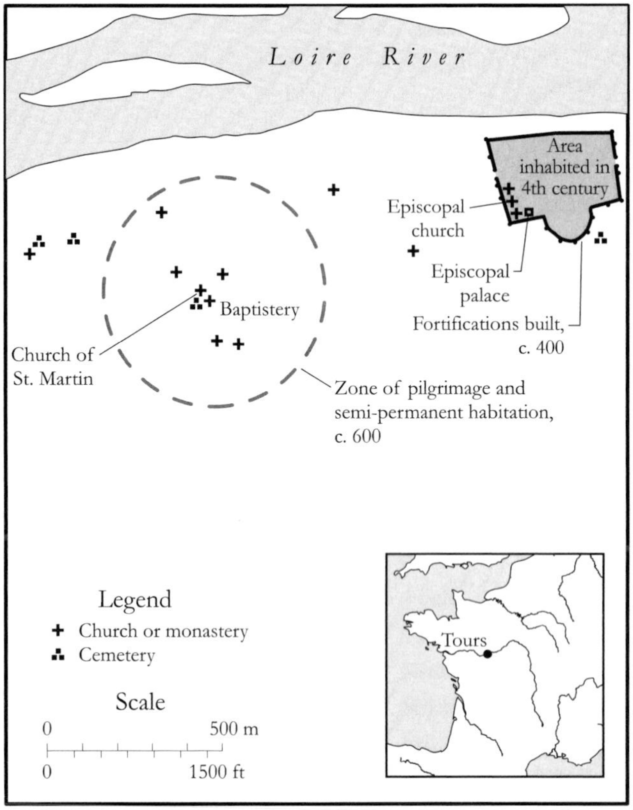

Map 1.4: Tours, *c.*600

The parents did not consent for long. In 378 the Visigoths rebelled against the Romans, killing Emperor Valens at the battle of Adrianople. Thereafter, again bound as federates to serve the Romans, the Visigoths under Alaric began in about 397 to seek a place for permanent settlement. Moving first to Greece, then to Italy, taking Rome for a few days in 410, the Visigoths settled in Gaul, south of the Loire, in 416. By 484 they had taken most of Spain as well.

Meanwhile, beginning late in 406, perhaps also impelled by the Huns, other barbarian groups—Alans, Vandals, and Sueves—entered the Empire by crossing the Rhine River. They first moved into Gaul, then into Spain. The Vandals crossed into North Africa; the Sueves remained in Spain, but most of their kingdom was conquered by the Visigoths in the course of the sixth century. When, after Attila's death in 453, the empire that he had created along the Danubian frontier collapsed, still other groups moved into the Roman empire—Ostrogoths, Rugi, Gepids—each with a "deal" from the Roman government, each with the hope of working for Rome and reaping its rewards. In 476 the last Roman emperor in the West, Romulus Augustulus, was deposed by Odoacer, a barbarian (from one of the lesser tribes, the Sciri) leading Roman troops. Odoacer promptly had himself declared King of Italy and, in a bid to "unite" the empire, sent Augustulus' imperial insignia to Emperor Zeno (*r*.474-491). But Zeno in his turn authorized Theodoric, king of the Ostrogoths, to attack Odoacer in about 490. Theodoric's conquest of Italy succeeded. Not much later the Franks, long used to fighting for the Romans, conquered Gaul under Clovis (*r*.481-511), a Roman official and king of the Franks, by defeating a provincial governor of Gaul and several barbarian rivals. Meanwhile other barbarian groups set up kingdoms of their own.

Around the year 500 the former Roman empire was no longer a scarf flung around the Mediterranean; it was a mosaic. (See Map 1.3.) Northwest Africa was now the Vandal Kingdom, Spain the Visigothic kingdom, Gaul the Kingdom of the Franks, and Italy the Kingdom of the Ostrogoths. The Anglo-Saxons occupied southeastern Britain; the Burgundians formed a kingdom centered in what is today Switzerland. Only the eastern half of the Empire—the long end of the scarf—remained intact.

THE NEW ORDER

What was new about the "new order" of the sixth century was less the rise of barbarian kingdoms than it was, in the West, the decay of the cities and corresponding liveliness of the countryside, the increased dominance of the rich, and the quiet domestication of Christianity. In the East, the Roman empire continued, made an ill-fated bid to expand, and finally retrenched as an autonomous entity: the Byzantine empire.

The Ruralization of the West

Where the barbarians settled, they did so with only tiny ripples of discontent from articulate Roman elites. It used to be thought that the Roman empire granted their invaders vast estates confiscated from Roman landowners. It now seems that the new tribal rulers were often content to live in cities or border forts, collecting land taxes rather than land.

For Romans, the chief objection to the new barbarian overlords was their Arian Christian beliefs. Clovis, king of the Franks, may have been the first Germanic king to overcome this problem. (If so, Sigismund, king of the Burgundians, was a close second.) Clovis flirted with Arianism early on, but he soon converted to the Catholic Christianity of his Gallic neighbors.

In other respects as well, the new rulers took over Roman institutions; they issued laws, for example. Under Alaric II (*r.*484–507) the Visigoths promulgated the *Breviary*, a compendium of Roman laws. Other barbarian law codes reflected more directly "tribal" customs, though in important ways these were indistinguishable from Roman provincial law. Sigismund, king of the Burgundians, issued a code of Burgundian laws in 517. A Frankish law code was compiled under King Clovis, fusing provincial Roman and Germanic procedures into a single whole.

Written in Latin, these laws revealed their Roman inspiration even in their language. Barbarian kings, some well educated themselves, often depended on Roman advisors to write up their letters and laws. In Italy, in particular, an outstanding group of Roman administrators, judges, and officers served Ostrogothic King Theodoric the Great (*r.*493–526). They included the encyclopedic Cassiodorus (490–583), author of the *Institutes of Christian Culture*, and the learned Boethius (480–524), who wrote the tranquil *Consolation of Philosophy* as he awaited execution for treason. Since the fourth century, Romans had become used to barbarian leaders; in the sixth, there was nothing very strange in having them as kings.

Far stranger was the disappearance of the urban middle class. The new taxes of the fourth century had much to do with this. The *curiales*—members of the town elites—had been used to collecting the taxes for their communities, making up any shortfalls, and reaping the rewards of prestige for doing so. In the fourth century, new land and head taxes impoverished the *curiales*, while very rich landowners, out in the countryside, surrounded by their bodyguards and slaves, simply did not bother to pay. Now the tax burdens fell on poorer people. Families pressed to pay taxes they could not afford escaped to the great estates of the rich, giving up their free status in return for land and protection. By the seventh century, the rich had won; the barbarian kings no longer bothered to collect general taxes.

The cities, most of them walled since the time of the crisis of the third century, were no longer thriving or populous, though they remained political and religious centers. For example, the episcopal complex at Tours (in Gaul) was within the walls of a fortification thrown up *c.*400. (See Map 1.4.) Although it still functioned as an institution of religion and government, almost no one lived there any longer. But outside the Roman city, in a cemetery that the Romans had carefully sited away from ordinary habitation, a new church rose over the relics of the local saint, Martin. This served as a magnet for the people of the surrounding countryside and even further away. A baptistery was constructed nearby, to baptize the infants of pilgrims and others who came to the tomb of Saint Martin hoping for a miracle. Sometimes people stayed for years. Gregory, bishop of Tours (*r.*573–594), our chief source for the history of Gaul in the sixth century, described Chainemund, a blind woman:

> She was a very pious woman, and full of faith she went to the venerable church of the blessed bishop Martin. She was ... also covered with abrasions on her entire body. For a sickness had attacked all her limbs with sores, and her appearance was so horrible and so repulsive to look at that she was considered by the people as a leper. Every day she felt her way and went to the church of the glorious champion. After almost three years, while she was standing in front of his tomb, her eyes were opened and she saw everything clearly. All the weakness in her limbs disappeared ... and a healthy skin grew back.[8]

With people like Chainemund flocking to the tomb, no wonder that archaeologists have found evidence of semi-permanent habitations right at the cemetery.

War and plague no doubt reduced the overall population, but it is impossible to gauge the precise toll. More calculable were changes in styles of life. The shift from urban to rural settlements brought with it a new localism. The active long-distance trade of the Mediterranean slowed down, though it did not stop. But now this trade penetrated very little beyond the coast. This is nicely illustrated by the story of pottery, a cheap necessity of the ancient world. In the sixth century we find fine mass-produced African red pottery on even the most humble tables along the Mediterranean Sea coast; but inland, most people had to make do with local handmade wares as regional networks of exchange eroded long-distance connections.

For some—the rich—the new disconnection of the rural landscape with the wider world had its charms. When they were inclined, they could still take advantage of luxury goods. In some regions they could even enjoy a life of splendid isolation:

> On the summit of the high rock a magnificent palace is built .... Marble columns hold up the imposing structure; from the top you can see boats gliding by on the surface of the river in summertime .... Water is channeled off along ducts following the contours of the mountain.... On these slopes, formerly sterile, Nicetius has planted juicy vines, and green vineshoots clothe the high rock that used to bear nothing but scrub. Orchards with fruit-trees growing here and there fill the air with the perfume of their flowers.[9]

The owner of this haven was Nicetius, bishop of Trier. He retreated to it when his pastoral cares gave him the chance. Bishops like Nicetius were among the rich; most rose to their episcopal status in their twilight years, after they had married and had sired children to inherit their estates. (Their wives continued to live with them but—or so it was hoped—not to sleep with them.) Great lay landlords, kings,

NORSE
SWEDES
FINNS
PICTS
SCOTS
North Sea
DANES
Baltic Sea
LITHUANIANS
PRUSSIANS
Atlantic Ocean
ANGLES
SAXONS
BRITONS
FRISIANS
SAXONS
Elbe
Oder
Vistula
EASTERN SLAVS
Austrasia
Tertry
Soissons
Reims
Cologne
Mainz
THURINGIANS
WESTERN SLAVS
Brittany
(Frankish Dependency)
Neustria
Seine
Loire
Metz
Frankish Kingdoms
Rhine
Tours
Poitiers
Aquitaine
Garonne
Burgundy
Rhône
Bavarians
(Frankish Dependency)
SLAVS
Dnieper
Suevian Kingdom
(Conquered by Visigoths, 584)
BASQUES
Ebro
Milan
Avar Khaganate
BULGARS
Visigothic Kingdom
Toledo
Córdoba
Lombard Kingdom
Adriatic Sea
SOUTHERN SLAVS
Danube
Black
Rome
Mediterranean Sea
Constantinople
Chalcedon
Nicaea
Eastern Roman Empire
Carthage
Ephesus
BERBERS
Antio
Damas
Jerusalem
Alexandria
GARAMANTES
BERBERS
Scale
0
800 km
0
500 mi
Lambert Conformal Conic projection.

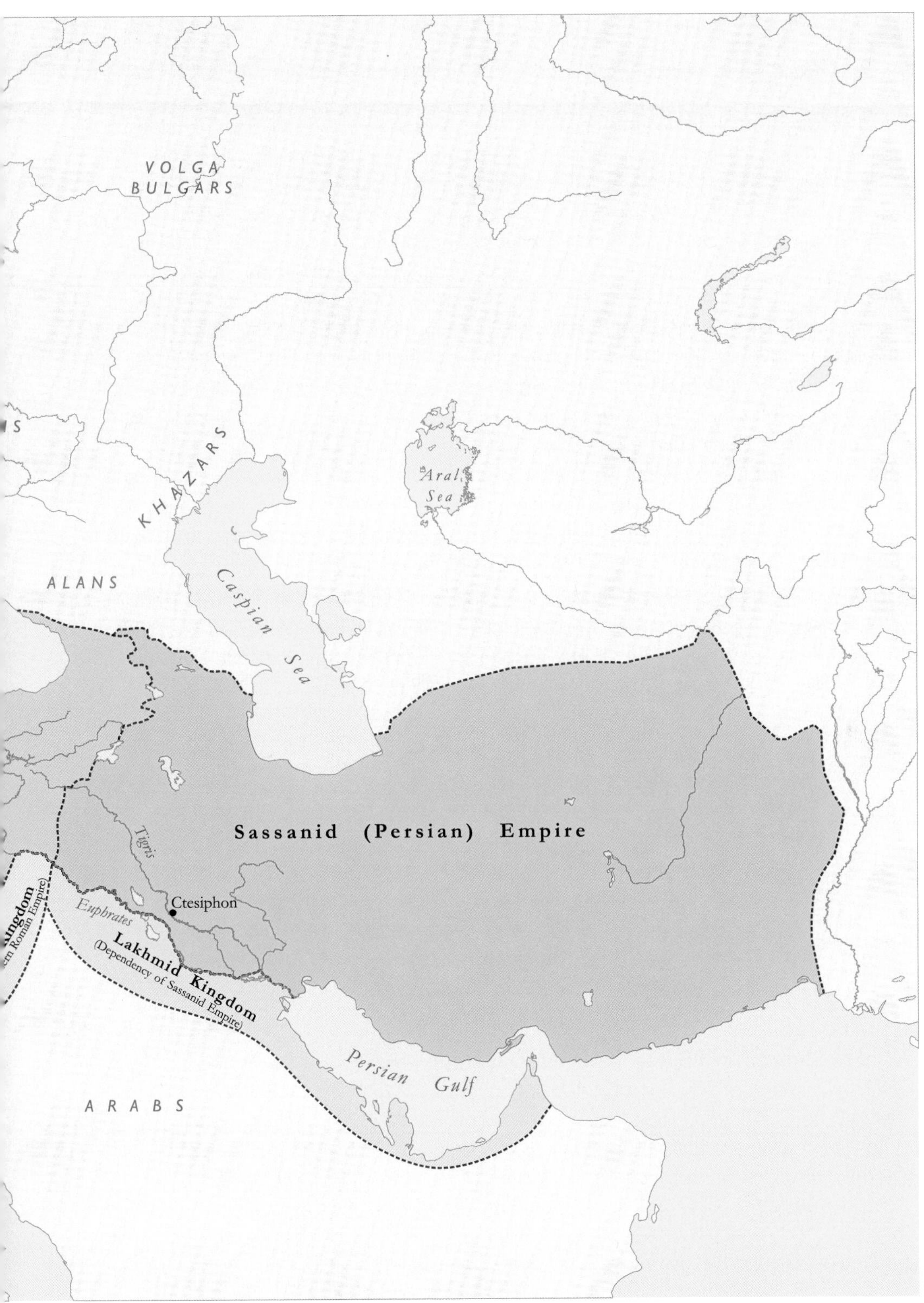

Map 1.5: Europe and the Eastern Roman Empire, *c.*600

queens, warriors, and courtiers controlled and monopolized most of the rest of the wealth of the West, now based largely on land.

Monasteries, too, were beginning to become important corporate landowners. In the sixth century many monks lived in communities just far enough away from the centers of power to be holy, yet near enough to be important. Monks were not quite laity (since they devoted their entire life to religion) yet not quite clergy (since they were only rarely ordained) but something in between and increasingly admired. It is often said that Saint Anthony was the "first monk," and though this may not be strictly true, it is not far off the mark. Like Anthony, monks lived a life of daily martyrdom, giving up their wealth, family ties, and worldly offices. Like Anthony, who towards the end of his life came out of the tombs he had once retreated to in order to be with others, monks lived in communities. Some communities were of men only, some of women, some of both (in separate quarters). Whatever the sort, monks lived in obedience to a "rule" that gave them a stable and orderly way of life.

The rule might be unwritten, as it was at Saint-Maurice d'Agaune, a monastic community set up in 515 by Sigismund on the eve of his accession to the Burgundian throne. The monks at Agaune, divided into groups that went to the church in relay, carried out a grueling regime of non-stop prayer every day. Built outside the Burgundian capital of Geneva, high on a cliff that was held to be the site of the heroic martyrdom of a Christian Roman legion, this monastery tapped into a holy landscape and linked it to Sigismund and his episcopal advisors.

Other rules were written. Caesarius, bishop of Arles (*r.*502–542) wrote one for his sister, the "abbess" (head) of a monastery of women. He wrote another for his nephew, the "abbot" of a male monastery. In Italy, Saint Benedict (*d.c.*555) wrote the most famous of the monastic rules some time around 540. With its adoption, much later, by the Carolingian kings of the ninth century, it became the monastic norm in the West. Unlike the rule of Agaune, where prayer was paramount, Benedict's Rule divided the day into discrete periods of prayer, reading, and labor. Nevertheless, the core of its program, as at Agaune, was the "liturgy"—not just the Mass, but an elaborate round of formal worship that took place seven times a day and once at night. At these specific times, the monks chanted—that is sang—the "Offices," much of which consisted of the psalms, a group of 150 poems in the Old Testament:

> The Morning Office [Lauds] on Sunday shall begin with Psalm 66 recited straight through without an antiphon [antiphons were additional chants, normally added before and after each psalm verse]. After that let Psalm 50 be said with "Alleluia," then Psalms 117 and 62, the Canticle of Blessing [a text taken from St. Luke's Gospel] and the Psalms of praise [Psalms 148–150]; then a lesson from the Apocalypse to be recited by heart. [More chants follow.][10]

By the end of each week the monks were to have completed all 150 psalms.

Benedict's monastery, Monte Cassino, was in the shadow of Rome, far enough to be an "escape" but near enough to link it to the papacy. Pope Gregory the Great (590-604), arguably the man most responsible for making the papacy the greatest power in Italy, took the time to write a biography of Benedict and praise his Rule. Monasteries, by their ostentatious rejection of wealth and power, became partners of the powerful. The monks were seen as models of virtue, and their prayers were thought to reach God's ear. It was crucial to ally with them.

Little by little the Christian religion was domesticated to the needs of the new order, even as it shaped that order to fit its demands. Chainemund was not afraid to go to the cemetery outside of Tours. There were no demons there; they had been driven far away by the power of Saint Martin. The fame of Saint Benedict, Gregory reported, drew "pious noblemen from Rome," who "left their sons with him to be schooled in the service of God."[11] Benedict's monasteries had become the perfectly acceptable alternatives to the old avenues to prestige: armies and schools. Saint Radegund, founder of a convent at Poitiers (not far from Tours), obtained a fragment of the Holy Cross as a relic for her nuns. It would be hard to find anything more precious. Thus sacred things were dispersed and diffused into the countryside, into city convents, into the texture of everyday life.

The Retrenchment of the East

After 476 there was a "new order" in the East as well, but it was much less obvious. For one thing, there was still an emperor. His subjects called themselves "Romans" and thought that they spoke "Romaic" (though we call their language Greek).

The east Roman towns continued to thrive, and their middle classes even experienced renewed prosperity and influence. The best of the small-town educated elite went off to Constantinople, where they found good jobs as administrators, civil servants, and financial advisors. While barbarian kings were giving in to the rich and eliminating general taxes altogether, the eastern emperors were collecting state revenues more efficiently than ever. When Hagia Sophia ("Holy Wisdom"), the great church of Constantinople, burned to the ground, Emperor Justinian (*r.*527-565) dipped into the treasury to hire 10,000 workers to rebuild it. They covered its domed ceiling with gold and used 40,000 pounds of silver for its decoration.

Nevertheless, the eastern Roman empire was not the old Roman empire writ small. It was becoming a "Middle Eastern state," more akin to Persia than to Gaul. When the Visigoths sacked Rome, the eastern Emperor Theodosius II (*r.*408-450) did not send an army; he built walls around Constantinople instead. When the roads

Plate 1.9: Mosaic from San Vitale, Ravenna (*c.*540–548). Flanked on one side by churchmen (holding a cross and a Bible) and on the other by military men (holding spears and a shield inscribed with the sign of Christ), Emperor Justinian is here depicted in an offertory procession. He himself carries the paten, which contains the eucharistic bread. By both his position in the composition and his role in the mass, he is thus made the link between heavenly and earthly orders.

fell into disrepair, Justinian let them decay—except for the one that led to the border with Persia. When the Slavs pressed on the Roman frontier in the Balkans, Justinian let them enter. Borrowing the ceremony and pomp of the Persian King of Kings for himself, Justinian was pleased to be represented in the mosaics of San Vitale at Ravenna (Plate 1.9) in a crown and jewels, his head surrounded by a gleaming halo, his ministers—both secular and ecclesiastic—flanking him on both sides. At San Vitale, he is almost an icon, a simplified, radically "abstracted" image of a person suffused with divinity.

Icons, perhaps originally the creation of the Coptic Christians of Egypt, were another Middle Eastern product crucial to the culture of the east Romans. Without denigrating relics, eastern Christians found that icons—whether painted, woven, or carved—gave them more important access to the sacred. In the sixth-century Egyptian tapestry shown in Plate 1.10, the Virgin, dressed in the purple robes of an empress, sits on a gem-encrusted throne with the Christ Child in her lap. Like the Eucharist, icons concentrated and transmuted spiritual into material substance.

Plate 1.10 (facing page): Woven Icon of the Virgin (6th cent.). Probably made in Egypt, this tapestry expresses the power and dignity of the Virgin through startling colors and simplified figures.

The fifth and sixth centuries brought retrenchment. For the first time emperors issued compendia of Roman laws. The *Theodosian Code*, which gathered together imperial "constitutions" (general laws) alongside "rescripts" (rulings on individual cases), was published in 438. The barbarian law codes of the sixth century attempted to match this achievement, but they were overshadowed by the great legal initiatives of Justinian, which included the *Codex Justinianus* (529), an imperial law code; an orderly compilation of Roman juridical thought called the *Digest* (533); and a textbook for lawyers known as the *Institutes* (534). From then on the laws of the eastern Roman empire were largely (though not wholly) fixed, though Justinian's books were soon eclipsed by short summaries in Greek, while in the West they had little impact until the twelfth century.

Under Justinian, this redefined Roman empire sought to recapture its past glory. It quickly took North Africa from the Vandals in 534. It added a strip of southeastern Spain in 552. Meanwhile Justinian's armies pressed on to wrench—but with great difficulty—Italy from the Ostrogoths. The first two enterprises were fairly successful; eastern Roman rule lasted in North Africa for another century. The last venture, however, was a disaster. The long war in Italy, which began in 535 and ended only in 552, devastated the country. Soon the Lombards, Germanic warriors employed by Justinian to help take Italy, returned to Italy on their own behalf. By 572 they were masters of part of northern Italy and, further south, of Spoleto and Benevento. (See Map 1.5.)

For the eastern Roman empire, the western undertaking was a sideshow. The empire's real focus was on the Sassanid empire of the Persians. The two "superpowers" confronted one another with wary forays throughout the sixth century. They thought that to the winner would come the spoils. Little did they imagine that

Ο ΑΓΙΟϹ ΜΙΧΑΗΛ
Η ΑΓΙΑ ΜΑΡΙΑ

the real winner in the Middle East would be a new and unheard of group: the Muslims.

★ ★ ★ ★

The crisis of the third century demoted the old Roman elites, bringing new groups to the fore. Among these were the Christians, who insisted on one God and one way to understand and worship him. Declared the official religion of the empire in 391, Christianity redefined the location of the holy: no longer was it in private households or city temples but in the precious relics of the saints and the Eucharist, in those who ministered on behalf of the church on earth (the bishops), and in those who led lives of ascetic heroism (the monks).

Politically the empire, once a vast conglomeration of conquered provinces, was in turn largely conquered by its periphery. In spite of themselves, the Romans had tacitly to acknowledge and exploit the interdependence between the center and the hinterlands. They invited the barbarians in, and then declined to recognize the needs of their guests. The repudiation came too late. The barbarians were part of the empire, and in the western half they took it over. In the next century they would show how much they had learned from their former hosts.

Chapter One Key Events

212	Roman Citizenship granted to all free inhabitants of the provinces
235-284	Crisis of the Third Century
284-305	Reign of Diocletian
306-337	Reign of Constantine
313	Edict of Milan
325	Council of Nicaea
378	Emperor Valens killed by Visigoths
391	Emperor Theodosius declares Christianity the official religion of the Roman empire
410	Visigoths sack Rome
453	Death of Attila
476	Deposition of Romulus Augustulus
*c.*540	Benedictine (St. Benedict's) *Rule* written
527-565	Emperor Justinian
590-604	Pope Gregory the Great

NOTES

1. "The Passion of SS. Perpetua and Felicitas," in *Medieval Saints: A Reader,* ed. Mary-Ann Stouck, Readings in Medieval Civilizations and Cultures 4 (Peterborough, ON, 1999), p.22.
2. Quoted in Ramsay MacMullen, *Christianizing the Roman Empire (A.D. 100-400)* (New Haven, 1984), p.95.
3. *The Confessions of Saint Augustine* 8.4, trans. Rex Warner (New York, 1963), p.166.
4. Quoted in W.H.C. Frend, *The Rise of the Monophysite Movement: Chapters in the History of the Church in the Fifth and Sixth Centuries* (Cambridge, 1972), p.xii.
5. Saint Athanasius, *The Life of Saint Antony*, trans. Robert T. Meyer, Ancient Christian Writers 10 (New York, 1978), p.32, spelling slightly modified.
6. *Acta Maximiliani* 3,4, ed. and trans. H. Musurillo, *The Acts of the Christian Martyrs* (Oxford, 1972), p.248, quoted in Peter Brown, *The Cult of the Saints: Its Rise and Function in Latin Christianity* (Chicago, 1981), p.33.
7. Charles Christopher Mierow, trans., *The Gothic History of Jordanes* (Princeton, 1915), pp.88-89.
8. Gregory of Tours, *The Miracles of the Bishop Saint Martin*, trans. Raymond Van Dam in his *Saints and Their Miracles in Late Antique Gaul* (New Jersey, 1993), p.210.
9. Fortunatus, quoted in Georges Duby, *The Early Growth of the European Economy: Warriors and Peasants from the Seventh to the Twelfth Century* (Ithaca, 1974), p.58, spelling and punctuation slightly modified.
10. *St. Benedict's Rule for Monasteries*, trans. Leonard J. Doyle (Collegeville, 1948), p.33.
11. Gregory the Great, "The Life and Miracles of Saint Benedict," in Stouck, p.177.

FURTHER READING

Bowersock, G.W., Peter Brown, and Oleg Grabar, eds. *Late Antiquity: A Guide to the Postclassical World.* Cambridge, MA, 1999.

Brown, Peter. *The Cult of the Saints.* Chicago, 1981.

—. *The World of Late Antiquity*, 150-750. London, 1971.

Geary, Patrick J. *The Myth of Nations: The Medieval Origins of Europe.* Princeton, 2002.

Heinzelmann, Martin. *Gregory of Tours: History and Society in the Sixth Century.* Trans. Christopher Carroll. Cambridge, 2001.

Jones, A.H.M. *The Later Roman Empire, 284-602*, 2 vols. Baltimore, 1986.

Kitzinger, Ernst. *Early Medieval Art.* Rev. ed. Bloomington, 1983.

Knight, Jeremy K. *The End of Antiquity: Archaeology, Society and Religion AD 235-700.* Charleston, SC, 1999.

MacMullen, Ramsay. *Christianity and Paganism in the Fourth to Eighth Centuries.* New Haven, 1997.

Moorhead, John. *Justinian.* London, 1994.

Pohl, Walter, with Helmut Reimitz, eds. *Strategies of Distinction: The Construction of Ethnic Communities, 300-800.* Leiden, 1998.

Wolfram, Herwig. *The Roman Empire and Its Germanic Peoples.* Trans. Thomas J. Dunlap. Berkeley, 1997.

TWO

THE EMERGENCE OF SIBLING CULTURES (*c*.600–*c*.750)

THE RISE OF Islam in the Arabic world and its triumph over territories that had for centuries been dominated by either Rome or Persia is the first astonishing fact of the seventh and eighth centuries. The second is the persistence of the Roman empire both politically, in what historians call the "Byzantine empire," and culturally, in the Islamic world and Europe. By 750 there were three distinct and nearly separate worlds: the Greek-speaking Byzantines, the Latin-writing Europeans, and the Arabic-writing Muslims. They professed different values, struggled with different problems, adapted to different standards of living. Yet all three bore the marks of common parentage—or, at least, of common adoption. They were sibling heirs of Rome.

SAVING BYZANTIUM

In the seventh century, the eastern Roman empire was so transformed that historians by convention call it something new, the "Byzantine empire," from the old Greek name for Constantinople: Byzantium. (Often the word "Byzantium" alone is used to refer to this empire as well.) War, first with the Sassanid Persians, then with the Arabs, was the major transforming agent. Gone was the ambitious imperial reach of Justinian; by 700, Byzantium had lost all its rich territories in North Africa and its tiny Spanish outpost as well. (See Map 2.1.) True, it held tenuously to bits and pieces of

Italy and Greece. But in the main it had become a medium-size state, in the same location but about two-thirds the size of Turkey today. Yet, if small, it was also tough.

Sources of Resiliency

Byzantium survived the onslaughts of outsiders by preserving its capital city, which was well protected by huge, thick, and far-flung walls that embraced farmland and pasture as well as the city proper. Within, the emperor (still calling himself Roman) and his officials serenely continued to collect the traditional Roman land taxes from the provinces left to them. This allowed the state to pay regular salaries to its soldiers, sailors, and court officials. The navy, well supplied with ships and proud of its prestigious weapon—Greek Fire, an oil hurled over the water that exploded on impact with enemy ships—patrolled the Mediterranean Sea. The armies of the empire, formerly posted as frontier guards, were now pulled back and set up as regional units

Map 2.1: The Byzantine Empire, *c.*700

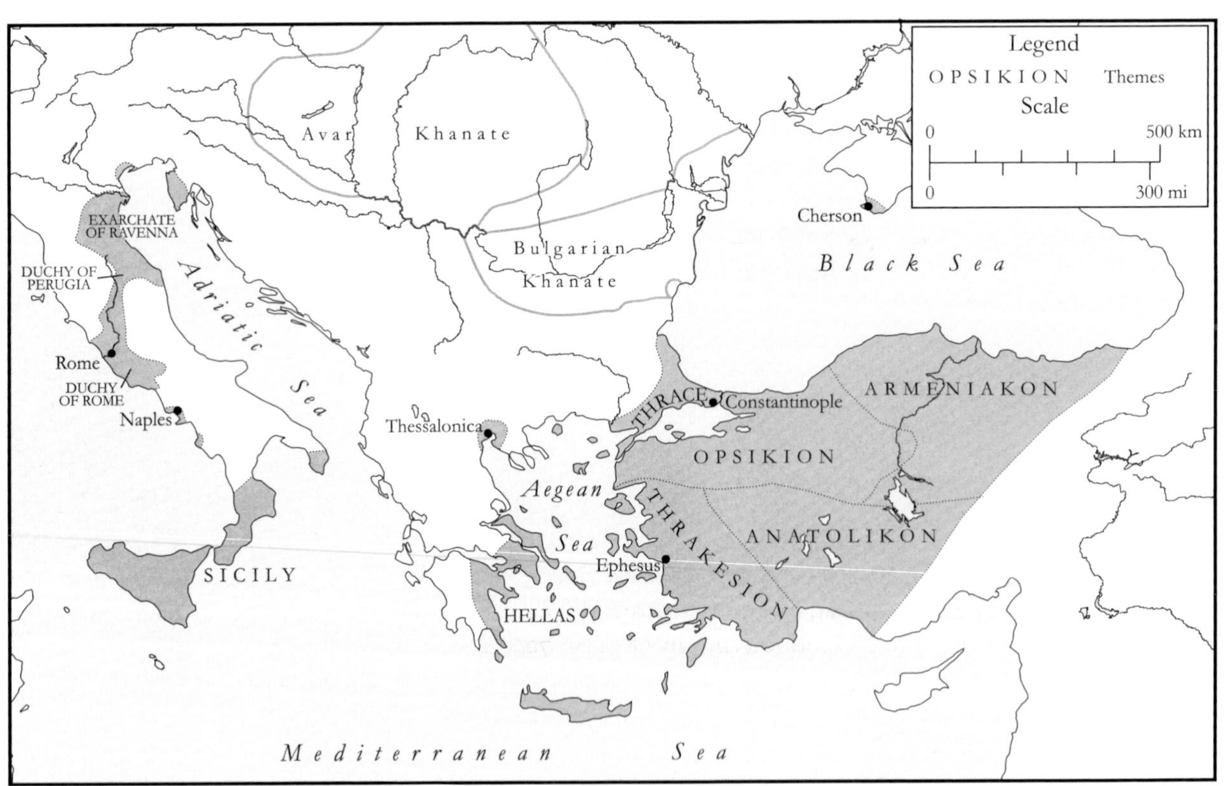

within the empire itself. These armies and their regions, both called "themes," were led by *strategoi* (*sing. strategos*), generals who were gradually given responsibility for both military and regional civil matters. They countered enemy raids while remaining close to sources of supplies and new recruits. Each soldier was given land in his theme to help him purchase his uniform and arms. In this way, the themes maintained the traditions of the imperial Roman army: well trained and equipped, Byzantium's troops served as reliable defenders of their newly compact state.

The Invaders and their Consequences

The Sassanid empire of Persia, its capital at Ctesiphon, its ruler styled "king of kings," was as venerable as the Roman empire—and as ambitious. (See Map 1.5 on pp.46-47.) King Chosroes II (*r.*591-628), not unlike Justinian a half-century before him, dreamed of recreating past glories. In his case the inspiration was the ancient empire of Xerxes and Darius, which had sprawled from a lick of land just west of Libya to a great swath of territory ending near the Indus River. Taking advantage of a dispute between two claimants to the imperial throne during the first decade of the seventh century, Chosroes marched into Byzantine territory in 607. By 613 he had taken Damascus, by 614 Jerusalem. The whole of Egypt fell to the Persians in 619. But Emperor Heraclius (*r.*610-641) rallied his troops and turned triumph into defeat; all territories taken by the Persians were back in Byzantine hands by 630. (For Heraclius and his successors, see list on p.330: Byzantine Emperors and Empresses.) On a map it would seem that nothing much had happened; in fact, the cities fought over were depopulated and ruined, and both Sassanid and Byzantine troops and revenues were exhausted.

Meanwhile, the Byzantines had to contend with Slavs and others north of the Danube. Again Map 1.5 makes the situation clear: Slavs—farmers and stock-breeders in the main—were pushing into the Balkans, sometimes accompanied by Avars, multiethnic horseback warriors and pastoralists. In 626, just before Heraclius wheeled around and bested the Persians on his frontiers, he was confronted with Avars and their Sassanid allies besieging—unsuccessfully, as it turned out—the very walls of Constantinople. It took another half-century for the Bulgars, a Turkic-speaking nomadic group, to become a threat, but in the 670s they began moving into what is today Bulgaria, defeating the Byzantine army in 681. By 700 the Balkan Peninsula was Byzantine territory no longer. (See Map 2.1 again.) The place where once the two halves of the Roman empire had met (see Map 1.1 on pp.20-21) was now a wedge that separated East from West.

An even more dramatic obliteration of the old geography took place further east, where attacks by Arab Muslims in the century after 630 ended in the conquest of Sassanid Persia and the further shrinking of Byzantium. We shall soon see how and why the Arabs poured out of Arabia. But we need first to know what the shrunken Byzantium was like.

Decline of Urban Centers

The city-based Greco-Roman culture on which the Byzantine empire was originally constructed had long been gradually giving way. Invasions and raids hastened this development. Urban centers, once bustling nodes of trade and administration, disappeared or reinvented themselves. Some became fortresses; others were abandoned; still others remained as skeletal administrative centers. The public activities of marketplaces, theaters, and town squares yielded to the pious pursuits of churchgoers or the private ones of the family. When warfare reduced cities to rubble, those that were rebuilt were remodeled along new lines.

Figure 2.1 (facing page): The Changing Face of Ephesus

The story of Ephesus is unique only in its details. (See Figure 2.1, noting the structures and labels in blue.) Ephesus had once been an opulent commercial and industrial center. Even after the turbulent centuries of the late Roman empire, Ephesus could still boast impressive vigor. Imagine it in about 600. Its vital center was the Embolos, a grand avenue paved with marble. (See Plate 2.1.) Extending the length of

Plate 2.1: The Embolos, Ephesus. The center of Late Antique Ephesus was this grand avenue, the Embolos, paved with marble and lined with columns, statues, and shops colorfully decorated with frescoes. After the seventh century, however, the street was largely abandoned.

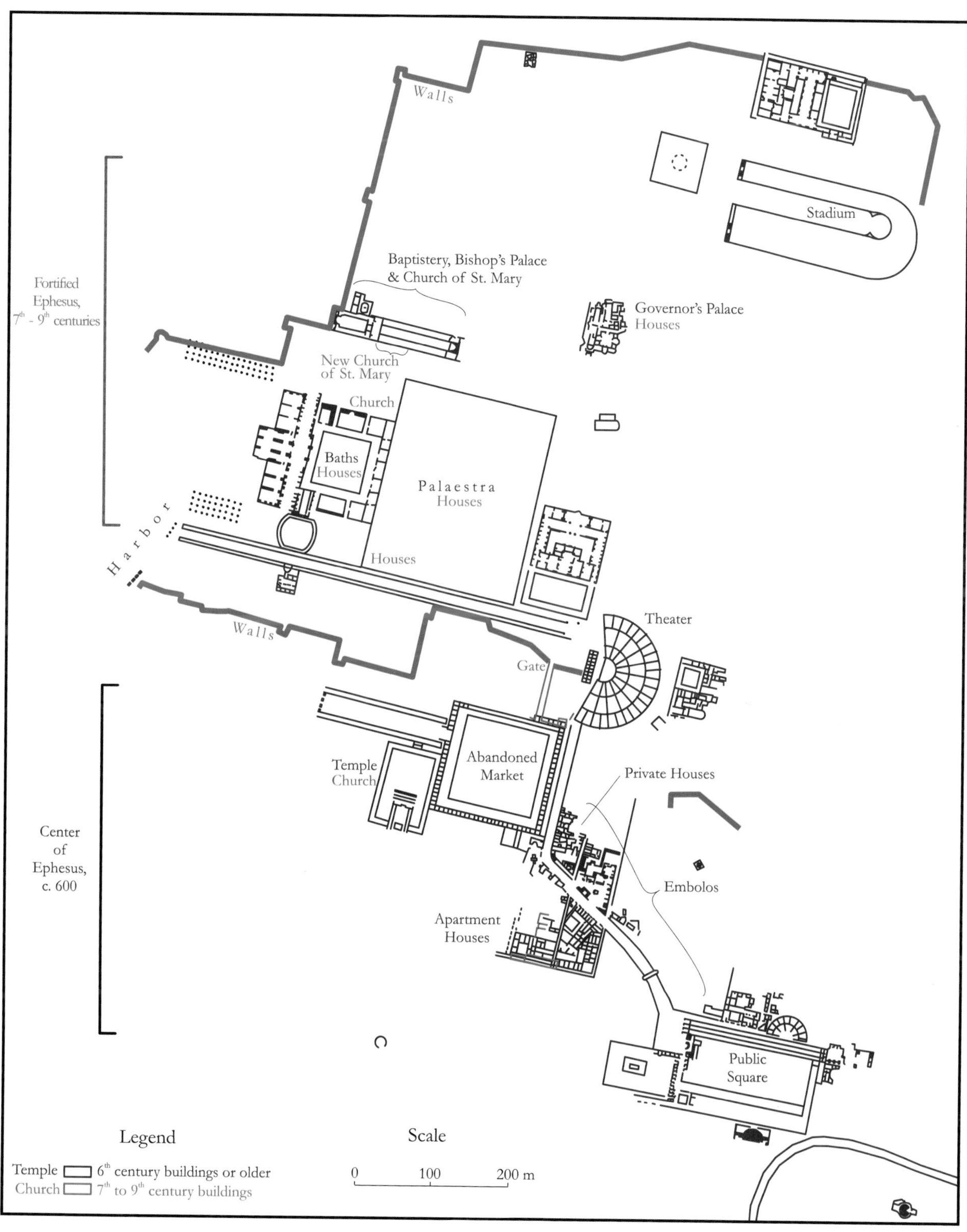

Walls
Stadium
Baptistery, Bishop's Palace
& Church of St. Mary
Fortified
Ephesus,
7th - 9th centuries
Governor's Palace
Houses
New Church
of St. Mary
Church
Baths
Houses
Palaestra
Houses
Harbor
Houses
Walls
Theater
Gate
Temple
Church
Abandoned
Market
Private Houses
Center
of
Ephesus,
c. 600
Embolos
Apartment
Houses
Public
Square
Legend
Temple 6th century buildings or older
Church 7th to 9th century buildings
Scale
0 100 200 m

more than three football fields, the Embolos began at its west end on an old (and no longer functioning) formal market square; it opened out at the east end onto another square; all along its length in between were statues, shops, and public buildings. Just behind the shops were private houses and apartments, evidence of a large and wealthy population.

There was no question of Ephesus's religious affiliation: the Embolos was well "Christianized" by numerous crosses carved as decorative motifs or scratched into the walls and paving stones. Although the church of Saint Mary, Ephesus's cathedral, was considerably north of the Embolos, there was at least one smaller church nearby, as well as a few chapels. The whole complex suggests a comfortable integration of old Roman institutions—baths, temples-turned-into-churches—with something new—an informal market jammed into the arcades of a street, itself fronting sprawling residential complexes.

By 700, little of this was left. The Persian wars disrupted Ephesus's trade and threatened its prosperity. Repeated visitations of bubonic plague began in the time of Justinian and recurred in virulent attacks until about 750. This was the first pandemic (widespread epidemic) in the historical record; Ephesus could not have been spared its grim demographic toll. An earthquake and fire in 614 struck decisive blows, destroying the Embolos and the luxurious houses built along its length. Arab attacks on Ephesus began in 654-655.

In the face of disaster, Ephesus was rebuilt, but not as before. The old vital center around the Embolos was abandoned. Walls, constructed around a much-reduced area to the north, enclosed the remaining population and a smaller cathedral. (See Figure 2.1 again, now noting the constructions and labels in green.) Old public baths were displaced by private houses, few of them elegant and many no more than huts. Exceptions to the decay were few: the bishop (housed just to the east of the new church of Saint Mary), his clergy, and local monasteries formed a rich and powerful upper stratum, as did imperial and military officials living in the vicinity.

Everywhere in Byzantium, cities became little more than fortresses in the course of the eighth century. Constantinople, with its walls, was only partially exceptional. As elsewhere, its population shrank, and formerly inhabited areas right within the city were abandoned or turned into farms. As the capital of church and state, however, Constantinople boasted an extraordinarily thriving imperial and ecclesiastical upper class. It also retained some trade and industry. Even in the darkest days of the seventh-century wars, it had taverns, brothels, merchants, and a money economy. Its factories continued to manufacture fine silk textiles. Even though Byzantium's economic life became increasingly rural in the seventh and eighth centuries, institutions vital to urban growth remained at Constantinople, ensuring a revival of commercial activity once the wars ended.

Ruralization

With the decline of cities came the rise of the countryside. Agriculture had all along been the backbone of the Byzantine economy. Apart from large landowners—the state, the church, and a few wealthy individuals—most Byzantines were free or semi-free peasant farmers. In the interior of Anatolia, on the great plateau that extends from the Mediterranean to the Black Sea, peasants must often have had to abandon their farms when Arab raiders came. Some may have joined the other pastoralists of the region, ready to drive their flocks to safety. Elsewhere (and, in times of peace, on the Anatolian plains as well), peasants worked small plots (sometimes rented, sometimes owned outright), herding animals, cultivating grains, and tending orchards.

The so-called Farmers' Law, which probably reflects rural conditions in at least some parts of the empire, paints a picture of autonomous village communities composed of small households. Since the *curiales* of the cities were gone, rural families now felt directly the impact of imperial rule, especially taxes. In turn, the state adopted an agenda of "family values," narrowing the grounds for divorce, setting new punishments for marital infidelity, and prohibiting abortions. New legislation gave mothers new power over their offspring and made widows the legal guardians of their minor children. These families no longer wanted their children to learn the classics—the Greek poets and philosophers—but rather the Bible. They used the psalms as a primer; from there their children might move on to hagiography (saints' lives), dogmatic treatises, and devotional works.

Iconoclasm

Such piety was partly a response to crisis. What had provoked God's anger, unleashing war, plague, earthquakes? What would appease him? The armies thought that they knew: they attributed Arab victories to the biblical injunction against graven images. Islam prohibited representations of the divine; Byzantine soldiers listened. They thought that icons revived pagan idolatry. As iconoclastic (anti-icon or, literally, icon breaking) feeling grew, some churchmen became outspoken in their opposition to icons, while others, especially monks, defended them.

Byzantine emperors, who were religious as well as political figures, sided with their troops. They had other reasons to oppose icons as well. As mediators between people and God, icons undermined the emperor's exclusive place in the divine and temporal order. In 726, in the wake of a terrifying volcanic eruption in the middle of the Aegean Sea, Emperor Leo III the Isaurian (*r.*717-741) had his officers tear down the great golden icon of Christ at the gateway of the imperial palace and replace it with a cross. A crowd of women protested in fury. Thus was launched the long iconoclastic period. Leo ordered all icons destroyed, and the ban lasted until 787. It was revived, in modified form, between 815 and 843.

Iconoclasm had a thousand intimate consequences. Anyone with a portable icon at home had to destroy or adore it in secret. The effects on the monasteries were dramatic: their treasuries were raided and properties confiscated. Most extreme was one zealous *strategos*, Michael Lachanodracon, who forced all the monks in his theme to marry or suffer blinding and exile. In this way, iconoclasm destroyed communities that might otherwise have served as centers of resistance to imperial power. That was perhaps incidental. The most important point was that it made the Byzantines, in the eyes of its defenders, the "people of God."

THE RISE OF THE "BEST COMMUNITY": ISLAM

The Muslims also considered themselves God's people. In the Qur'an, the "recitation" of God's words, Muslims are "the best community ever raised up for mankind ... having faith in God" (3:110). The community's common purpose is "submission to God," the literal meaning of "Islam." The Muslim (a word that derives from "Islam") is "one who submits." Beginning in Arabia under the leadership of Muhammad, within less than a century Islam had created a new world power.

Origins of Islam

"One community" was a revolutionary notion for the disparate peoples of Arabia (today Saudi Arabia), who first converted to this new religion in the course of the early seventh century. Pre-Islamic Arabia supported Bedouins: nomads (the word "arab" is derived from the most prestigious of these, the camel-herders) and semi-nomads. But by far the majority of the population was neither; it was sedentary. To the southwest, where rain was adequate, farmers worked the soil. Elsewhere people settled at oases, where they raised date palms (a highly prized food); some of these communities were prosperous enough to support merchants and artisans. Both the nomads and the settled population were organized as tribes—groups whose members thought themselves ultimately bound together by a common father.

Herding goats, sheep, or camels, the nomads and semi-nomads lived in small groups, largely making do with the products (leather, milk, meat) of their animals, and raiding one another for booty—including women. "Manliness" was the chief Bedouin virtue; it meant not sexual prowess (though polygyny—having more than one wife at a time—was practiced) but bravery, generosity, and a keen sense of honor. Lacking written literature, the nomads were proud of their oral culture of storytelling and poetry.

Islam began as a religion of the sedentary, but it soon found support and military strength among the nomads. It began at Mecca, a commercial center, the launching pad of caravans organized to sell Bedouin products—mainly leather goods and raisins—to the more urbanized areas at the Syrian border. (See Map 2.2.) Mecca was also a holy place. Its shrine, the Ka'ba, was rimmed with hundreds of idols. Within its sacred precincts, where war and violence were prohibited, pilgrims bartered and traded.

Within this commercial and religious center, Muhammad, the prophet of Islam, was born in about 570. Orphaned as a child, he came under the guardianship of his uncle, a leader of the Quraysh tribe, which dominated Mecca and controlled access to the Ka'ba. Muhammad became a trader, married, had children, and seemed comfortable and happy. But he sought something more: he would sometimes leave home, escaping to a nearby cave to pray.

Map 2.2: The Islamic World by 750

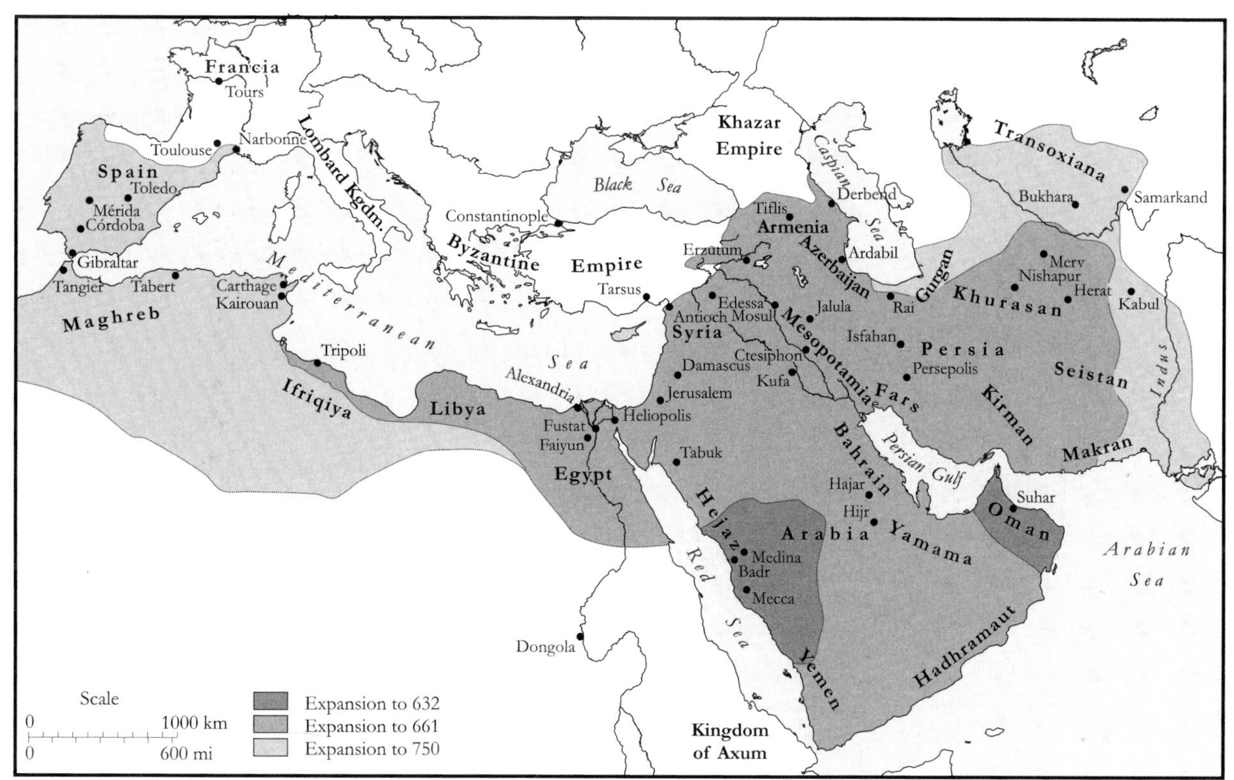

In about 610, on one such retreat, Muhammad heard a voice calling on him to worship God (the Arabic word for God is Allah). After he solemnly assented, the voice gave him further messages—they continued, intermittently, for the rest of his life. Later, when they had been written down and arranged—a process that was completed in the seventh century, but after Muhammad's death—these messages became the Qur'an, the holy book of Islam. The Qur'an is understood to be God's revelation as told to Muhammad by the angel Gabriel, then recited in turn by Muhammad to others. Its first chapter—or sura—is the Fatihah:

> In the name of Allah, most benevolent, ever-merciful.
> All praise be to Allah,
> 1. Lord of all the worlds.
> 2. Most beneficent, ever-merciful,
> 3. King of the Day of Judgement.
> 4. You alone we worship, and to You alone turn for help.
> 5. Guide us (O Lord) to the path that is straight,
> 6. The path of those You have blessed,
> 7. Not of those who have earned Your anger, nor those who have gone astray.[1]

The Qur'an continues with a far longer sura, followed by others (114 in all) of gradually decreasing length. For Muslims the Qur'an covers the gamut of human experience—the sum total of history, prophecy, and the legal and moral code by which men and women should live—as well as the life to come.

Banning infanticide, Islam gave girls and women new dignity. It allowed for polygyny, but this was limited to four wives at one time, all to be treated equally. It mandated dowries and offered some female inheritance rights. At first women even prayed with men, though that practice ended in the eighth century.

It is striking that Islam emphasized the nuclear family at just about the same moment as the Byzantines did. In the Arab world this new emphasis worked to downgrade the tribe. In Islam there are three essential social facts: the individual, God, and the *ummah*, the community of the faithful. There are no intermediaries between the divine and human realms, no priests, Eucharist, relics, or icons.

Not all welcomed the new religion. Muhammad's insistence that paganism be abandoned threatened Quraysh tribal interests, so bound up with the Ka'ba. Its leaders tried to thwart his missionary efforts. When some of Muhammad's followers at Medina, an oasis about 200 miles to the northeast of Mecca, invited him to join them, he agreed. In 622 he made the *Hijra*, or flight from Mecca to Medina, where he was greeted not only as a religious but also as a secular leader. This joining of the political and religious spheres set the pattern for Islamic government thereafter. After Muhammad's death, the year of the *Hijra*, 622, became the year 1 of the Islamic calendar, marking the establishment of the Islamic era.

Muhammad consolidated his position as a religious and secular leader by asserting hegemony over three important groups. At Medina itself he took control by ousting and sometimes killing his main competitors, the Jewish clans of the city. With regard to the Meccans, to whom he was related, he fought a series of battles; the battle of Badr (624), waged against a Meccan caravan, marked the first Islamic military victory. After several other campaigns, Muhammad triumphed and took over Mecca in 630, offering leniency to most of its inhabitants, who in turn converted to Islam. Meanwhile, Muhammad allied himself with numerous nomadic groups, adding their contingents to his army. Warfare was thus integrated into the new religion as a part of the duty of Muslims to strive in the ways of God; *jihad*, often translated as "holy war," in fact means "striving." Through a combination of military might, conversion, and negotiation, Muhammad united many, though by no means all, Arabic tribes under his leadership by the time of his death in 632.

In time, new, defining practices for Muslims were instituted. There was the *zakat*, a tax to be used for charity; Ramadan, a month of fasting to mark the battle of Badr; the *hajj*, a yearly pilgrimage to Mecca; and the *salat*, formal worship at least three times a day (later increased to five), including the *shahadah*, or profession of faith: "there is no god but God, and Muhammad is His prophet." The place of worship was known as a "mosque." Breaking with Jewish practices, Muhammad had the Muslims turn their prayers away from Jerusalem, the center of Jewish worship, and towards Mecca instead. Detailed regulations for these practices, sometimes called the "five pillars of Islam," were worked out in the eighth and early ninth centuries.

Out of Arabia

"Strive, O Prophet," says the Qur'an, "against the unbelievers and the hypocrites, and deal with them firmly. Their final abode is Hell; And what a wretched destination." Cutting across tribal allegiances, Muhammad's *ummah* was itself a formidable "supertribe" dedicated to victory over the enemies of God. Led by caliphs, literally the "successors" of Muhammad, armies of Muslims moved into Sassanid and Byzantine territories, toppling or crippling the once great ancient empires. (See Map 2.2.) They captured the Persian capital, Ctesiphon, in 637 and continued eastward to take Persepolis in 648, Nishapur in 651, and then, beyond Persia, Kabul in 664, and Samarkand in 710. To the west, they picked off, one by one, the great cities of the Byzantine empire: Antioch and Damascus in 635, Alexandria in 642, Carthage

Plate 2.2: The Great Mosque at Damascus (8th cent.). Mosaics such as these, symbolizing Umayyad rule over civilization (with its buildings and cities) and nature (with its rivers and vegetation) once covered most of the interior and exterior walls of the Great Mosque at Damascus. Very likely Byzantine mosaicists were imported to do the work; certainly the style is Byzantine. Thus the Islamic world under the Umayyads absorbed and made its own the traditions of Rome.

in 698. By the beginning of the eighth century, Islamic warriors held sway from Spain to India.

It was an astonishing triumph, but one not hard to understand with the benefit of hindsight. The Arabs were formidable fighters, and their enemies were relatively weak. The Persian and Byzantine empires were militarily exhausted from their years of fighting one another. Nor were their populations particularly loyal; some—Jews and Christians in Persia, Monophysites in Syria—even welcomed the invaders. In large measure they were proved right: the Muslims made no attempt to convert them. Setting up "garrison cities" to guard their conquests, the new Islamic rulers taxed their subjects but did not persecute them. The men and women of North Africa and Spain went back to work and play much as they had done before the invasions. Safe in his monastery near Jerusalem, Saint John of Damascus (*c.*657-*c.*749) thundered against iconoclasm. He would never have been able to do so in the Byzantine empire. Maps of the Islamic conquest divide the world into Muslims and Christians. But the "Islamic world" was only slightly Islamic; Muslims constituted a minority of the population. Even as their religion came to predominate, they were themselves absorbed, at least to some degree, into the cultures that they had conquered.

The Culture of the Umayyads

Dissension, triumph, and disappointment accompanied the naming of Muhammad's successors. The caliphs were not chosen from the old tribal elites but rather from a new inner circle of men close to Muhammad. The first two caliphs, Abu-Bakr and Umar, ruled without serious opposition. They were the fathers of two of Muhammad's wives. But the third caliph, Uthman, husband of two of Muhammad's daughters and great-grandson of the Quraysh leader Umayyah, aroused resentment. (See Genealogy 2.1: Muhammad's Relatives and Successors.) His family had come late to Islam, and some of its members had even once persecuted Muhammad. The Umayyad opponents supported Ali, the husband of Muhammad's daughter Fatimah. After a group of discontented soldiers murdered Uthman, civil war broke out between the Umayyads and Ali's faction. It ended when Ali was killed in 661 by one of his own erstwhile supporters. The caliphate remained thereafter in Umayyad hands until 750.

Yet the *Shi'ah*, the faction of Ali, did not forget their leader. They became the "Shi'ites," faithful to Ali's dynasty, mourning his martyrdom, shunning the "mainstream" caliphs of the other Muslims ("Sunni" Muslims, as they were later called), awaiting the arrival of the true leader—the *imam*—who would spring from the house of Ali.

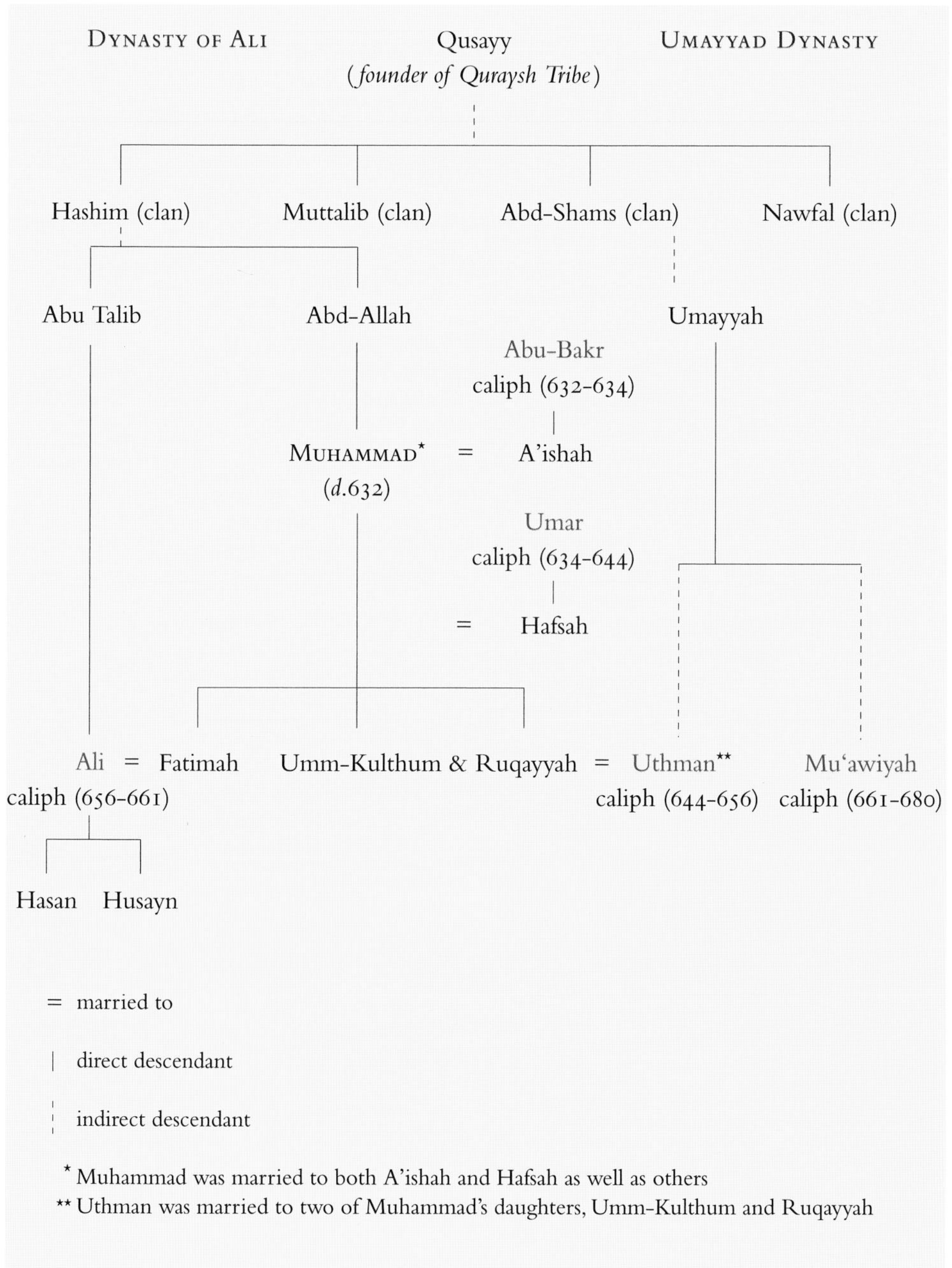

Genealogy 2.1: Muhammad's Relatives and Successors

Scale
0
500 km
0
300 mi
Scotland
Ireland
Bernicia
Lindisfarne
Hadrian's Wall
Jarrow
Wearmouth
Whitby
Northumbria
Deira
Anglo-Saxon England
Wales
Mercia
East Anglia
Hwicce
Thames
West Saxons
London
Kent
North Sea
Baltic Sea
Elbe
Saxony
Dorestad
Oder
Quentovic
Austrasia
Moselle
Seine
Paris
Metz
Brittany
Neustria
Rhine
Danube
Bavaria
Loire
Tours
Alamannia
Francia
Poitiers
Burgundy
Aquitaine
Lombard Kingdom
Pavia
Gascony
Kingdom of Asturias
Basques
Roncesvalles
Pamplona
Ebro
Septimania
(To Francia, 751)
Provence
Exarchate
Pentapolis
Adriatic Sea
Duchy of Spoleto
Islamic Spain
Corsica
Rome
Duchy of Rome
Duchy of Benevento
Sardinia
Tyrrhenian Sea
Calabria
Mediterranean Sea
Sicily

Meanwhile, the Umayyads made Damascus, an important Syrian city, their capital. Here they adopted many of the institutions of the culture that they had conquered: they issued coins, employed former Byzantine officials as administrators, and hired artists trained in the Byzantine style and expert in the Byzantine medium of mosaic to decorate their new Great Mosque. (See Plate 2.2.) It is true that Arabic, the language of the Qur'an, eventually became the new official language. But into this language began to flow translations of Greek writings, bringing the new culture into contact with older traditions. At the same time, Muslim scholars determined the definitive form of the Qur'an and compiled pious narratives about the Prophet's sayings, or *hadith*. In the course of the seventh and eighth centuries, a new literate class—composed mainly of the old Persian and Syrian elite now converted to Islam and schooled in Arabic—created new forms of prose and poetry. A commercial revolution in China helped to vivify commerce in the Islamic world. At hand was a cultural flowering in a land of prosperity.

Map 2.3 (facing page): Western Europe, *c.*750

THE MAKING OF WESTERN EUROPE

No reasonable person in the year 750 would have predicted that, of the three heirs of the Roman empire, Western Europe would be the one eventually to dominate the world. While Byzantium cut back, reorganized, and forged ahead, while Islam spread its language and rule over territory that stretched nearly twice the length of the United States today, Western Europe remained an impoverished backwater. Fragmented politically and linguistically, its cities (left over from Roman antiquity) mere shells, its tools primitive, its infrastructure—what was left of Roman roads, schools, and bridges—collapsing, Europe lacked identity and cohesion. That these and other strengths did indeed eventually develop over a long period of time is a tribute in part to the survival of some Roman traditions and institutions and in part to the inventive ways in which people adapted those institutions and made up new ones to meet their needs and desires.

Impoverishment and Its Variations

Taking in the whole of Western Europe around this time means dwelling long on its variety. Dominating the scene was Francia. To its south were Spain (ruled first by the Visigoths, and then, after *c.*715, by the Muslims) and Italy (divided between the pope, the Byzantines, and the Lombards). To the north, joined to rather than separated from the Continent by the lick of water called the English Channel, the British Isles were home to a plethora of tiny kingdoms, about three quarters of which were native ("Celtic") and the last quarter Germanic ("Anglo-Saxons").

There were clear differences between the Romanized south—Spain, Italy, southern Francia—and the north. (See Map 2.3.) Travelers going from Anglo-Saxon England to Rome would have noticed them. There were many such travelers: some, like the churchman Benedict Biscop, were voluntary pilgrims; others were slaves on forced march. Making their way across England, voyagers such as these would pass fenced wooden farmsteads, each with a rectangular "hall" for eating and sleeping, a few outbuildings serving as sheds, and perhaps a sunken house, its floor below the level of the soil, its damp atmosphere suitable for weaving. (Even royal complexes were made of wood and looked much like humble farmsteads: see Figure 2.2.) Most farms were built in clusters of four to five, making up tiny hamlets. The farmstead, including its land, represented a family farm. Fields were planted with barley (used to make a thick and nourishing beer) as well as oats, wheat, and rye. The richest peasants had iron-coulter plows to turn the thick and heavy soils. There were many animals: sheep, goats, horses, cattle, pigs, and dogs. Little of this belonged outright to the men and women who farmed the soil and tended the animals. For the most part, great lords—under whose "protection" the workers toiled—owned the land and commanded a share of the produce. But all was not pastoral or agricultural in England: here and there, and especially towards the south, were commercial settlements—real emporia.

Crossing the Channel, travelers would enter northern Francia, also dotted with emporia (such as Quentovic and Dorestad) but also boasting old Roman cities, now mainly religious centers. Paris, for example, was to a large extent an agglomeration of churches: Montmartre, Saint-Laurent, Saint-Martin-des-Champs—perhaps 35 churches were jammed into an otherwise nearly abandoned city. Outside, the countryside was farmed by villagers who lived much like their Anglo-Saxon counterparts, though here and there stone was beginning to be used to construct farm buildings. Moving eastward, our voyagers would pass through thick forests and land more often used as pasture for animals than for cereal cultivation. Along the Moselle River they would find villages with fields, meadows, woods, and water courses, a few supplied with mills and churches. Some of the peasants in these villages would be tenants or slaves of a lord; others would be independent farmers who owned all or part of the land that they cultivated.

Southern Francia and much of Italy, by contrast, would have been home to vineyards and olive groves. Here the great hulks of Roman cities, with their amphitheaters, baths, and walls, dominated the landscape, though (as at Byzantium) their populations were much diminished. The countryside here had once been organized into great estates farmed by slave gangs. There were still a few of these, but for the most part slaves and other peasants were settled on their own plots of land, though, as elsewhere, most were not landowners but rather tenant farmers, owing a proportion of their produce to an aristocratic lord. Fewer animals roamed here; there was more emphasis on grain. The soil was lighter, easily worked with scratch plows—if any were to be had! Our travelers would normally have seen peasants using only hoes, spades, and weeders.

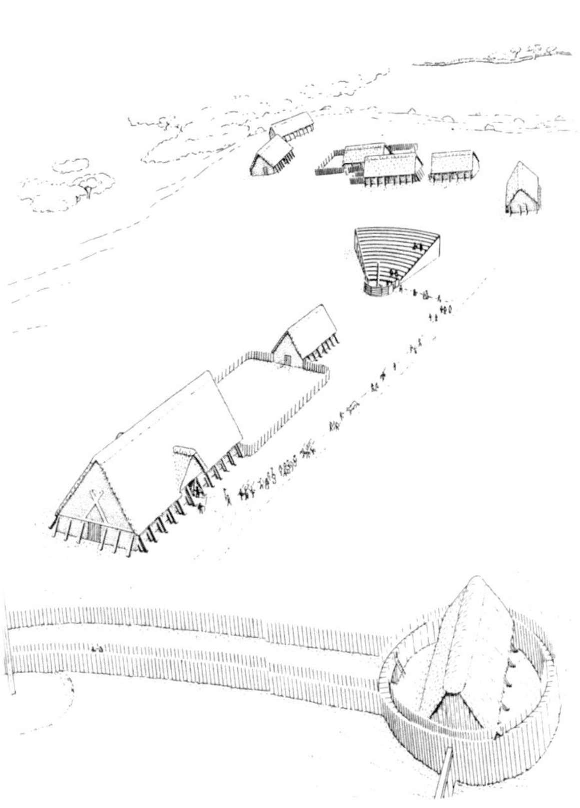

Figure 2.2: Yeavering, Northumberland. In this artist's reconstruction of an early seventh-century Anglo-Saxon royal complex in the north of England, the use of one-story rectangular halls reflects the architecture of the previous Roman-British settlers in the region.

By 700, there was little left of the old long-distance Mediterranean commerce of the ancient Roman world. But, although this was an impoverished society, it was not without wealth or lively patterns of exchange. In the first place, money was still minted, but increasingly in silver rather than gold. The change of metal was due in part to a shortage of gold in Europe. But it was also a nod to the importance of small-scale commercial transactions—sales of surplus wine from a vineyard, say, for which small coins were the most practical. In the second place, North Sea merchant-sailors—carrying, for example, ceramic plates and glass vessels—had begun to link northern Francia, the east coast of England, Scandinavia, and the Baltic Sea. Brisk trade gave rise to new emporia and revivified older Roman cities along the coasts. In the third place, a gift economy, that is, an economy of give and take, was flourishing. Booty was taken, tribute demanded, harvests hoarded, and coins struck, all to be redistributed to friends, followers, dependents, and the church. Kings and other rich and powerful men and women amassed gold, silver, ornaments, and jewelry in their treasuries and grain in their storehouses to give out in ceremonies that marked their power and added to their prestige. Even the rents that peasants paid to their lords, mainly in kind, were often couched as "gifts."

Politics and Culture

If variations were plentiful in even so basic a matter as material and farming conditions, the differences were magnified by political and cultural conditions. We need now to take Europe kingdom by kingdom.

Francia

Francia comes first because it was the major player, a real political entity that dominated what is today France, Belgium, the Netherlands, Luxembourg, and much of Germany. In the seventh century, it was divided into three related kingdoms—Neustria, Austrasia, Burgundy—each of which included parts of a fourth, southern region, Aquitaine. By 700, however, the political distinctions between them were melting, and Francia was becoming one kingdom.

The line of Clovis—the Merovingians—ruled these kingdoms. (See Genealogy 2.2: The Merovingians.) The dynasty owed its longevity to biological good fortune and excellent political sense: it allied itself with the major lay aristocrats and ecclesiastical authorities of Gaul—men and women of high status, enormous wealth, and marked local power. To that alliance, the kings brought their own sources of power: a skeletal Roman administrative apparatus, family properties, appropriated lands once belonging to the Roman state, and the profits and prestige of leadership in war.

The royal court—which moved with the kings as they traveled from one palace to another, as they had no capital city—was the focus of political life. Here gathered talented young men, clerics-on-the-rise, aristocratic scions. The most important courtiers had official positions: there was, for example, the referendary and the cupbearer. Highest of all was the "mayor of the palace," who controlled access to the king and brokered deals with aristocratic factions.

Queens were an important part of the court as well. One of them, Balthild (*d.*680), had once been among the unwilling travelers from England. Purchased there as a slave by the mayor of the palace of Neustria, she parlayed her beauty into marriage with the king himself. (Merovingian kings often married slaves or women captured in war. By avoiding wives with powerful kindred, they staved off challenges to their royal authority.) Balthild's biographer described how kindly she cared for the young men at court: "to the princes she showed herself a mother, to the priests as a daughter, and to the young and the adolescents as the best possible nurse." When her husband, King Clovis II, died, Balthild served as regent for her minor sons, acting, in effect, as king during this time. She arranged, "through the advice of the great magnates," (as her biographer put it) that one of her sons become king of Austrasia, and she maintained the prestige of the royal line through her extraordinary generosity:

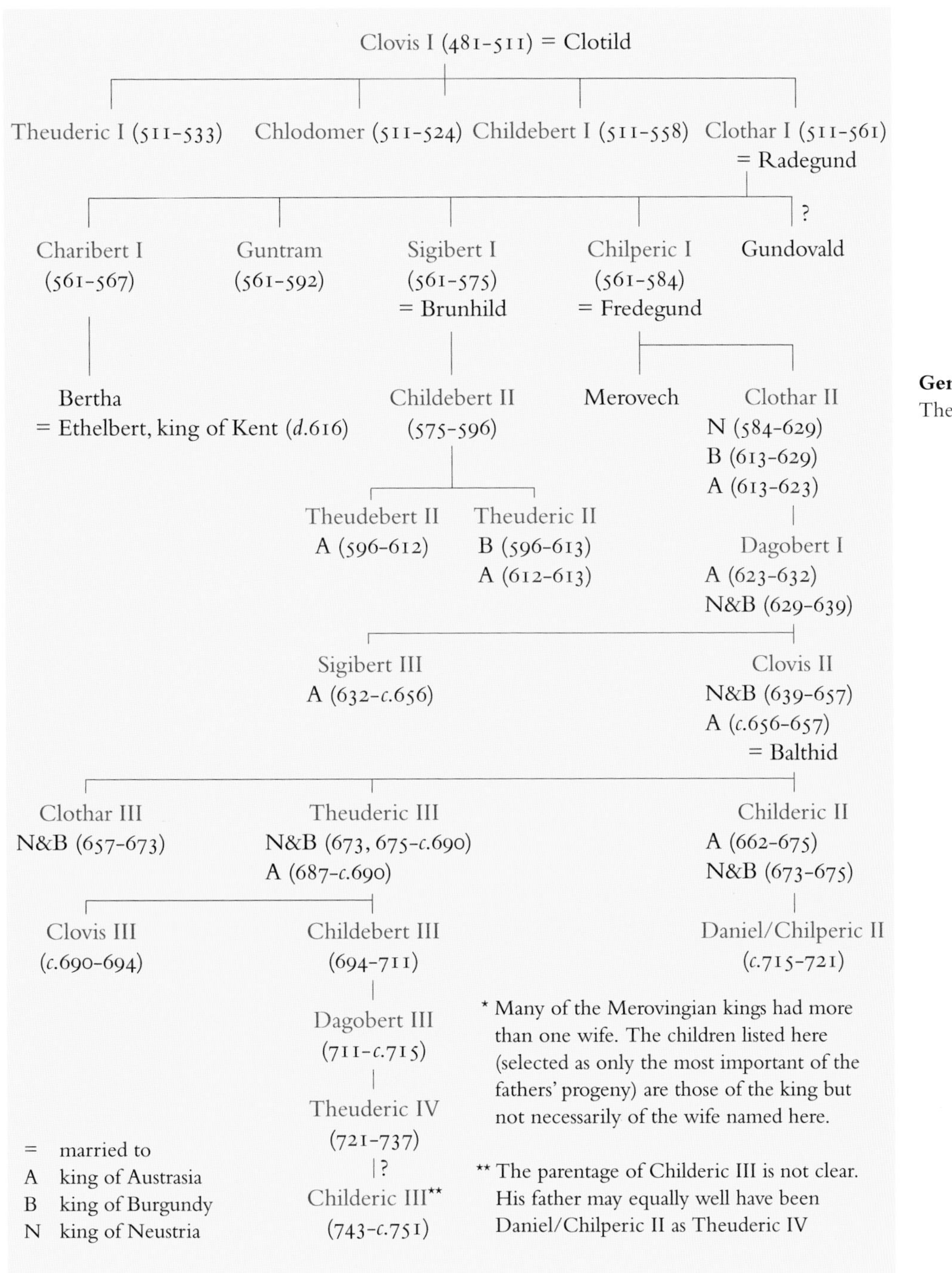

Geneology 2.2: The Merovingians*

"Who, then, is able to say how many and how great were the sources of income, the entire farms and the large forests she gave up by donating them to the establishments of religious men ...?"[2] By the end of her life, she was counted a saint.

Important as the court was as a focus of power, aristocrats usually stayed at "home," though in fact they might (like kings) have many homes, scattered in many regions. Tending to their estates, honing their skills in the hunt, aristocratic men regularly led armed retinues to war. They proved their worth in the regular taking of booty and rewarded their faithful followers afterwards at generous banquets.

Or they bedded down. The bed—or rather the production of children—was the focus of marriage, the key to the survival of aristocratic families and the transmission of their property and power. Though churchmen had many ideas about the value of marriage, they had nothing to do with the ceremony; no one married in church. Rather, marriage was a family affair, and a very expensive one. There was more than one form of marriage: in the most formal, the husband-to-be gave to his future bride a handsome dowry of clothes, bedding, livestock, and land. Then, after the marriage was consummated, he gave his wife a morning gift of furniture and perhaps the keys to the house. Very rich men often had, in addition to their wife, one or more "concubines" at the same time. These enjoyed a less formal type of marriage, receiving a morning gift but no dowry.

The wife's role was above all to maintain the family. We have already seen how important the metaphor of motherhood was for Balthild, even in connection with unrelated men at court. A woman passed from one family (that of her birth) to the next (that of her marriage) by parental fiat. When they married, women left the legal protection of their father for that of their husband. Did women have any freedom of action? Yes. For one thing, they had considerable control over their dowries. Some participated in family land transactions: sales, donations, exchanges. Upon the death of their husbands, widows received a portion of the household property. Although inheritances generally went from fathers to sons, many fathers left bequests to their daughters, who could then dispose of their property more or less as they liked. In 632, for example, the nun Burgundofara, who had never married, drew up a will giving to her monastery the land, slaves, vineyards, pastures, and forests that she had received from her two brothers and her father. In the same will, she gave other property near Paris to her brothers and sister.

Burgundofara's generous piety was extraordinary only in degree. The world of kings, queens, and aristocrats intersected with that of the church. The arrival (*c.*590) on the Continent of the fierce Irish monastic reformer Saint Columbanus (543–615) marked a new level of association between the two. Columbanus's brand of monasticism, which stressed exile, devotion, and discipline, made a powerful impact on Merovingian aristocrats. They flocked to the monasteries that he established in both

Francia and Italy, and they founded new ones themselves on their own lands in the countryside. In Francia alone there was an explosion of monasteries: between the years 600 and 700, an astonishing 320 new houses were established, most of them outside of the cities. Some of the new monks and nuns were grown men and women, others were young children, given to a monastery by their parents. This latter practice, called oblation, was not only accepted but even considered essential for the spiritual well-being of both children and their families.

Irish monasticism introduced aristocrats on the Continent to a deepened religious devotion. Those who did not actively join or patronize a monastery still read, or listened to others read, books preaching penance, and they chanted the Psalms. The Merovingian laity developed a culture of domestic piety at about the same time as the Byzantines did.

Deepened piety did not, in this case, lead to the persecution of others—something that (as we shall see) happened in later centuries. In particular, where Jews were settled in Western Europe—along the Mediterranean coast and inland, in Burgundy, for example—they remained integrated into every aspect of secular life. They used Hebrew in worship, but otherwise they spoke the same languages as Christians and used Latin in their legal documents. Their children were often given the same names as Christians (and Christians often took Biblical names, such as Solomon); they dressed as everyone else dressed; and they engaged in the same occupations. Many Jews planted and tended vineyards, in part because of the importance of wine in synagogue services, in part because the surplus could easily be sold. Some were rich landowners, with slaves and dependent peasants working for them; others were independent peasants of modest means. While there certainly were urban Jews, most, like their Christian neighbors, lived on the land.

The British Isles

Roman Britain had been as habituated to barbarian defenders—in this case Saxons—as the rest of the empire. When all the Roman garrisons left England in 410 for service elsewhere, the Saxons gradually took over in the southeast, helped by massive invasions of their brethren from the Continent. The old and new tribes together are called "Anglo-Saxons"; where they conquered—in the southeastern lowlands of the British Isles—most Christians were absorbed as slaves into the pagan culture of the invaders. Elsewhere—in what is today the north and west of England, Scotland, and Ireland—Celtic kingdoms survived. Wales was already Christian when, in the course of the fifth century, Ireland and Scotland were converted by missionaries. (Saint Patrick, apostle to the Irish, is only the most famous of these.) These Celtic kingdoms supported relatively non-hierarchical church organizations. Rural monasteries often served as the seats of bishoprics as well as centers of population and settlement. Abbots and abbesses, often members of powerful families, enjoyed considerable power and prestige.

The Anglo-Saxon quadrant was reintroduced to Christianity from two different directions: the Celtic north and the Roman south. The Anglo-Saxon king of Northumbria Oswald (*r.*633-641), a convert to Christianity during his period of exile in Ireland, called for missionaries to come to his kingdom to preach. Monks and a bishop arrived from Ireland, setting up a monastery at Lindisfarne, just off the coast of Northumbria, and, as the historian and monk Bede (673?-735) put it about a century later,

Plate 2.3 (facing page): Belt Buckle from Sutton Hoo (early 7th cent.). Beginning in 1939 and continuing through the 1980s, archaeologists excavated seventeen curious mounds at Sutton Hoo, a barren stretch of land in southeast England. Their finds included numerous Anglo-Saxon cremations and burials, the bones of horses, spears, shields, helmets, large open boats, jewelry, silver bowls, and many other objects, including this heavy buckle made of gold.

> from that time, as the days went by, many came from the country of the Irish into Britain and to those English kingdoms over which Oswald reigned, preaching the word of faith with great devotion .... Churches were built in various places and the people flocked together with joy to hear the Word.[3]

In the south, Christianity arrived from the Continent, most spectacularly in 597 when missionaries sent from Rome by Pope Gregory the Great came to the court of King Ethelbert of Kent (*d.*616). Under their leader, Augustine (not the fifth-century bishop of Hippo!), the missionaries converted the king. He was primed for the change, having long before married a Christian Merovingian princess, who arrived in Kent with a bishop in her entourage.

Augustine had in mind more than the conversion of a king: he wanted to set up an English church on the Roman model, with ties to the pope and a clear hierarchy. He divided England into territorial units (dioceses) headed by an archbishop and bishops. Augustine himself became archbishop of Canterbury. There he set up the model English ecclesiastical complex: a cathedral, a monastery, and a school to train young clerics.

There was nothing easy or quick about the conversion of England. Everywhere paganism maintained its attractive hold. And once converted, as we have seen, the Christians of the north and south differed in their interpretation of the religious life and in the organization of the church. Above all, they clashed in their calculations of the date of Easter. Everyone agreed that they could not be saved unless they observed the day of Christ's Resurrection properly and on the right date. But what was the right date? Each side was wedded to its own view. A turning point came at the Synod of Whitby, organized in 664 by the Northumbrian King Oswy to decide between the Roman and Irish dates. When Oswy became convinced that Rome spoke with the very voice of Saint Peter, the heavenly doorkeeper, he opted for the Roman calculation of the date and embraced the Roman church as a whole.

As Christianization proceeded in Anglo-Saxon England, a particularly learned and eclectic clerical culture emerged there. The pull of Rome—symbol, in these clerics' view, of the Christian religion itself—was palpable. Benedict Biscop (*c.*630-690), a Northumbrian aristocrat-turned-abbot and founder of two important English monasteries, Wearmouth and Jarrow, made numerous arduous trips to Rome. He brought back saints' relics, liturgical vestments, and even a cantor to teach his monks the proper melodies in a time before written musical notation existed. Above all, he went to Rome to fetch books. In Anglo-Saxon England, as in Ireland, both of which lacked a strong classical foundation, books were precious and exotic objects.

From this fact came a flowering of manuscript illumination. The Anglo-Saxons, like other barbarian (and, indeed, Celtic) tribes, had artistic traditions particularly well suited to decorating flat surfaces. Belt-buckles, helmet nose-pieces, brooches and other sorts of jewelry of the rich were adorned with semi-precious stones and enlivened with decorative patterns, often made up of intertwining snake-like animals. A particularly fine example is a buckle from Sutton Hoo (see Plate 2.3), perhaps the greatest archaeological find for the Anglo-Saxon period. The style was quickly adapted to Christian needs.

Books, which were artefacts of Roman origin, inspired Anglo-Saxon artists to combine their decorative traditions with the classical pictorial style. The resulting illumination was perfectly suited to flat pages. Consider the Lindisfarne Gospels, probably made at the monastery of Lindisfarne in the first third of the eighth century. (The Gospels are the four canonical accounts of Christ's life and death in the New Testament.) The artist of this sumptuous book was clearly uniting Germanic, Irish, and Roman artistic traditions when he introduced each Gospel with three full-page illustrations: first, a portrait of the "author" (the evangelist); then an entirely ornamental "carpet" page; finally, the beginning words of the Gospel text. Plates 2.4 to 2.6 illustrate the sequence for the Gospel of Luke. The figure of Luke (see Plate 2.4), though clearly human, floats in space. His "throne" is a square of ribbons, his drapery a series of loopy lines. The artist captures the essence of an otherworldly saint without the distraction of three-dimensionality. The carpet page (see Plate 2.5), with its interlace panels, has some of the features of the Sutton Hoo brooch as well as Irish interlace patterns. It is more than decorative,

Plate 2.4

+ lucas uitulus ⁊

on ginneð god spell æft lucas

incipit euangelium secundum lucan ...

forðon

QUONIAM

æc forð

QUIDEM

monigo cunnendo

MULTI CONA

woeron ðte him ge

TI SUNT ORDINA

endebrednudon ðitt gesaga

RE NARRATIONEM

however: the design clearly evokes a cross. The next page (see Plate 2.6) begins with a great letter, Q (for the first word, "quoniam"), as richly decorated as the cross of the carpet page; gradually, in the course of the next few words, the ornamentation diminishes. In this way, after the fanfare of author and carpet pages, the reader is ushered into the Gospel text itself.

The amalgamation of traditions in England is perhaps most clearly illustrated by the so-called Franks Casket, probably made in Northumbria around the same time as—or a bit later than—the Lindisfarne Gospels. Carved out of whale bone, this box is decorated with scenes from Roman, Jewish, Christian, and Germanic tales. On the left side of the front panel (Plate 2.7), the princess Beadohild is tricked by Weyland the Smith into bearing his son, the hero Widia. Weyland, an otherworldly figure of incredible skill at the forge, was celebrated in the Anglo-Saxon poems *Beowulf* and *Deor*. On the right side of the same panel, the Magi bring gifts to Christ, seated on Mary's lap. That, of course, was a story from the Gospels. The two scenes thus pull together two traditions, playing on the theme of mothers who bear the son of an otherworldly father.

Just as the Anglo-Saxons held on to their legends after they were Christianized, so they retained their language. In England, the vernacular—the language of the people, as opposed to Latin—was quickly turned into a written language and used in every aspect of English life, from government to entertainment. But much the same was true in Ireland; the uniqueness of Anglo-Saxon culture should not be exaggerated. The model for the Franks Casket probably came from a similar one carved earlier in Francia or Italy, and certainly a similar cultural creativity and fusion of diverse elements was equally characteristic of early medieval Ireland and Scotland.

The South: Spain and Italy

It is just possible that the exemplar for the Franks Casket came from Spain, which boasted an equally lively mix of cultures. Here, especially in the south and east, some Roman cities had continued to flourish after the Visigothic invasions. Merchants from Byzantium regularly visited Mérida, for example (see Map 2.2), and the sixth-century bishops there constructed lavish churches and set up a system of regular food distribution. Under King Leovigild (*r.*569-586) all of Spain came under Visigothic control. Under his son Reccared (*r.*586-601), the monarchy converted from Arian to Catholic Christianity. This event (587) cemented the ties between the king and the Hispano-Roman population, which included the great landowners and leading bishops. Two years later, at the Third Council of Toledo, most of the Arian bishops followed their king by announcing their conversion to Catholicism, and the assembled churchmen enacted decrees for a united church in Spain.

Preceding pages:

Plate 2.4: Saint Luke, Lindisfarne Gospels (1st third of 8th cent.?). Inspired by Late Roman traditions, the artist—who was also the scribe of this book—introduced the Gospel of Luke with an author's portrait. The winged calf perched on Luke's halo is his symbol.

Plate 2.5: Carpet Page, Lindisfarne Gospels (1st third of 8th cent.?). Anglo-Saxon and Celtic artistic ornamental traditions lie behind this elaborate cross, which follows Luke's portrait in **Plate 2.4** and faces the first text page depicted in **Plate 2.6**.

Plate 2.6 (facing page): First Text Page, Gospel of Saint Luke, Lindisfarne Gospels (1st third of 8th cent.?). The third page in the Luke Gospel sequence begins the text itself: "Quoniam quidem multi conati sunt ordinare narrationem," "Since many have undertaken to put in narrative order..."

Plate 2.7: Franks Casket (1st half of 8th cent.). Made up of panels of carved whalebone, the Franks Casket combines not only various literary traditions but also some artistic ones. The whole idea of having figural scenes on a casket was classical, but the style here is Anglo-Saxon. Compare the style of cloaks and figures on the left (the Weyland scene) with Luke in **Plate 2.4**.

Thereafter, the bishops and kings of Spain cooperated to a degree unprecedented in other regions. While the king gave the churchmen free rein to set up their own hierarchy (with the bishop of Toledo at the top) and to meet regularly at synods to regulate and reform the church, the bishops in turn supported the king. They even anointed him, daubing him with holy oil in a ritual that paralleled the ordination of priests and echoed the anointment of kings in the Old Testament. While the bishops in this way made the king's cause their own, their lay counterparts, the great landowners, helped supply the king with troops.

Unlike the Merovingians, the Visigothic kings were not able to establish a stable dynasty. The minority of a king's son almost always sparked revolts by rival families, and the child's deposition was often accompanied by wholesale slaughter of his father's followers and confiscation of their lands. This may help to explain why Visigothic courtiers painted a particularly lustrous picture of their kings, resplendent and dazzling, their throne "radiant with shining gold," and why royal laws punished treason by death or blinding.[4]

It was precisely the centralization of the Visigothic kingdom that proved its undoing. In 711, a small raiding party of Arabs killed the Visigothic king and thereby dealt the whole state a decisive blow. Between 712 and 715, armies led by Arabs took over the peninsula.

But this was less an Arab or Islamic conquest than a Berber one. The generals who led the invasion of Spain were Arab, to be sure; but their fighters were Berbers from North Africa. Perhaps a million people settled in Spain in the wake of the invasions, the Arabs generally taking the better lands in the south, the Berbers getting less rich properties in the center and north. Few Berbers were Muslims, while most of the conquered population consisted of Christians (and some Jews). The Islamic presence, then, was minuscule. The history of Spain would for many centuries thereafter be one of conversion, acculturation, and war.

Unlike Visigothic Spain, Lombard Italy presented no united front. In the center of the peninsula was the papacy, always hostile to the Lombard kings of the north. (See Map 2.3.) To Rome's east and south were the dukes of Benevento and Spoleto. Although theoretically the Lombard king's officers, in fact they were virtually independent rulers. Although many Lombards were Catholics, others, including important kings and dukes, were Arian. The "official" religion varied with the ruler in power. Rather than signal a major political event, then, the conversion of the Lombards to Catholic Christianity occurred gradually, ending only in the late seventh century. Partly as a result of this slow development, the Lombard kings, unlike the Visigoths, Franks, or even Anglo-Saxons, never enlisted the wholehearted support of any particular group of churchmen.

Yet the Lombard kings did not lack advantages. They controlled extensive estates, and they made use of the Roman institutions that survived in Italy. The Lombard kings made the cities their administrative bases, assigning dukes to rule from them and setting up one, Pavia, as their capital. Recalling emperors like Constantine and Justinian, the kings built churches and monasteries at Pavia, maintained city walls, and minted coins. Revenues from tolls, sales taxes, port duties, and court fines filled their coffers.

Emboldened by their attainments in the north, the Lombard kings tried to make some headway against the independent dukes of southern Italy. But that threatened to surround Rome with a unified Lombard kingdom. The pope, fearing for his own position, called on the Franks for help.

The Pope: Man in the Middle

By the end of the sixth century, the pope's position was ambiguous. Bishop of Rome, he wielded real secular power within the city as well as a measure of spiritual leadership farther afield. Yet in other ways he was just a subordinate of Byzantium. Pope Gregory the Great (590-604), whom we have already met a number of times, laid the foundations for the papacy's later spiritual and temporal ascendancy. (See Popes and Antipopes to 1500 on pp. 216-19.) During Gregory's tenure, the pope became the greatest landowner in Italy; he organized Rome's defense and paid for its army; he heard court cases, made treaties, and provided welfare services. The missionary expedition he sent to England was only a small part of his involvement in the rest of Europe. A prolific author of spiritual works and Biblical exegesis, Gregory digested and simplified the ideas of Church Fathers such as Saint Augustine, making them accessible to a wider audience. His practical handbook for clerics, *Pastoral Care*, went hand-in-hand with his practical church reforms in Italy, where he tried to impose regular episcopal elections and enforce clerical celibacy.

On the other hand, even Gregory was only one of many bishops in the former Roman empire, now ruled from Constantinople. For a long time the emperor's views on dogma, discipline, and church administration prevailed at Rome. However, this authority began to unravel in the seventh century. In 692, Emperor Justinian II convened a council that determined 102 rules for the church. When he sent the rules to Rome for papal endorsement, Pope Sergius I (687-701) found most of them acceptable, but he was unwilling to agree to the whole because it permitted priestly marriages (which the Roman church did not want to allow), and it prohibited fasting on Saturdays in Lent (which the Roman church required). Outraged by Sergius's refusal, Justinian tried to arrest the pope, but Italian armies (theoretically under the emperor's command) came to the pontiff's aid instead. Justinian's arresting officer was reduced to cowering under the pope's bed. Clearly Constantinople's influence and authority over Rome had become tenuous. Sheer distance as well as diminishing imperial power in Italy meant that the popes had in effect become the leaders of non-Lombard Italy.

The gap between Byzantium and the papacy widened in the early eighth century when Emperor Leo III tried to increase the taxes on papal property to pay for his wars against the Arabs. The pope responded by leading a general tax revolt. Meanwhile, Leo's fierce policy of iconoclasm collided with the pope's tolerance of images. For the pope, holy images could and should be venerated, though not worshiped.

Increasing friction with Byzantium meant that when the pope felt threatened by the Lombard kings, as he did in the mid-eighth century, he looked elsewhere for support. Pope Stephen II (752-757)

> besought the pestilential king of the Lombards for the flocks God had entrusted to him and for the lost sheep—[in short,] for the entire exarchate of Ravenna and for the people of the whole of this province of Italy, whom that impious king had deceived with devilish trickery and was now occupying. He was getting nowhere with him; and in particular he saw that no help would come his way from the imperial power [at Byzantium].... He sent word incessantly to the king of the Franks [Pippin III]: the king must dispatch his envoys here to Rome; he must have them summon [the pope] to come to [the king].[5]

Pippin listened to the pope's entreaties and marched into Italy with an army to fight the Lombards. The new Frankish/ papal alliance would change the map of Europe in the coming decades.

★ ★ ★ ★

The "fall" of the Roman empire meant the rise of its children. In the east the Muslims swept out of Arabia—and promptly set up a Roman-style government where they conquered. The bit in the east that they did not take—the part ruled from Constantinople—still considered itself the Roman empire. In the west, impoverished kingdoms looked to the city of Rome for religion, culture, and inspiration. However much East and West, Christian and Muslim, would come to deviate from and hate one another, they could not change the fact of shared parentage.

Chapter Two Key Events

570-632	Life of Muhammad
587	Reccared, Visigothic king, converts to Catholic Christianity
590	Saint Columbanus arrives on the Continent
590-604	Pope Gregory the Great
597	Augustine arrives at the court of King Ethelbert
607-630	Sassanid-Byzantine wars
622	Hijra; Muhammad's migration from Mecca to Medina
624	Battle of Badr
633	Beginning of Islamic conquests outside of Arabia
661	Death of Ali
661-750	Umayyad caliphate
664	Synod of Whitby
681	Bulgars enter Byzantine territory
711-715	Conquest of Spain by Islamic-led armies
726-787, 815-843	Iconoclasm at Byzantium

NOTES

1. *Al-Qur'an: A Contemporary Translation*, trans. Ahmed Ali (Princeton, 1993), p.11.
2. *Late Merovingian France: History and Hagiography 640-720,* ed. and trans. Paul Fouracre and Richard A. Gerberding (Manchester, 1996), quotations on pp.121-23.
3. Bede, *The Ecclesiastical History of the English People*, ed. Judith McClure and Roger Collins (Oxford, 1994), p.114.
4. The "radiant throne" is from Eugenius of Toledo, quoted in Geneviève Bührer-Thierry, "'Just Anger' or 'Vengeful Anger'? The Punishment of Blinding in the Early Medieval West," in *Anger's Past: The Social Uses of an Emotion in the Middle Ages*, ed. Barbara H. Rosenwein (Ithaca, NY, 1998), p.79.
5. *The Lives of the Eighth-Century Popes (Liber Pontificalis): The Ancient Biographies of Nine Popes from AD 715 to AD 817*, trans. Raymond Davis, Translated Texts for Historians, 13 (Liverpool, 1992), pp.58-59.

FURTHER READING

Barford, P.M. *The Early Slavs: Culture and Society in Early Medieval Eastern Europe*. Ithaca, 2001.

Charles-Edwards, T.M. *Early Christian Ireland*. Cambridge, 2001.

Donner, Fred McGraw. *The Early Islamic Conquests*. Princeton, 1981.

Foss, Clive. *Ephesus after Antiquity: A Late Antique, Byzantine and Turkish City*. Cambridge, 1979.

Foster, Sally M. *Picts, Gaels and Scots: Early Historic Scotland*. London, 1996.

Haldon, J.F. *Byzantium in the Seventh Century: The Transformation of a Culture*. Cambridge, 1990.

Hodgson, Marshall G.S. *The Venture of Islam: Conscience and History in a World Civilization*, 1: *The Classical Age of Islam*. Chicago, 1974.

Mayr-Harting, Henry. *The Coming of Christianity to Anglo-Saxon England*. University Park, PA, 1991.

Noble, Thomas F.X. *The Republic of St. Peter: The Birth of the Papal State, 680-825*. Philadelphia, 1984.

Peters, F.E. *Muhammad and the Origins of Islam*. Albany, 1994.

Whittow, Mark. *The Making of Byzantium, 600-1025*. Berkeley, 1996.

Wood, Ian. *The Merovingian Kingdoms, 450-751*. London, 1994.

THREE

CREATING NEW IDENTITIES (*c*.750–*c*.900)

IN THE SECOND half of the eighth century the periodic outbreaks of plague that had devastated half of the globe for two centuries came to an end. In its wake came a gradual but undeniable upswing in population, land cultivation, and general prosperity. At Byzantium an empress took the throne, in the Islamic world the Abbasids displaced the Umayyads, in Francia the Carolingians deposed the Merovingians. New institutions of war and peace, learning, and culture developed, giving each state—Byzantium, the Islamic caliphate, Francia—its own characteristic identity (though with some telling similarities).

BYZANTIUM: FROM TURNING WITHIN TO CAUTIOUS EXPANSION

In 750 Byzantium was a state with its back to the world. Its iconoclasm isolated it from other Christians, its theme structure focused its military operations on internal defense, its abandonment of classical learning set it apart from its past. By 900, all this had changed. Byzantium was iconophile (icon-loving), aggressive, and cultured.

New Icons, New Armies, New Territories

Within Byzantium, iconoclasm sowed dissension. In the face of persecution and humiliation, men and women continued to venerate icons, even in the very bedrooms of the imperial palace. The impasse was ended by a woman. In 780, upon the death of Leo IV, his widow, Irene, in effect became head of the Byzantine state as regent for her son Constantine VI. Long a secret iconophile, Irene immediately moved to replace important iconoclast bishops. Then she called a council at Nicaea (787), the first there since the famous one of 325. The meeting went as planned, and the assembled bishops condemned iconoclasm. Few Byzantines lamented its passing. A later revival of iconoclasm (815-843), though long, was half-hearted; with some exceptions, icons and their venerators were tolerated. After 843, Byzantium would henceforth be confidently iconophile.

At first the end of iconoclasm displeased the old guard in the army, but a canny ruler like Irene knew how to appoint loyal generals and defuse opposition. By her day, the army had been reformed and the theme organization supplemented by an even more responsive force. In the mid-eighth century, Emperor Constantine V (*r.*741-775) had created new crack regiments, the *tagmata* (*sing. tagma*). These were mobile troops, not tied to any theme. Many were composed of cavalry, the elite of fighting men; others—infantry, muleteers—provided necessary backup. At first deployed largely around Constantinople itself to shore up the emperors, the *tagmata* were eventually used in cautious frontier battles. Under the ninth- and tenth-century emperors, they helped Byzantium to expand.

To the west, in the Balkans, Emperor Nicephorus I (*r.*802-811) remodeled the old thematic territories and added new ones. Leading his army against the Slavs, he took the region around Serdica (today Sofia, Bulgaria). His successes prompted the Bulgarians to attack. To secure the area, Nicephorus uprooted thousands of families from Anatolia and sent them to settle in the Balkans. Reshaping old themes and adding new ones, Nicephorus created fortified centers to anchor the settlers. Although he intended to recreate an earlier Byzantium, his policies in fact ensured the future fission between Greek- and Slavic-speaking Balkan states.

Nicephorus's later foray into Bulgarian territory further north in the Balkans proved disastrous. Marshaling a huge army and escorted by the luminaries of his court, the emperor plundered the Bulgarian capital, Pliska, then coolly made his way west. But the Bulgarians blockaded his army as it passed through a narrow river valley, fell on the imperial party, and killed the emperor. The toll on the fleeing soldiers and courtiers was immense, but even more memorable was the imperial humiliation. Krum, the Bulgarian khan (ruler), lined Nicephorus's skull with silver and used it as a ceremonial drinking cup. Further defeats in the region in the late ninth century led to yet more shuffling of themes. The end result may be seen in Map 3.1, to which Map 2.1 on p.60 (Byzantium at its smallest) should be compared.

Another glance at the two maps reveals a second region of modest expansion, this time on Byzantium's eastern front. In the course of the ninth century the Byzantines had worked out a strategy of skirmish warfare in Anatolia. When Arab raiding parties attacked, the *strategoi* evacuated the population, burned the crops, and, while sending out a few troops to harass the invaders, largely waited out the raid within their local fortifications. But by 860, the threat of Arab invading armies—apart from raiding parties—was largely over (though the threat of Muslim navies—on Sicily and in southern Italy, for example—remained very real). In 900, Emperor Leo VI (*r.*886-912) was confident enough to go on the offensive, sending the *tagmata* in the direction of Tarsus. The raid was a success, and in its wake at least one princely family of Armenia, which was allied with the Arabs, was persuaded to enter imperial service and cede its principality to Byzantium. Reorganized as the theme of Mesopotamia, it was the first of a series of new themes that Leo created in an area that had been largely a no-man's-land between the Islamic and Byzantine worlds.

Map 3.1: The Byzantine Empire, *c.*917

But the rise of the *tagmata* eventually had the unanticipated consequence of downgrading the themes. The soldiers of the themes got the "grunt work"—the inglorious job of skirmish warfare with the Arabs, for example—without the honor and (probably) extra pay. The *tagmata* were the professionals, gradually taking over most of the fighting, especially as the need to defend the interior of Anatolia receded. By the same token, the troops of the themes became increasingly inactive.

Educating Without and Within

No longer turned in on itself, the Byzantine empire first brought most of the Slavic regions into its orbit, not with troops but via missionaries. The whole of the eastern and northern Balkans was ripe for conversion. Here Byzantium's competitors were the Roman church and the Franks, who preached the Catholic brand of Christianity. The Slavic principalities tried to manipulate the two sides—the Catholics and the Orthodox Byzantines—to their own advantage, but in the end they were pulled into one world or the other.

Plate 3.1 (facing page): Byzantine Book Cover (886-912). After the end of iconoclasm in 843, two distinct artistic styles flourished at Byzantium, easily seen by comparing this plate to **Plate 3.2**. The frontal, formal, hierarchical, and decorative style represented by this enameled book cover harks back to late imperial work, such as that of the Hippodrome obelisk base in **Plate 1.7** on p.37.

The prince of Moravia (a new Slavic state bounded by Francia to the west and the Bulgarian khanate to the east) made a bid for autonomy from Frankish hegemony by calling on Byzantium for missionaries. The imperial court was ready. Two brothers, Constantine (later called Cyril) and Methodius, set out in 863, armed with translations of the Gospels and liturgical texts. Born in Thessalonica, they well knew about the Slavic languages, which had been purely oral. Constantine devised an alphabet using Greek letters to represent the sounds of one Slavic dialect (the "Glagolitic" alphabet), and then added Greek words and grammar where the Slavic lacked Christian vocabulary and suitable expression. The resulting language, later called Old Church Slavonic, was an effective tool for conversion. Its use shows that Byzantium, relentlessly centralizing as it was in most matters, was willing in a few others to work with regional traditions. The Catholic church, by contrast, was more rigid: it insisted that the Gospels and liturgy be in Latin. Despite this, Moravia ended in the Catholic camp, but the Byzantine brand of Christianity prevailed in Bulgaria, Serbia, and later (see Chapter 4) Russia.

The creation of an alphabet in the mid-ninth century was part of a pattern of scholarly and educational initiatives. Constantinople had always had private schools, books, and teachers to train its civil servants. But in the eighth century the number of bureaucrats was steadily dwindling, the schools were decaying, and the books, painstakingly written out on papyrus, were disintegrating. Education had lost its prestige—except for the religious education of the Psalms.

Ninth-century confidence reversed the trend; fiscal stability and surplus wealth in

the treasury greased the wheels. Emperor Theophilus (*r.*829-842) opened a public school in the palace, headed by Leo the Mathematician, a master of geometry, mechanics, medicine, and philosophy. Controversies over iconoclasm sent churchmen scurrying to the writings of the Church Fathers to find passages that supported their cause. With the end of iconoclasm, the monasteries, staunch defenders of icons, garnered renewed prestige and gained new recruits. Because their abbots insisted that they read Christian texts, the monks had to get new manuscripts in a hurry. Practical need gave impetus to the creation of a new kind of script: minuscule. This was made up of lower case letters, written in cursive, the letters strung together. It was faster and easier to write than the formal capital uncial letters that had previously been used. Separating words by spaces, as they had not been before, made them easier to read. Papyrus was no longer easily available from Egypt, so the new manuscripts were made out of parchment—animal skins scraped and treated to create a good writing surface. Far more expensive than papyrus, parchment was nevertheless much more durable, making possible their preservation over the long haul.

Plate 3.2 (facing page): Ezechiel in the Valley of Dry Bones, Homilies of Gregory Nazianzen (880-886). The style of this miniature is inspired by classical art. However, depicting Ezechiel talking to an archangel is new. It reflects iconophile delight in the post-843 permission to portray the human vision of divinity.

A general cultural revival was clearly underway by the middle of the century. As a young man, Photius, the patriarch of Constantinople (*r.*858-867, 877-886), dictated summaries of hundreds of books he had read, including works of history, literature, and philosophy. As patriarch he gathered a circle of scholars around him; wrote sermons, homilies, and theological treatises; and tutored Emperor Leo VI. For his own part, Constantine-Cyril, the future missionary to the Slavs, was reportedly such a brilliant student in Thessalonica that an imperial official invited him to the capital:

> When he arrived at Constantinople, he was placed in the charge of masters to teach him. In three months he learned all the grammar and applied himself to other studies. He studied Homer and geometry and with Leo [the Mathematician] and Photius dialectic and all the teachings of philosophy, and in addition [he learned] rhetoric, arithmetic, astronomy, music, and all the other "Hellenic" [i.e., pagan Greek] teachings.[1]

The resurrection of "Hellenic" books helped inspire an artistic revival. Sometimes called the Macedonian Renaissance, after the ninth- and tenth-century imperial dynasty that fostered it, the new movement found its models in both the abstract, transcendental style of the pre-iconoclastic period and the natural, plastic style of classical art.

Even during the somber years of iconoclasm, artistic activity did not entirely end at Byzantium. But the new exuberance and sheer numbers of mosaics, manuscript illuminations, ivories, and enamels after 870 suggest a new era. Plate 3.1 illustrates the return to the abstract style: Christ and the saints and archangels who surround him on this book cover have no weight or volume. Like Justinian and his ministers in Plate 1.9 (p.50-51), they stare out beyond their viewers to another, otherworldly reality. At about the same time, however, classical styles were also making a comeback. On the left of Plate 3.2 the prophet Ezekiel stands in a landscape of bones, the hand of God reaching toward him to tell him that the bones will rise and live again (Ezek. 37:1-11). On the right the prophet stands next to an angel. The figures have depth and weight; they turn and interact. It is true that their drapery flutters and loops unnaturally, giving the scene a nonclassical excitement; and it is true that the angel "floats," one foot in front of the prophet, one arm a bit behind him. But it is in just this way that the Byzantines adapted classical traditions to their overriding need to represent transcendence.

Not surprisingly, the same period saw the revival of monumental architecture. Already Emperor Theophilus was known for the splendid palace that he built on the outskirts of Constantinople, and Basil I (*r.*867-886) was famous as a builder of churches. Rich men from the court and church imitated imperial tastes, constructing palaces, churches, and monasteries of their own.

THE SHIFT TO THE EAST IN THE ISLAMIC WORLD

Just as at Byzantium the imperial court determined both culture and policies, so too the Islamic world of the ninth century was centered on the caliph and his court. The Abbasids, who ousted the Umayyad caliphs in 750, moved their center of power to Iraq (part of the former Persia) and stepped into the shoes of the Sassanid king of kings, the "shadow of God on earth." Yet in fact much of their time was spent less in imposing their will than in conciliating different interest groups.

The Abbasid Reconfiguration

Years of Roman rule had made Byzantium relatively homogeneous. Nothing was less true of the Islamic world, made up of regions wildly diverse in geography, language, and political, religious, and social traditions. Each tribe, family, and region had its own expectations and desires for a place in the sun. The Umayyads paid little heed. Their power base was Syria, formerly a part of Byzantium. There they rewarded their hard-core followers and took the lion's share of conquered land for themselves. They expected every other region to send its taxes to their coffers at Damascus. This annoyed regional leaders, even though they probably managed to keep most of the taxes that they raised. Moreover, with no claims to the religious functions of an *imam*, the Umayyads could never gain the adherence of the followers of Ali. Soon still other groups began to complain. Where was the equality of believers preached in the Qur'an? The Umayyads privileged an elite; Arabs who had expected a fair division of the spoils were disappointed. So too were non-Arabs who converted to Islam: they discovered that they had still to pay the old taxes of their non-believing days.

The discontents festered, and two main centers of resistance emerged: Khurasan (today eastern Iran) and Iraq. (See Map 3.2.) Both had been part of the Persian empire; the rebellion was largely a coming together of old Persian and newly "Persianized" Arab factions. In the 740s this defiant coalition at Khurasan decided to support the Abbasid family. This was an extended kin group with deep-rooted claims to the caliphate, tracing its lineage back to the very uncle who had cared for the orphaned Muhammad. With militant supporters, considerable money, and the backing of a powerful propaganda organization, the Abbasids organized an army in Khurasan and, marching it undefeated into Iraq, picked up more support there. In

Map 3.2: The Islamic World, *c.*800

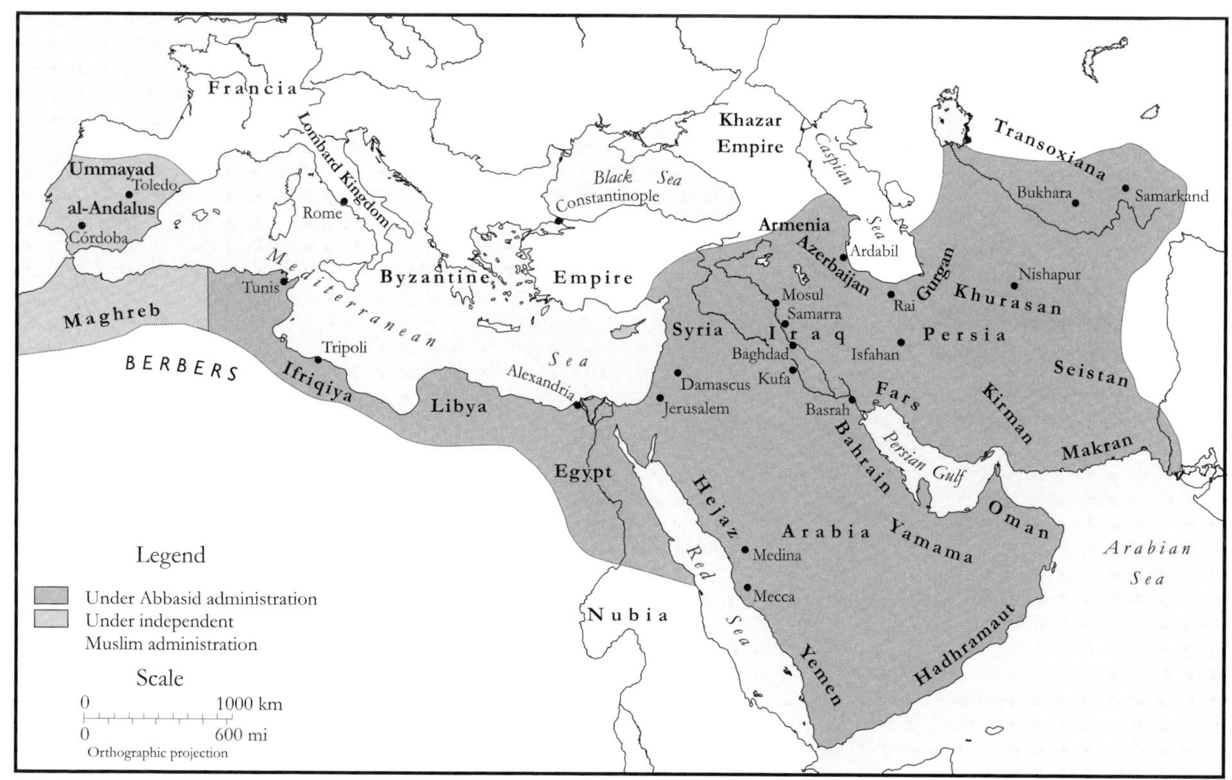

749 they defeated the Umayyad governor at Kufa, and al-Saffah was solemnly named the first Abbasid caliph. Less than a year later the last Umayyad caliph, abandoned by almost everyone and on the run in Egypt, was killed in a short battle.

The new dynasty seemed to signal a revolution. (See list of Islamic Rulers on p.220.) Most importantly, the Abbasids recognized the crucial centrality of Iraq and built their capital cities there: Baghdad was begun in 762, Samarra in the 830s, in the aftermath of a bitter civil war. The Abbasids had to recognize the quasi-independence of various regions—Syria, Egypt, and (at times) Khurasan—allowing some provincial governorships to become hereditary. They took the title of *imam* and even, at one point, wore the green color of the Shiʿites.

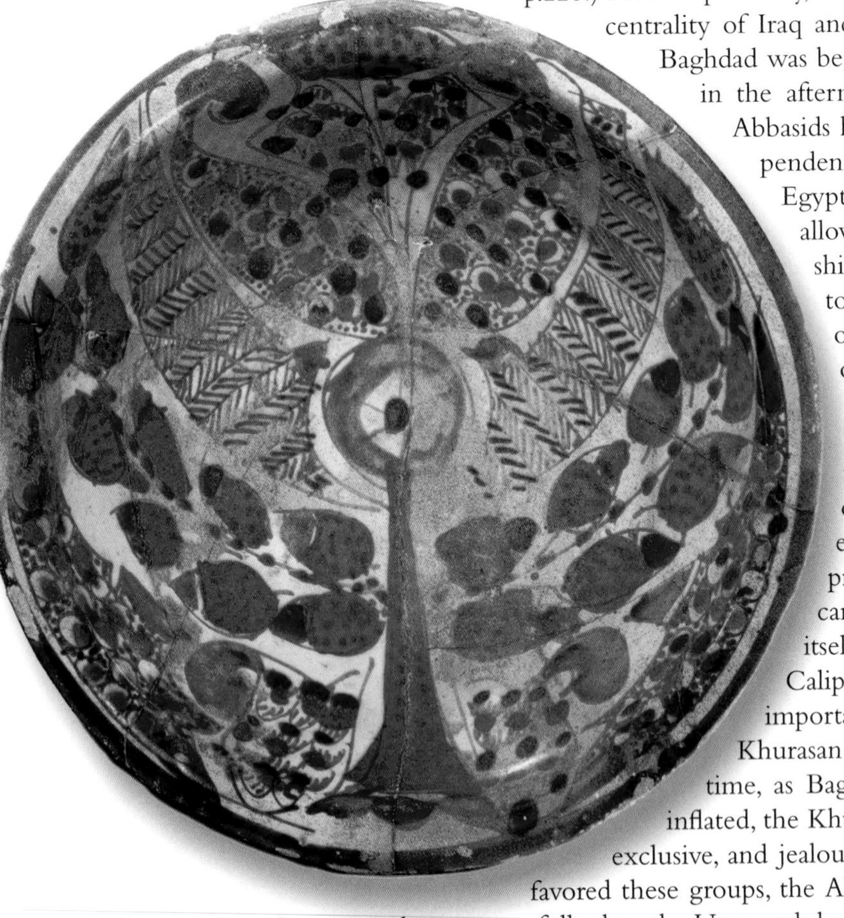

Yet as the Abbasids became entrenched, they in turn created their own elite, under whom other groups chafed. In the eighth century most of their provincial governors, for example, came from the Abbasid family itself. When building Baghdad, Caliph al-Mansur (*r.*754-775) allotted important tracts of real estate to his Khurasan military leaders. In the course of time, as Baghdad prospered and land prices inflated, the Khurasani came to constitute a new, exclusive, and jealous elite. At the same time as they favored these groups, the Abbasids succeeded in centralizing their control even more fully than the Umayyads had done. This is clearest in the area of taxation. The Umayyads had demanded in vain that all taxes come to them. But the Abbasid al-Muʿtasim (*r.*833-842) was able to control and direct provincial revenues to his court in Iraq.

Control, however, was uneven. Until the beginning of the tenth century, the Abbasid caliphs generally could count on ruling Iraq (their "headquarters"), Syria, Khurasan, and Egypt. But they never had the Iberian peninsula; they lost Ifriqiya (today Tunisia) by about 800; and they never controlled the Berbers in the soft underbelly of North Africa. In the course of the tenth century, they would lose effective control even in their heartlands. That, however, was in the future (see Chapter 4).

Whatever control the Abbasids had depended largely on their armies. Unlike the Byzantines, the Abbasids did not need soldiers to stave off external enemies or to expand outwards. (The Byzantine strategy of skirmish warfare worked largely because the caliphs led raids to display their prowess, not to take territory. The serious naval wars that took Sicily from Byzantium were launched from Ifriqiya, independent of the caliphs.) Rather, the Abbasids needed troops to collect taxes in areas already conquered but weakly controlled.

Well into the ninth century the caliphs' troops were paid, but not mustered, by them. Generals recruited their own troops from their home districts, tribes, families, and clients. When the generals were loyal to the caliphs, this military system worked well. In the dark days of civil war, however, when two brothers fought over the caliphate (811-819), no one controlled the armies. After al-Ma'mun (*r.*813-833) won this civil war, he had no reliable army to back him up. His brother and successor, al-Mu'tasim, found the solution in a new-style, private army. He bought and trained his own slaves, many of them Turks and thus unrelated to other tribal groups. These men were given governorships as well as military posts. They were the reason that al-Mu'tasim was able to collect provincial taxes so effectively. He could not foresee that in time the Turks would come to constitute a new elite, one that would eventually help to overpower the caliphate itself.

Plate 3.3 (facing page): Dish from Iraq (9th cent.). Boasting an elaborate, multi-colored floral design that contrasts with its plain white background, this plate reflects the luxurious tastes of the Abbasid elite.

With the Abbasid transformation came wealth. The Mediterranean region had always been a great trade corridor. In the ninth century, Baghdad, at the crossroad of east and west, drew that trade into a wider network. All of Iraq partook in the commercial buoyancy:

> From India are imported tigers, panthers, elephants, panther skins, rubies, white sandal, ebony, and coconuts. From China are imported silk stuffs, silk, chinaware, paper, ink, peacocks, racing horses, saddles, felts, cinnamon, Greek unblended rhubarb … racing horses, female slaves, knicknacks with human figures … hydraulic engineers, expert agronomists, marble workers, and eunuchs. From Arabia: Arab horses, ostriches, pedigreed she-camels … From Egypt: trotting donkeys, suits of fine cloth, papyrus, balsam, and—from its mines—topazes of superior quality. From the land of the Khazars [on the lower Volga River]: slaves of both sexes, coats of mail, [and] helmets.[2]

The porcelains from China inspired Islamic artisans to add tin to their own glazes to achieve a bright white color, over which they added decorative effects, from simple designs that used just one color to elaborate patterns created with metallic luster. (See Plate 3.3.) Dining off of such finely decorated plates and bowls was part of the elites' newly luxurious lifestyle: their clothes were made of richly woven fabrics, their homes were furnished with fine rugs (on both floors and walls) and perfumed with elaborately carved censers.

With revenues from commerce and (above all) taxes from agriculture in their coffers, the caliphs paid their armies, salaried their officials (drawn from the many talented men—but, in this relentlessly male-dominated society, not women—in the Persian, Arab, Christian, and Jewish population), and presided over a cultural revival even more impressive than the one at Constantinople.

New Cultural Forms

Plate 3.4 (facing page): Córdoba, Great Mosque (late 10th cent.). The Great Mosque of Córdoba was built in several phases. The view here is of an area added in 987. Note the two tiers of arches—the first set on pre-Islamic columns, the second on long piers—giving the building a sense of both height and liveliness.

Under the Abbasids (most spectacularly, under Harun al-Rashid [*r.*786-809] of *Arabian Nights* fame), science, law, and literature flourished. The caliphs launched scientific studies via a massive translation effort that brought the philosophical, medical, mathematical, and astrological treatises of the Indian and Greek worlds into Islamic culture. They encouraged new literary forms—the refined and learned prose and poetry of *adab* literature—as part of the education of gentlemen at court. Books of all sorts were relatively cheap (and therefore accessible) in the Islamic world because they were written on paper.

Shoring up the regime with astrological predictions; winning theological debates with the pointed weapons of Aristotle's logical and scientific works; understanding the theories of bridge-building, irrigation, and land-surveying with Euclid's geometry—these were just some of the motives behind the translations and original scientific work of the period. The movement had general support. Patrons of scientific writing included the caliphs, their wives, courtiers, generals, and ordinary people with practical interests. Muhammad ibn Musa (*d.*850), author of a book on algebra (the word itself is from the Arab *al-jabr*), explained the many sensible uses of his topic:

> people constantly require [it] in cases of inheritance, legacies, partition, lawsuits, and trade, and in all their dealings with one another where surveying, the digging of canals, [and] geometrical computation ... are concerned.[3]

The same scholar also wrote the first Arabic treatise on the Indian method of calculation (Indian numerals are what *we* call Arabic numerals) and the use of the zero, essential for distinguishing 100 from 1, for example.

Similarly practical were the treatises on law (*fiqh*) that began to appear in the Abbasid period. They included commentaries on religious obligations, rules of war, and forms of taxation. Eminent jurists founded schools to perpetuate their ideas.

By contrast, *adab* literature was impractical, though "political" in the sense that it paved a man's way at court. It strove after an ideal of beauty and elegance. Knowledge was important, but only in the service of wit and style. The highest form of *adab* was poetry. When performed, it was sung, and thus was closely tied to music. *Adab* poets wrote verses of praise, satire, nostalgia, suffering, deep religious feeling, worldly loves and hates, and wry comments on the human condition:

> She said, "I love you"; "you're a liar," I said,
> "cheat someone else who cannot scrutinize
> these words which I can't accept!
> For truly I say, no one loves an old man!
> It's like saying, 'We have tethered the wind',
> or like saying, 'Fire is cold' or 'water is aflame'."[4]

Map 3.3 (facing page): Europe, *c.*814

Al-Andalus: A Society in the Middle

The poet who wrote those lines was al-Ghazal (775-864), a great practitioner of *adab*—in Spain! In the eighth and ninth centuries, Islamic Spain was a miniature caliphate minus the caliph. In the mid-eighth century Abd al-Rahman I, a Umayyad prince on the run from the Abbasids, managed to gather an army, make his way to Iberia, defeat the provincial governor at Córdoba, and (in 756) proclaim himself "emir" (commander) of al-Andalus. His dynasty would govern Islamic Spain for two and a half centuries, and one of his descendants, Abd al-Rahman III (*r.*912-961) would even take the title caliph. Nevertheless, like the Abbasid caliphs, the Umayyad rulers of Spain headed a state poised to break into its regional constituents.

Al-Andalus under the emirs was hardly Muslim and even less Arab. As the caliphs came to rely on Turks, so the emirs relied on a professional standing army of non-Arabs, the *al-khurs*, the "silent ones"—men who could not speak Arabic. They lived among a largely Christian—and partly Jewish—population; even by 900, only about 25 per cent of the people in al-Andalus were Muslims. This had its benefits for the regime, which taxed Christians and Jews heavily. Although, like Western European rulers, they did not have the land tax that the Byzantine emperors and caliphs could impose, the emirs did draw some of their revenue from Muslims, especially around their capital at Córdoba. (See Map 3.3.)

Money allowed the emirs to pay salaries to their civil servants and to sponsor a culture of science and literature of their own. Al-Ghazal was only one of the poets

Norway
Sweden
Scotland
North Sea
Baltic Sea
Denmark
Haithabu
Ireland
York
Anglo-Saxon England
London
OBODRITES
Frisia
Elbe
Vistula
Saxony
Meerssen
Cologne
St.-Amand
Aachen
Hersfeld
Oder
English Channel
Herstal
Meuse
Austrasia
Fulda
CZECHS
Atlantic Ocean
Quierzy
Laon
Soissons
Würzburg
Paris
Attigny
Seine
Dniester
Brittany
Neustria
Verdun
Regensburg
Moravian Empire
Orléans
Sens
Rhine
Danube
Passau
Loire
Theiss
Prut
Tours
Francia
Poitiers
Burgundy
Aquitaine
Lyon
Kingdom of Italy
Drava
Bulgarian Empire
Milan
Pavia
Verona
Sava
Vienne
Venice
Kingdom of Asturias
Oviedo
Po
CROATS
Garonne
Rhône
Genoa
León
Ravenna
Adriatic Sea
Danube
Duero
Ebro
Spoleto
Rome
Duchy of Benevento
Benevento
Barcelona
Tagus
al-Andalus
Naples
Guadiana
Córdoba
Guadalquiver
Byzantine Empire
Mediterranean Sea
Maghreb
Ifriqiya
Libya
Legend
Carolingian Kingdom 768
Conquests of Charles the Great
Scale
0
500 km
0
300 mi

and musicians patronized by the court. Like the others, his poems—blunt and to the point—were not quite what a poet from, say, Baghdad would write. The culture of al-Andalus reflected its unique ethnic and religious mix. The Great Mosque in Córdoba is a good example. Begun under Abd al-Rahman I and expanded by his successors, it drew on the design of the Roman aqueduct at Mérida for its rows of columns connected by double arches. (See Plate 3.4.) For the shape of the arches, however, it borrowed a form—the "Visigothic" horseshoe arch—from the Christians. For the decorative motif of alternating light and dark stones, it looked to the Great Mosque of Damascus.

The cultural "mix" went beyond buildings and poems. Some Christians and Muslims intermarried; Muslim men were allowed to take Christian wives. Even religious practices may have melded a bit. The Christians who lived in al-Andalus were called "Mozarabs"—"would-be Arabs"—by Christians elsewhere. It used to be thought that the martyrdom of 48 Christians at Córdoba between 850 and 859 was proof of implacable hostility between Christians and Muslims there. But recent research suggests that the story of the martyrs was hugely exaggerated by its idiosyncratic author, Eulogius. It is likely that Christians and Muslims on the whole got along fairly well. Christians dressed like Muslims, worked side-by-side with them in government posts, and used Arabic in many aspects of their life. At the time of the supposed martyrdoms, there were in the region of Córdoba alone at least four churches and nine monasteries.

Still, some Andalusian Christians were not content—Eulogius was one—and they were glad to have contact with the north. For to the north of al-Andalus, beyond the Duero River, were tiny Christian principalities. Partaking in the general demographic and economic growth of the period, they had begun to prosper a little. One, Asturias, became a kingdom. There Alfonso II (*r.*791-842) and his successors established a capital city—first at Oviedo, then, at the beginning of the tenth century, at León. They built churches, encouraged monastic foundations, collected relics, patronized literary efforts, and welcomed Mozarabs from the south. The kings themselves looked to models still further north—to Francia, where Charlemagne and his heirs ruled as kings "by grace of God."

AN EMPIRE IN SPITE OF ITSELF

Between Byzantium and the Islamic world was Francia. While the other two were both politically centralized, subject to sophisticated tax systems, and served by salaried armies and officials, Francia inherited the centralizing traditions of the Roman empire without its order and efficiency. Francia's kings could not collect a land tax, the backbone of the old Roman and the more recent Byzantine and Islamic fiscal systems. There were no salaried officials or soldiers in Francia. Yet the new dynasty of kings there, the Carolingians, managed to muster armies, expand their kingdom, encourage a revival of scholarship and learning, command the respect of emperors and caliphs, and forge an identity for themselves as leaders of the Christian people (by which they meant Roman Catholics). Their successes bore striking resemblance to contemporary achievements at Constantinople and Baghdad. How was this possible? The answer is at least threefold. They took advantage of the same gentle economic upturn that seems to have taken place generally; they exploited to the full the institutions of Roman culture and political life that remained to them; at the same time, they were willing to experiment with new institutions and take advantage of unexpected opportunities.

The Making of the Carolingians

The Carolingian take-over was a "palace coup." After a battle (at Tertry, 687) between Neustrian and Austrasian noble factions, one powerful family with vast estates in Austrasia came to monopolize the high office of mayor in both places. In the first half of the eighth century these mayors took over much of the power and most of the responsibilities of the kings.

Charles Martel (mayor 714-741) gave the name Carolingian (from *Carolus*, Latin for Charles) to the dynasty. In 732 he won a battle near Poitiers against an army led by the Muslim governor of al-Andalus:

> He utterly destroyed their armies, scattering them like stubble before the fury of his onslaught; and in the power of Christ he utterly destroyed them. So did he triumph over all his enemies in this his glorious day of victory![5]

Thus did a contemporary chronicler laud the event with phrases borrowed from the Bible and the Church Fathers. The battle ended plundering raids from al-Andalus. But, as the chronicler said, Charles had other enemies: he spent most of his time fighting vigorously against regional Frankish aristocrats intent on carving out independent lordships for themselves. Playing powerful factions against one another, rewarding supporters, defeating enemies, and dominating whole regions by controlling monasteries and bishoprics that served as focal points for both religious piety and land donations, the Carolingians created a tight network of supporters.

Moreover, they chose their allies well, reaching beyond Francia to the popes and to Anglo-Saxon churchmen, who (as we have seen) were closely tied to Rome. When the Anglo-Saxon missionary Boniface (*d.*754) wanted to preach in Frisia (today the Netherlands) and Germany, the Carolingians readily supported the move as a prelude to their own conquest. Many of the areas Boniface missionized had long been Christian but their practices were local rather than tied to Rome. Boniface came from England as a papal ambassador: he set up a hierarchical church organization and founded monasteries dedicated to the "Roman" *Rule* of Saint Benedict (see p.48) rather than to the Columbanian or other traditions. His newly appointed bishops were loyal to Rome and the Carolingians, not to regional aristocracies. They knew that their power came from papal and royal fiat rather than from local power centers.

Men like Boniface opened the way to a more direct alliance between the Carolingians and the pope. Charles Martel's son Pippin III (*d.*768) and his supporters made it a reality. In 751 they petitioned a willing Pope Zachary to legitimize their deposition of the last Merovingian king. The Carolingians returned the favor a few years later when the pope asked for their help against the encircling Lombards. This marked a signal moment: before 754 the papacy had been part of the Byzantine Empire; afterward, it was part of the West. In that year the papacy and the Frankish king formed a close alliance based on "a bond of love and devotion and peace."[6] Two years later, in the so-called Donation of Pippin, the new king forced the Lombards to give some cities back to the pope. The arrangement recognized that the papacy was now ruler in central Italy of a territory that had once belonged to Byzantium. It was probably around this time that members of the papal chancery (writing office) forged a document, the "Donation of Constantine," that declared the pope the recipient of Constantine's crown, cloak, and military rank, along with "all provinces, palaces, and districts of the city of Rome and Italy and of the regions of the West."

The chronicler of Charles Martel had already tied his hero's victories to Christ. The Carolingian partnership with Rome and Romanizing churchmen added to the dynasty's Christian aura. Anointment provided the finishing touch. Churchmen daubed the Carolingian kings with holy oil, reminding contemporaries of David, king of the Israelites: "Then Samuel took the horn of oil and anointed him in the midst of his brethren; and the spirit of the Lord came upon David from that day forward" (1 Sam [or Vulgate 1 Kings] 16:13)

Charlemagne

The most famous Carolingian king was Charles (*r.*768–814), called "the Great" ("le Magne" in Old French). Large, tough, wily, and devout, he was almost everyone's model king. Einhard, his courtier and scholar, saw him as a Roman emperor: he patterned his *Life of Charlemagne* on the *Lives of the Caesars*, written in the second century by Suetonius. Alcuin, the king's courtier and an even more famous scholar, emphasized Charlemagne's religious side, nicknaming him "David." Empress Irene at Constantinople saw Charlemagne as a suitable husband for herself (though the arrangement eventually fell through). An anonymous Italian poet emphasized Charlemagne's achievements: "noble in wit, intrepid in the midst of war, the bearer of two diadems [the crowns of Francia and Lombardy]."[7]

War indeed was the key to both Charlemagne's image and real success. While the Byzantine and Islamic rulers clung tightly to what they had, Charlemagne expanded, waging wars of plunder and conquest. He invaded Italy, seizing the Lombard crown and annexing northern Italy in 774. He moved his armies northward, fighting the Saxons for more than thirty years, forcibly converting them to Christianity, and annexing their territory. To the southeast, in a series of campaigns against the Avars, Charlemagne captured their strongholds, forced them to submit to his overlordship, and made off with cartloads of plunder. (Once they were defeated, around 800, the Bulgars and Moravians moved in.) His expedition to al-Andalus gained him a band of territory north of the Ebro River, a buffer between Francia and the Islamic world. Even his failures were the stuff of myth: a Basque attack on Charlemagne's army as it returned from Spain became the core of the epic poem *Song of Roland*.

Conquests like these depended on a good army. Charlemagne's was led by his *fideles*, faithful aristocrats, and manned by free men, many the "vassals" (clients) of the aristocrats. The king had the *bannum*, the right to call his subjects to arms (and, more generally, to command, prohibit, punish, and collect fines when his ban was not obeyed). Soldiers provided their own equipment; the richest went to war on horseback, the poorest had to have at least a lance, shield, and bow. There was no standing army; men had to be mobilized for each expedition. No *tagmata*, themes, or Turkish slaves were to be found here! Yet, while the empire was expanding, it was a very successful system; men were glad to go off to war when they could expect to return enriched with booty.

By 800, Charlemagne's kingdom stretched 800 miles east to west, even more north to south when Italy is counted. (See Map 3.3.) On its eastern edge was a strip of "buffer regions" extending from the Baltic to the Adriatic; they were under Carolingian overlordship. Such hegemony was reminiscent of an empire, and Charlemagne began to act according to the model of Roman emperors, sponsoring building programs to symbolize his authority, standardizing weights and measures, and acting as a patron of intellectual and artistic efforts. He built a capital "city"—a palace complex, in fact—at Aachen, complete with a chapel patterned on San Vitale, the church built by Justinian at Ravenna (see p.52). So keen was he on his Byzantine models that he had columns, mosaics, and marbles from Rome and Ravenna carted up north to use in his own buildings.

Further drawing on imperial traditions, Charlemagne issued laws in the form of "capitularies," summaries of decisions made at assemblies held with the chief men of the realm. He appointed regional governors, called "counts," to carry out his laws, muster his armies, and collect his taxes. Chosen from Charlemagne's aristocratic supporters, they were compensated for their work by temporary grants of land rather than with salaries. This was not Roman; but Charlemagne lacked the fiscal apparatus of the Roman emperors (and of his contemporary Byzantine emperors and Islamic caliphs), so he made land substitute for money. To discourage corruption, he appointed officials called *missi dominici* ("those sent out by the lord king") to oversee the counts on the king's behalf. The *missi*, chosen from the same aristocratic class as bishops and counts, traveled in pairs across Francia, making "diligent investigation whenever any man claims that an injustice has been done to him by anyone."[8]

Thus Charlemagne set up institutions meant to echo those of the Roman empire. It was a brilliant move on the part of Pope Leo III (795-816) to harness the king's imperial pretensions to papal ambitions. In 799, accused of adultery and perjury by a hostile faction at Rome, Leo narrowly escaped blinding and having his tongue cut out. Fleeing northward to seek Charlemagne's protection, he returned home under escort, the king close behind. Charlemagne arrived in late November 800 to an imperial welcome orchestrated by Leo. On Christmas Day of that year, Leo put an imperial crown on Charlemagne's head, and the clergy and nobles who were present acclaimed the king "Augustus," the title of the first Roman emperor. In one stroke the pope managed to exalt the king of the Franks, downgrade Irene at Byzantium, and enjoy the role of "emperor maker" himself.

About twenty years later, when Einhard wrote about this coronation, he said that the imperial titles at first so displeased Charlemagne "that he declared that he would not have set foot in the church the day that they were conferred, although it was a great feast-day, had he foreseen the plan of the pope."[9] In fact, Charlemagne continued to use the title "king" for about a year; then he adopted a new one that was both long and revealing: "Charles, the most serene Augustus, crowned by God, great and peaceful emperor who governs the Roman empire and who is, by the mercy of God, king of the Franks and the Lombards." According to this title, Charlemagne was not the Roman emperor crowned by the pope but rather God's emperor, who governed the Roman empire along with his many other duties.

Charlemagne's Heirs

When Charlemagne died, only one of his sons remained alive: Louis, nicknamed "the Pious." (See Genealogy 3.1: The Carolingians.) Emperor he was (from 814 to 840), but over an empire that was a conglomeration of territories, not a unit. He had to contend with the revolts of his sons, the depredations of outside invaders, the regional interests of counts and bishops, and above all an enormous variety of languages, laws, customs, and traditions, all of which tended to pull his empire apart. He contended with gusto, his chief unifying tool being Christianity. Calling on the help of the monastic reformer Benedict of Aniane, Louis imposed the *Rule* of Saint Benedict on all the monasteries in Francia. Monks and abbots served as his chief advisors. Louis's imperial model was Theodosius I, who had made Christianity the official religion of the Roman empire. Organizing inquests by the *missi*, he looked into allegations of exploitation of the poor, standardized the procedures of his chancery, and put all Frankish bishops and monasteries under his control.

Charlemagne had used his sons as "sub-kings." Louis politicized his family still more. Early in his reign he had his wife crowned empress, named his firstborn son, Lothar, emperor and co-ruler, and had his other sons, Pippin and Louis (later called "the German"), agree to be sub-kings under their older brother. It was neatly planned. But when Louis's first wife died he married Judith, daughter of one of the most powerful kindreds (the Welfs) in the kingdom. In 823 she and Louis had a son, Charles (later "Charles the Bald"), and this (plus the death of Pippin in 838) upset the earlier arrangement. A family feud became bitter civil war as brothers fought one another and their father for titles and kingdoms. After Louis's death a peace was hammered out in the Treaty of Verdun (843). (See Map 3.4a.) The empire was divided into three parts, an arrangement that would roughly define the future political contours of Western Europe. The western third, bequeathed to Charles the Bald (*r.*840-877), would eventually become France, and the eastern third, given to Louis the German (*r.*840-876), would become Germany. The "Middle Kingdom," which became Lothar's portion (*r.*817-855) along with the imperial title, had a different fate: parts of it were absorbed by France and Germany, while the rest eventually coalesced into the modern states of Belgium, the Netherlands, Luxembourg, Switzerland, and Italy. All this was far in the future. As the brothers had their own children, new divisions were tried: one in 870 (the Treaty of Meerssen), for example, and another in 880. (See Map 3.4b and Map 3.4c.) After the deposition of Emperor Charles the Fat (888), as one chronicler put it,

> the kingdoms which had obeyed his will, as if devoid of a legitimate heir, were loosened from their bodily structure into parts and now awaited no

lord of hereditary descent, but each set out to create a king for itself from its own inner parts.[10]

Genealogy 3.1 (facing page): The Carolingians*

Below left to right:

Map 3.4a: Partition of 843 (Treaty of Verdun)

Map 3.4b: Partition of 870 (Treaty of Meerssen)

Map 3.4c: Partition of 880

Dynastic problems were not the primary cause of the breakup of the Carolingian empire, however. Nor were the invasions by outsiders—Vikings, Muslims, and, starting in 899, Hungarians—which harassed the Frankish Kingdom throughout the ninth century. These certainly weakened the kings: without a standing army, they were unable to respond to the lightning raids, and what defense there was fell into the hands of local leaders, such as counts. The Carolingians lost prestige and money as they paid out tribute to stave off further attacks. But the invasions were not all bad; to some degree they even helped fortify the king. The Carolingian empire atomized because linguistic and other differences between regions—and familial and other ties within regions—were simply too strong to be overcome by directives from a central court. Only today is a unified Europe more than a distant ideal. Anyway, as we shall see, fragmentation had its own strengths and possibilities.

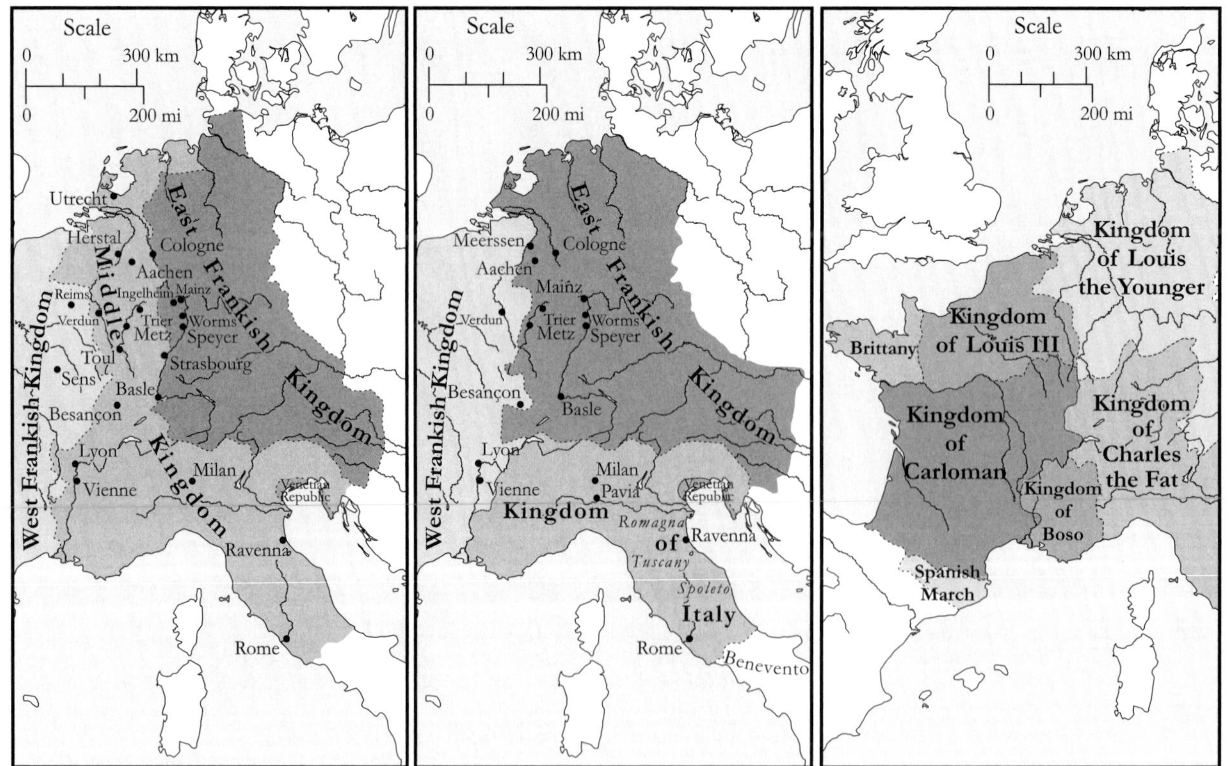

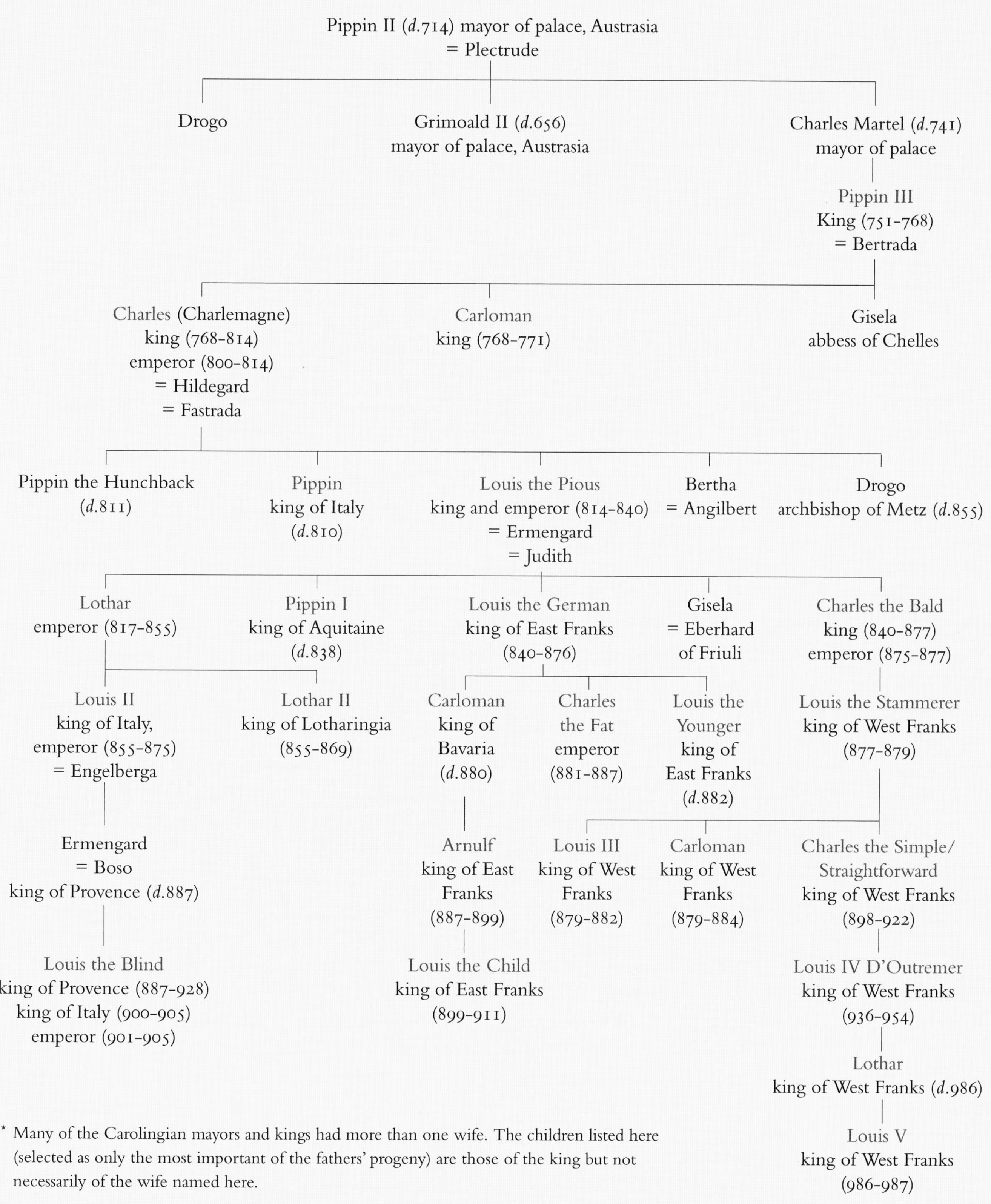

* Many of the Carolingian mayors and kings had more than one wife. The children listed here (selected as only the most important of the fathers' progeny) are those of the king but not necessarily of the wife named here.

The Wealth of a Local Economy

The Carolingian economy was based on plunder, trade, and agriculture. After the Carolingians could push no further, and the booty raids of Charlemagne's day came to an end, trade and land became the chief resources of the kingdom. To the north, in Viking trading stations such as Haithabu (see Map 3.3), archaeologists have found Carolingian glass and pots alongside Islamic coins and cloth, showing that the Carolingian economy meshed with that of the Abbasid caliphate. Silver from the Islamic world probably came north from the Caspian Sea, up the Volga River (through what is today Russia) to the Baltic Sea. (You can figure out the likely route on the map at the front of this book.) There the coins were melted down, the silver traded to the Carolingians in return for wine, jugs, glasses, and other manufactured goods. The Carolingians turned the silver into coins of their own, to be used throughout the empire for small-scale local trade. Baltic sea emporia such as Haithabu supplemented those—Quentovic and Dorestad, for example (see Map 2.3 on p.74)—that served the North Sea trade.

Nevertheless, the backbone of the Carolingian economy was land. A few written records, called *polyptychs*, document the output of the Carolingian great estates—"villae," as they were called in Latin, "manors," as we term them. On the far-flung and widely scattered manors of rich landowners—churches, monasteries, kings, and aristocrats—a major reorganization and rationalization was taking place. The most enterprising landlords instituted a three-field rather than a two-field cultivation system. It meant that two-thirds of the land rather than one-half was sown with crops each year, yielding a tidy surplus.

Consider Villeneuve-Saint-Georges, one of the many manors belonging to the monastery of Saint-Germain-des-Prés (today right in the heart of Paris). This "new villa" was no compact farm but rather a conglomeration of essential parts: its lands, woods, meadows, and vineyards dotted the countryside. All were worked by peasant families, some legally free, some unfree, each settled on its own *mansus*, or "manse," including a house, a garden, small bits of several fields, and so on. The peasants farmed the land that belonged to them, and they also worked the *demesne*, the very large manse of their lord (in this case the monastery of Saint-Germain):

> Actard, villein *(colonus)*, and his wife, also a villein (*colona*), named Eligilde, "men" of Saint-Germain, have with them six children .... They hold a free *manse* containing five *bonniers* of arable land and two *ansanges*, four *arpents* of vineyard, 4½ *arpents* of meadow. They provide four silver sous for military service and the other year two sous for the livery of meat, and the third year, for the livery of fodder, a ewe with a lamb. Two *muids* of

wine for the right of pannage, four deniers for the right of wood; for cartage a measure of wood, and 50 shingles. They plough four perches for the winter grain, and two perches for the spring. Manual and animal services, as much as is required of them....[11]

Actard and his family were "free peasants," with a fairly large "free" manse that included arable, vineyard, and meadow. They owed Saint-Germain many dues—some in money (sous), some in kind (like the ewe and lamb)—and labor services such as plowing Saint-Germain's *demesne*. Nearby lived other peasants, some with the status of slaves. They too had manses, but smaller ones, and they owed more dues and labor. Some of the women were required to feed the chickens or busy themselves in the *gynecaeum*, the women's workshop, where they made and dyed cloth and sewed garments.

Clearly the labor was onerous and the accounting system complex and unwieldy; but manors organized on the model of Saint-Germain made a profit. Like Saint-Germain and other lords, the Carolingian kings benefitted from their own extensive manors. Nevertheless, farming was still too primitive to return great surpluses, and as the lands belonging to the king were divided up in the wake of the partitioning of the empire, Carolingian dependence on manors scattered throughout their kingdom proved to be a source of weakness.

The Carolingian Renaissance

With profits from its manors, Saint-Germain-des-Prés put together a fine library of manuscripts. Some were copied right at the monastic scribal workshop (the *scriptorium*); others came from as near by as Saint-Amand (about 150 miles to the north) and as far away as Italy. Saint-Germain's library had books of liturgy (one book that came from Saint-Amand was a Sacramentary, a set of texts for the Mass), Latin grammars, and medical manuscripts. It had monk-scholars who used the books (sometimes writing in the margins) and expounded on them to their young pupils.

Saint-Germain was not unusual. The monastery of Saint-Amand, for example, was an even more important center of manuscript production. It produced Gospels, works of the Church Fathers, and grammars. Above all, the *scriptorium* of Saint-Amand made beautifully illustrated liturgical books, tailor-made for various other churches. Such liturgical manuscripts required particular expertise, for they were becoming books of music as well as text. The development of written music was a response to royal policy. Before Charlemagne's day, the melodies used for the Mass and the Divine Office were not at all uniform. Various churches in different places

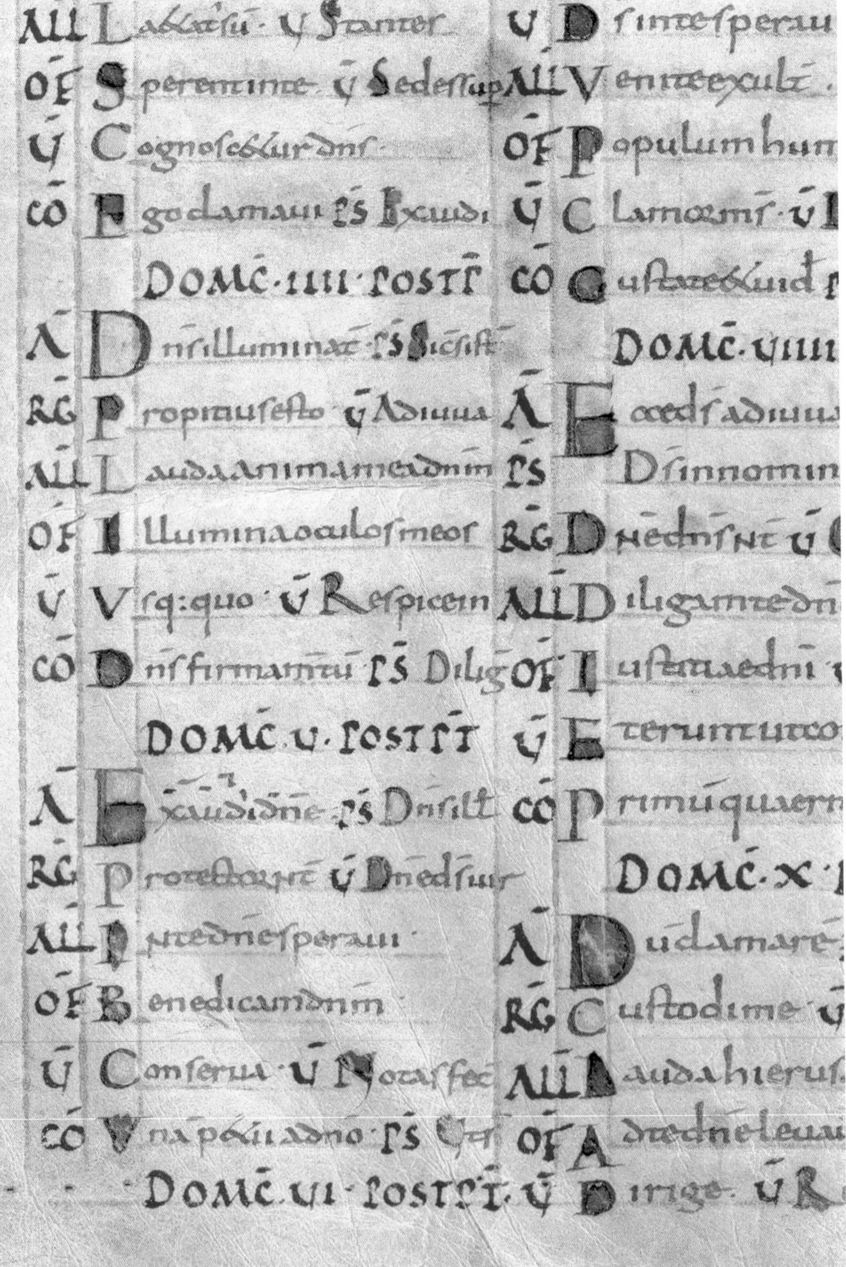

Plate 3.5: Sacramentary of Saint-Germain-des-Prés (early 9th cent.). The scribe of this list of *incipits* (the "first words") of mass chants provided a musical reminder of one (seven lines from the bottom, on the left) by adding neumes above the first words, "Exaudi Domine," "Hear, O Lord."

sang the tunes as they had learned them; music was part of local oral traditions. But since Charlemagne's time the melodies used for the Mass and the Divine Office were required to be "Roman," not Frankish. This reform—the imposition of the so-called "Gregorian chant"—posed great practical difficulties. It meant that every monk and priest had to learn a year's worth of Roman music; but how? A few cantors were imported from Rome; but without a system of musical notation, it was easy to forget new tunes. The monks of Saint-Amand were part of a musical revolution: they invented one of the first systems of musical notation. In the Sacramentary that they made for Saint-Germain they added "neumes," precursors of "notes," above some lines of text to indicate a melodic pattern. On the manuscript leaf shown in Plate 3.5, the neumes hover over a few words in the first column, 7 lines from the bottom of the page.

The same Sacramentary reveals another key development: the use of minuscule writing. As at Byzantium, and at about the same time, the Carolingians experimented with letter forms that were quicker to write and easier to read. "Caroline minuscule" lasted into the eleventh century, when it gave way to a more angular script called "Gothic." But the Carolingian letter forms were rediscovered in the fifteenth century—by scholars who thought that they represented ancient Roman writing!—and they became the model for modern lower-case printed fonts.

Like monasteries, cathedrals too were centers of cultural production in the Carolingian period. Würzburg, for example, had a *scriptorium*, library, and school for young clerics. As enterprising about its books as Saint-Germain was about its manors, Würzburg made lists of its library's holdings. By the mid-ninth century these were substantial: Gospels, writings of the Church Fathers, liturgical manuscripts, grammars, biblical commentaries, and even books of canon (church) law. The bishops of Würzburg were avid collectors. When one of them wanted Hraban Maur's Bible commentaries, he sent his request for a copy along with a pile of blank parchment (there was no paper or papyrus in the West) to the monastery of Fulda, where Hraban was abbot. Meanwhile, Würzburg helped Fulda and other places build their own libraries, lending Fulda, for example, a manuscript of Gregory the Great's *Homilies* so that the monks there could copy it.

The Carolingian court was behind much of this activity. Most of the centers of learning, scholarship, and book production began under men and women who at one time or another had been part of the royal court. Alcuin (*c.*732-804), perhaps the most famous of the Carolingian intellectuals, was "imported" by Charlemagne from England—where, as we have seen, monastic scholarship flourished—to head up his palace school. Chief advisor to the king and tutor to the entire royal family, Alcuin eventually became abbot of Saint-Martin of Tours, grooming a new generation of teachers, including Hraban Maur (780-856). More unusual but equally telling was the

Plate 3.6

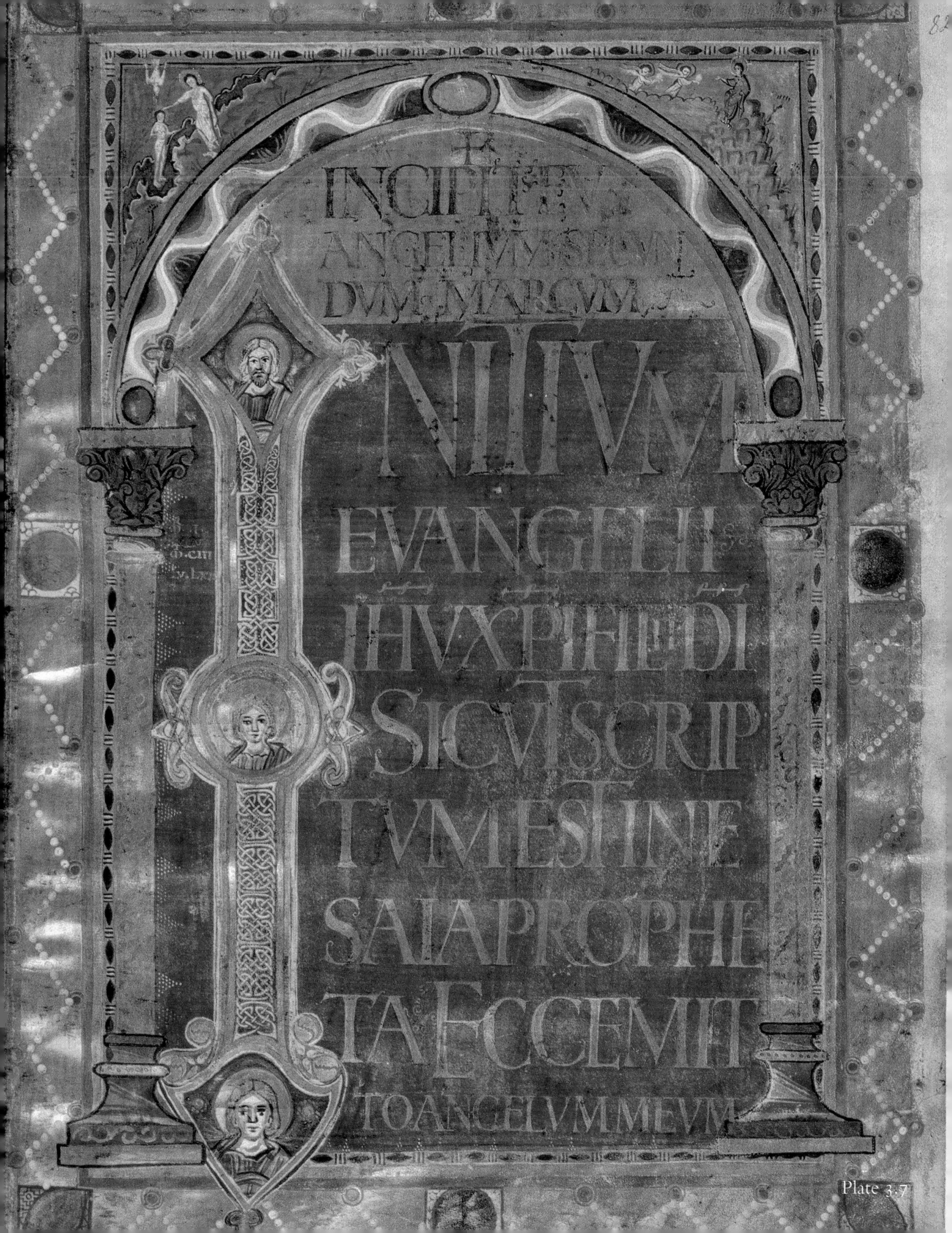

82

INCIPIT EV
ANGELIUM SECUN
DUM MARCUM

INITIUM
EVANGELII
IHU XPI FILII DI
SICUT SCRIP
TUM EST IN E
SAIA PROPHE
TA ECCE MIT
TO ANGELUM MEUM

Plate 3.7

experience of Gisela, Charlemagne's sister. She too was a key royal advisor, the one who alerted the others at home about Charlemagne's imperial coronation at Rome in 800. She was also abbess of Chelles, a center of manuscript production in its own right. Chelles had a library, and its nuns were well educated. They wrote learned letters and composed a history (the "Prior Metz Annals") that treated the rise of the Carolingians as a tale of struggle between brothers, sons, and fathers eased by the wise counsel of mothers, aunts, and sisters.

Preceding pages:

Plate 3.6: Saint Mark, Soissons Gospels (800-810). Compare this "author portrait" of St. Mark with that of St. Luke in **Plate 2.4** on p.84. Consider the different elements that each artist has used to render the portraits both figural and decorative.

Plate 3.7: First Text Page, Soissons Gospels (800-810). Compare this Carolingian first text page of the Gospel of Mark with the first text page of the Anglo-Saxon Gospel of Luke in **Plate 2.6** on p.86. In the Carolingian text, the letter forms are resolutely Roman looking, as if cut in stone. This classical allusion is reinforced by the artist's lavish use of purple (the Roman imperial color) and gold leaf. This is a manuscript meant for an emperor—Charlemagne.

Women and the poor make up the largely invisible half of the Carolingian Renaissance. But without doubt some were part of it. One of Charlemagne's capitularies ordered that the cathedrals and monasteries of his kingdom should teach reading and writing to all who could learn. There were enough complaints (by rich people) about peasants who had "made it" that we may be sure that some talented sons of the poor were getting an education. A few churchmen expressed the hope that schools for "children" would be established even in small villages and hamlets. Were they thinking of girls as well as boys? Certainly one woman—admittedly noble—in the mid-ninth century in the south of France proves that education was available to some women. We would never know about Dhuoda had she not worried enough about her absent son to write him a *Handbook* of advice. Only incidentally does it become clear in the course of her deeply felt moral text that Dhuoda was drawing on an excellent education: she clearly knew the Bible, writings of the Church Fathers, Gregory the Great, and "moderns," like Alcuin. Her Latin was fluent and sophisticated. And she understood the value of books:

> I, Dhuoda, am far away from you, my son William. For this reason I am anxious and filled with longing to do something for you. So I send you this little work written down in my name, that you may read it for your education, as a kind of mirror.[12]

The original manuscript of Dhuoda's text is not extant. Had it survived, it would no doubt have looked like other "practical texts" of the time: the "folios" (pages) would have been written in Caroline minuscule, each carefully planned to set off the poetry—Dhuoda's own and quotes from others—from the prose; the titles of each chapter (there are nearly a hundred, each very short) would have been enlivened with delicately colored capital letters. The manuscript would probably not have been illuminated; fancy books were generally made for royalty, for prestigious ceremonial occasions, or for books that were especially esteemed, such as the Gospels.

There were many such lavish productions. In fact, Carolingian art and architecture mark a turning point. For all its richness, Merovingian culture had not stressed artistic expression, though some of the monasteries inspired by Saint Columbanus produced a few illuminated manuscripts. By contrast, the Carolingians, admirers and

Plate 3.8: Saint Mark, Coronation Gospels (*c.*800). Two portraits of St. Mark (this and the one in **Plate 3.6**), done at about the same time, and in about the same place, could hardly be in more disparate styles. They attest to the eclectic and wide-ranging artistic endeavors of the Carolingians.

imitators of Christian Rome, vigorously promoted a vast, eclectic, and ideologically motivated program of artistic work. They were reviving the Roman empire. We have already seen how Charlemagne brought the very marble of Rome and Ravenna home to Aachen to build his new palace complex. A similar impulse inspired Carolingian art.

As with texts, so with pictures: the Carolingians revered and imitated the past while building on and changing it. Their manuscript illuminations were inspired by a vast repertory of models: from the British Isles (where, as we have seen, a rich synthesis of decorative and representational styles had a long tradition), from late-antique Italy (which yielded its models in old manuscripts), and from Byzantium (which may have inadvertently provided some artists, fleeing iconoclasm, as well as manuscripts).

Plate 3.9 (facing page): Utrecht Psalter (*c.*820–835). Never completed, the Utrecht Psalter was commissioned by Archbishop Ebbo of Reims and executed at a nearby monastery. Providing a visual "running commentary" on every psalm, it may have been meant for Emperor Louis the Pious and his wife Queen Judith.

In Plate 3.6 and Plate 3.7, facing pages from a Carolingian manuscript made in the early ninth century, the artist has borrowed from the Anglo-Saxons by pairing his evangelist portrait of Mark with the beginning of Mark's Gospel text. The interlace motif of the large I in Plate 3.7 is also insular. But insofar as the figure of Saint Mark is sturdy, with clothes clinging to a body of convincing roundness, the artist has used a Byzantine model (compare Plate 3.2). And yet the real inspiration for this Mark is neither English nor Byzantine but entirely original. The evangelist's lively twist—his attention caught by the lion (Mark's symbol) about to give him the Word—and the bright, exuberant colors and designs that frame him are pure Carolingian invention. Like the artist of the Lindisfarne Gospels, the anonymous Mark artist has synthesized figural and decorative elements to suit the flat pages of a book; but the two syntheses are nothing alike.

Quite different, yet equally characteristic of Carolingian art, is the Saint Mark of Plate 3.8, made in the late eighth century. Here is a somber, utterly corporeal evangelist. He sits between mountains, with tinted sky above, light playing on his face. Were it not for his halo, he would be simply a man with a scroll. The colors are soft; the drapery subdued. No one was producing art like this outside of Francia. Its closest comparison is with Pompeiian wall paintings (see Plates 1.1 and 1.2 on pp. 31 and 32).

Both of these styles, the first richly decorative, the second subtly naturalistic, would have long lives in the West. It may even be said that they were the direct ancestors of the entire Western artistic tradition. One more model with a long life must be added: the Utrecht Psalter (Plate 3.9), a book containing all 150 Psalms and 16 other songs known as canticles. Fleeting precedents for this extraordinary manuscript of narrative art exist. For example, Plate 3.7 has lithe figures in the top corners to illustrate Bible stories: on the left is the baptism of Christ, on the right angels minister to Christ after the Temptation. The Utrecht Psalter, produced *c.*820–835, takes this impulse to its logical conclusion. It precedes each poem with drawings that depict its important elements in unified composition. In Plate 3.9, the illustration for Psalm 8, the artist

CIRCUMDABITTE
TPROPTERHANCINALTŪ
REGREDERE · DNSIUDI
CATPOPULOS
UDICAMEDNESECUN
DŪIUSTITIAMMEĀ · ET
SECUNDUMINNOCEN
TIAMMEAMSUPERME
ONSUMMETURNEQUITI
APECCATORŪETDIRI
GESIUSTUM · ETSCRUTANS
CORDAETRENESDS
USTUMADIUTORIUM
MEUMADNO · QUISAL

VIII · INFINEM

UOSFACITRECTOSCORDE
DSIUDEXIUSTUSETFORTIS
ETPATIENS · NUMQUIDI
RASCETURPERSINGU
LOSDIES
NISICONUERSIFUERITIS
GLADIUMSUUMUIBRA
BITARCUMSUUMTE
TENDITETPARAUITILLŪ
ETINEOPARAUITUASA
MORTIS · SAGITTASSU
ASARDENTIBUSEFFECIT ·
ECCEPARTURITINIUS
TITIAM · CONCEPITDO

PROTORCOLARIBUS

LOREMETPEPERITINIQUI
TATEM
LACUMAPERUITETEFFODIT
EUM · ETINCIDITINFOUE
AMQUAMFECIT
CONUERTETURDOLOR
EIUSINCAPUTEIUS · ET
INUERTICEMIPSIUSINI
QUITASEIUSDESCENDET
CONFITEBORDNOSECUN
DUMIUSTITIAMEIUS ·
ETPSALLAMNOMINI
DNIALTISSIMI ;

PSALMUSDAUID

DNEDNSNOSTER
QUAMADMIRABILE
ESTNOMENTUUM
INUNIUERSATERRA ·
QNMELEUATAESTMAG
NIFICENTIATUA · SU
PERCAELOS ·
XOREINFANTIUMETLAC

TANTIUM · PERFECISTI
LAUDEMPROPTERINI
MICOSTUOS · UTDESTRU
ASINIMICUMETULTORĒ ·
QNMUIDEBOCAELOSTU
OSOPERADIGITORŪ
TUORUM · LUNAMETS
TELLASQUAETUFUNDASTI ·

QUIDESTHOMOQUOD
MEMORESEIUS · AUT
FILIUSHOMINISQUO
NIAMUISITASEUM ·
MINUISTIEUMPAULOMI
NUSABANGELIS · GLO
RIAETHONORECORO
NASTIEUM · ETCONS

has, for example, sketched sheep and oxen on the bottom left, birds flying and fish swimming on the bottom right, to render literally verses 8 and 9:

> Thou hast subjected all things under his feet, all sheep and oxen: moreover the beasts also of the fields. / The birds of the air, and the fishes of the sea, that pass through the paths of the sea.

The ambition, style, wit, and narrative thrust of the Utrecht Psalter inspired much art in the Middle Ages and beyond.

* * * *

In the course of the eighth and ninth centuries, the three heirs of Rome established clearly separate identities, each largely bound up with its religious affiliation. Byzantium saw itself as the radiating center of Orthodox faith; the Caliphate was the guarantor of Islam; Francia was "the assembly of Christian people." From this perspective, there were few commonalities. Yet today we are struck more by the similarities than the differences. All were centralizing monarchies shored up by military might. All had a bit of wealth, though the East certainly had more than the West. All had pretensions to God-given power. And all used culture and scholarship to give luster and expression to their political regimes. All may also have known, without explicitly admitting it, how strong were the forces of dissolution.

Chapter Three Key Events

714–741	Charles Martel "Mayor of the Palace" in Francia
732	Charles Martel's victory over Muslim-led army near Poitiers
750	Abbasid caliphate begins
751	Deposition of last Merovingian king; Pippin III elevated to kingship and anointed
754	Death of Boniface
756	"Donation of Pippin"
756	Emirate of Córdoba established
762	Baghdad begun
768–814	Reign of Charlemagne (Charles the Great)
787	Second Council of Nicaea; end of the first phase of iconoclasm
c. 790–*c.* 900	Carolingian Renaissance
c. 790–*c.* 1050	Renaissance in Islamic world
800	Charlemagne crowned emperor
814–840	Reign of Louis the Pious
843	End of iconoclasm in Byzantine empire
847	Treaty of Verdun
c. 860	Arab invasions of Byzantium end
863	Missionary expedition of Constantine (Cyril) and Methodius begins
c. 870–*c.* 1025	Macedonian Renaissance at Byzantium

NOTES

1. Quoted in *Byzantium: Church, Society, and Civilization Seen through Contemporary Eyes*, ed. Deno John Geanakoplos (Chicago, 1984), p.409.
2. "Imports of Iraq" in *Medieval Trade in the Mediterranean World: Illustrative Documents,* trans. Robert S. Lopez and Irving W. Raymond (New York, 1997), p.28.
3. *Algebra of Mohammed ben Musa* as quoted in Dimitri Gutas, *Greek Thought, Arabic Culture: The Graeco-Arabic Translation Movement in Baghdad and Early 'Abbasid Society (2nd-4th/8th-10th Centuries)* (London, 1998), p.113.
4. Quoted in Salma Khadra Jayyusi, "Andalusi Poetry: The Golden Period," in *The Legacy of Muslim Spain* (Leiden, 1994), 1:327.
5. *The Fourth Book of the Chronicle of Fredegar with its Continuations*, trans. J.M. Wallace-Hadrill (London, 1960), p.91.

6. Quoted in Thomas F.X. Noble, *The Republic of St. Peter: The Birth of the Papal State, 680-825* (Philadelphia, 1984), p.263.
7. "Epitaph for Adalhaid," in *Carolingian Civilization: A Reader*, ed. Paul Dutton (Peterborough, 1993), p.46.
8. "The General Capitulary for the Missi from 802," in *Carolingian Civilization*, p.61.
9. "Einhard's *Life of Charlemagne*," in *Carolingian Civilization*, p.38.
10. "Regino's Reasons for the End of the Carolingian Line," in *Carolingian Civilization*, p.507.
11. "Polyptyque of Saint-Germain-des-Prés," quoted in Georges Duby, *Rural Economy and Country Life in the Medieval West*, trans. Cynthia Postan (Philadelphia, 1998), p.368.
12. *Handbook for William: A Carolingian Woman's Counsel for Her Son by Dhuoda*, trans. Carol Neel (2nd ed., Washington, 1991), p.2.

FURTHER READING

Beckwith, John. *The Art of Constantinople: An Introduction to Byzantine Art, 330-1453*. London, 1968.

Chazelle, Celia. *The Crucified God in the Carolingian Era: Theology and Art of Christ's Passion*. Cambridge, 2001.

Collins, Roger. *Charlemagne*. Toronto, 1998.

Fine, John V.A. *The Early Medieval Balkans. A Critical Survey from the Sixth to the Late Twelfth Century*. Ann Arbor, 1991.

Fouracre, Paul. *The Age of Charles Martel*. Harlow, Essex, 2000.

Ganshof, François Louis. *Frankish Institutions under Charlemagne*. Trans. Bryce and Mary Lyon. New York, 1970.

Herrin, Judith. *Women in Purple: Rulers of Medieval Byzantium*. Princeton, 2002.

James, Edward. *Britain in the First Millennium*. London, 2001.

Kennedy, Hugh. *The Abbasid Caliphate: A Political History*. London, 1981.

—. *Muslim Spain and Portugal: A Political History of al-Andalus*. London, 1996.

—. *The Prophet and the Age of the Caliphates: The Islamic Near East from the Sixth to the Eleventh Century*. London, 1986.

McCormick, Michael. *Origins of the European Economy: Communications and Commerce, AD 300-900*. Cambridge, 2001.

McKitterick, Rosamond, ed. *Carolingian Culture: Emulation and Innovation*. Cambridge, 1994.

—. *The Carolingians and the Written Word*. Cambridge, 1989.

Nelson, Janet L. *Charles the Bald*. London, 1992.

—. *The Frankish World, 750-900*. London, 1996.

Treadgold, Warren. *The Byzantine Revival, 780-842*. Stanford, 1988.

Verhulst, Adriaan. *The Carolingian Economy*. Cambridge, 2002.

Whittow, Mark. *The Making of Byzantium, 600-1025*. Berkeley, 1996.

FOUR

POLITICAL COMMUNITIES REORDERED (*c*.900–*c*.1050)

THE LARGE-SCALE CENTRALIZED governments of the ninth century dissolved in the tenth. The fission was least noticeable at Byzantium, where, although important landowning families emerged as brokers of patronage and power, the primacy of the emperor was never effectively challenged. Quite the opposite happened in the Islamic world, where new dynastic groups quickly established themselves as regional rulers. In Western Europe, Carolingian kings ceased to control land and men, while new political entities—some extremely local and weak, others quite strong and unified—emerged in their wake. Everywhere political reordering brought new military elites to the fore.

BYZANTIUM: THE STRENGTHS AND LIMITS OF CENTRALIZATION

By 1025 the Byzantine empire once again shadowed the Danube and touched the Euphrates. To the north it had a new and restless neighbor: Kievan Rus. The emperors at Constantinople maintained the traditional cultural importance of the capital city by carefully orchestrating the radiating power of the imperial court. Nevertheless, the centralized model of the Byzantine state was challenged by powerful men in the countryside, who gobbled up land and dominated the peasantry.

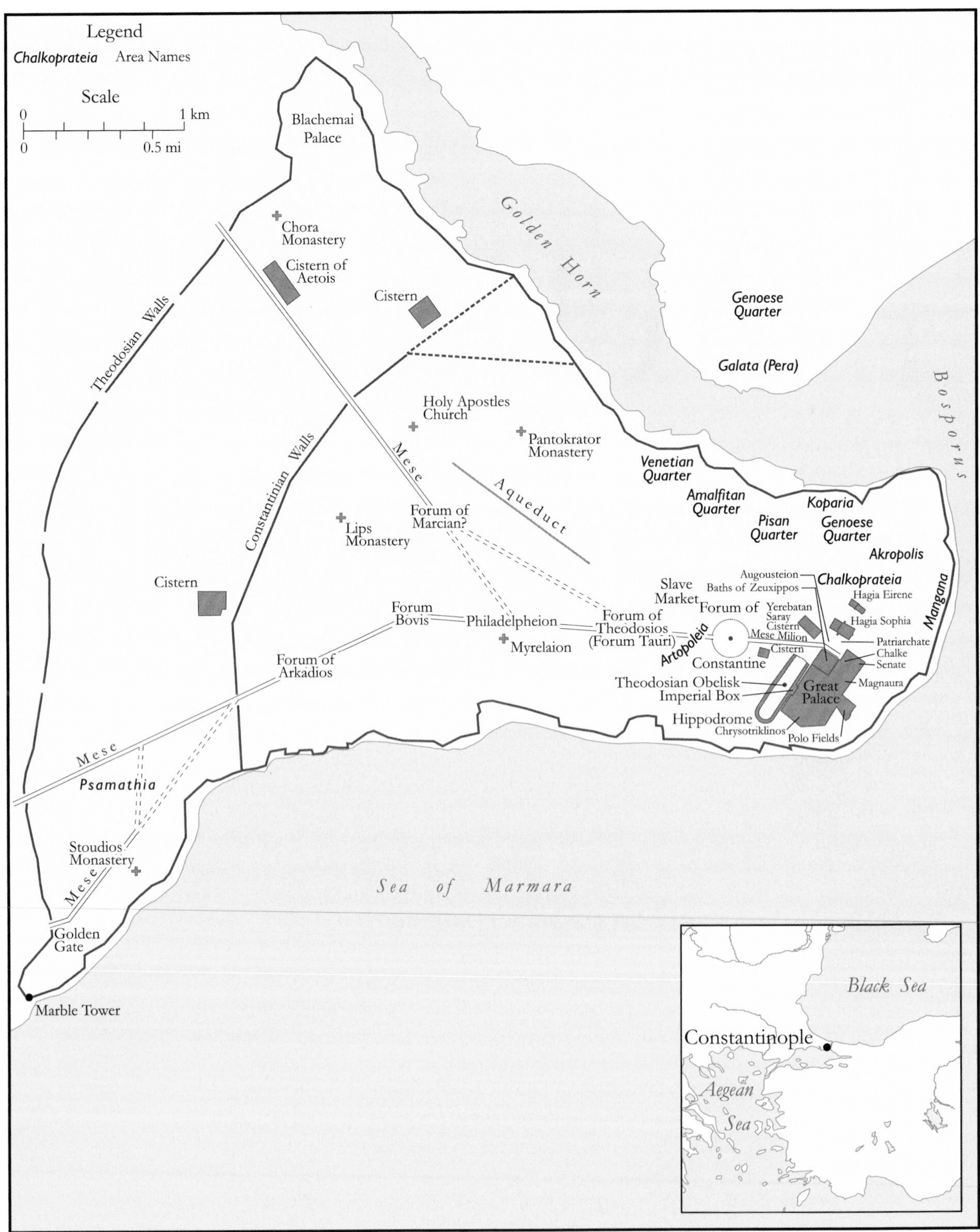

Legend
Chalkoprateia Area Names
Scale
0
1 km
0
0.5 mi
Blachemai Palace
Chora Monastery
Cistern of Aetois
Cistern
Golden Horn
Genoese Quarter
Galata (Pera)
Bosporus
Theodosian Walls
Constantinian Walls
Holy Apostles Church
Pantokrator Monastery
Mese
Aqueduct
Venetian Quarter
Amalfitan Quarter
Koparia
Pisan Quarter
Genoese Quarter
Akropolis
Forum of Marcian?
Lips Monastery
Cistern
Augousteion
Chalkoprateia
Baths of Zeuxippos
Hagia Eirene
Mangana
Slave Market
Forum of Constantine
Yerebatan Saray Cistern
Hagia Sophia
Mese Milion
Patriarchate
Cistern
Chalke
Senate
Forum Bovis
Philadelpheion
Forum of Theodosios (Forum Tauri)
Artopoleia
Myrelaion
Forum of Arkadios
Theodosian Obelisk
Great Palace
Magnaura
Imperial Box
Hippodrome
Chrysotriklinos
Polo Fields
Mese
Psamathia
Stoudios Monastery
Mese
Sea of Marmara
Golden Gate
Marble Tower
Black Sea
Constantinople
Aegean Sea

The Imperial Court

The Great Palace of Constantinople, a sprawling building complex begun under Constantine, was expanded, redecorated, and fortified under his successors. (See Map 4.1.) It was more than the symbolic emplacement of imperial power; it was the central command post of the empire. Servants, slaves, and grooms; top courtiers and learned clergymen; cousins, siblings, and hangers-on of the emperor and empress lived within its walls. Other courtiers—civil servants, officials, scholars, military men, advisers, and other dependents—lived as nearby as they could manage. They were "on call" at every hour. The emperor had only to give short notice and all were to be at the Palace for impromptu but nevertheless highly choreographed ceremonies. These were in themselves instruments of power; the emperors manipulated courtly formalities to indicate new favorites or to signal displeasure.

Map 4.1 (facing page): Constantinople before *c.*1100

Highly visible at the Great Palace were corps of eunuchs, castrated men who acted as advisers, guards, and go-betweens for the empress and her female entourage. There were important empresses in the tenth and eleventh centuries, women like Zoë, the niece of Basil II (*r.*963-1025), who orchestrated the downfall of one emperor and the rise of another. Nevertheless, she did so only because she was the wife of the first and the lover of the second; hers was the power of the bedroom. The eunuchs at court reminded everyone that *real* power was not a matter of fecundity. It was a matter of proximity to the emperor. Eunuchs, who could not have children and therefore could not pass possessions and power to their heirs, were close to the emperor precisely because they could be trusted to be innocently near the empress, bearer of the emperor's children. No wonder that in the tenth century, Basil the Nothos, the castrated bastard son of one emperor, rose to become grand chamberlain (responsible for internal affairs) at the court of another.

About a century later, the grand chamberlain was not a eunuch but rather a professor, Michael Psellos. The Macedonian Renaissance, which had begun in the ninth century, continued apace in the tenth and eleventh, bringing people like Psellos to the fore. Under his direction a new school of philosophy at Constantinople, founded by Constantine IX (*r.*1042-1055), began to flourish. Beyond his philosophical interests, Psellos was a moralist, keen to explore the character and emotional life of powerful men and women. In his hands, a new sort of historical writing was born: not a universal chronicle covering Creation to the present, as had been the style, but rather opinionated accounts of recent events, personalities, and well-oiled political networks:

> Basil [II] surrounded himself with favorites who were neither remarkable for brilliance of intellect, nor of noble lineage, nor too learned. To them

were entrusted the imperial rescripts [orders], and with them he was accustomed to share the secrets of State.[1]

The impression that Psellos gives of a self-indulgent emperor presiding over a frivolous court is only part of the story, however. As Psellos himself recognized, Basil was a successful centralizer, amassing enormous wealth through taxes, confiscations, and tribute. Above all—something that Psellos only hinted at—he was a tough military man whose rule reshaped the geography of Byzantium.

A Wide Embrace and Its Tensions

Map 4.2: The Byzantine Empire, *c.*1025

The expansion of the Byzantine Empire, so cautiously begun in the ninth century, quickened under the tenth-century soldier-emperors Nicephorus Phocas and John Tzimisces. (See Map 4.2.) Crete, lost to the Muslims in the ninth century, was retaken in 961; Cyprus was reconquered in 965; Antioch, portal to Syria, in 969. Most

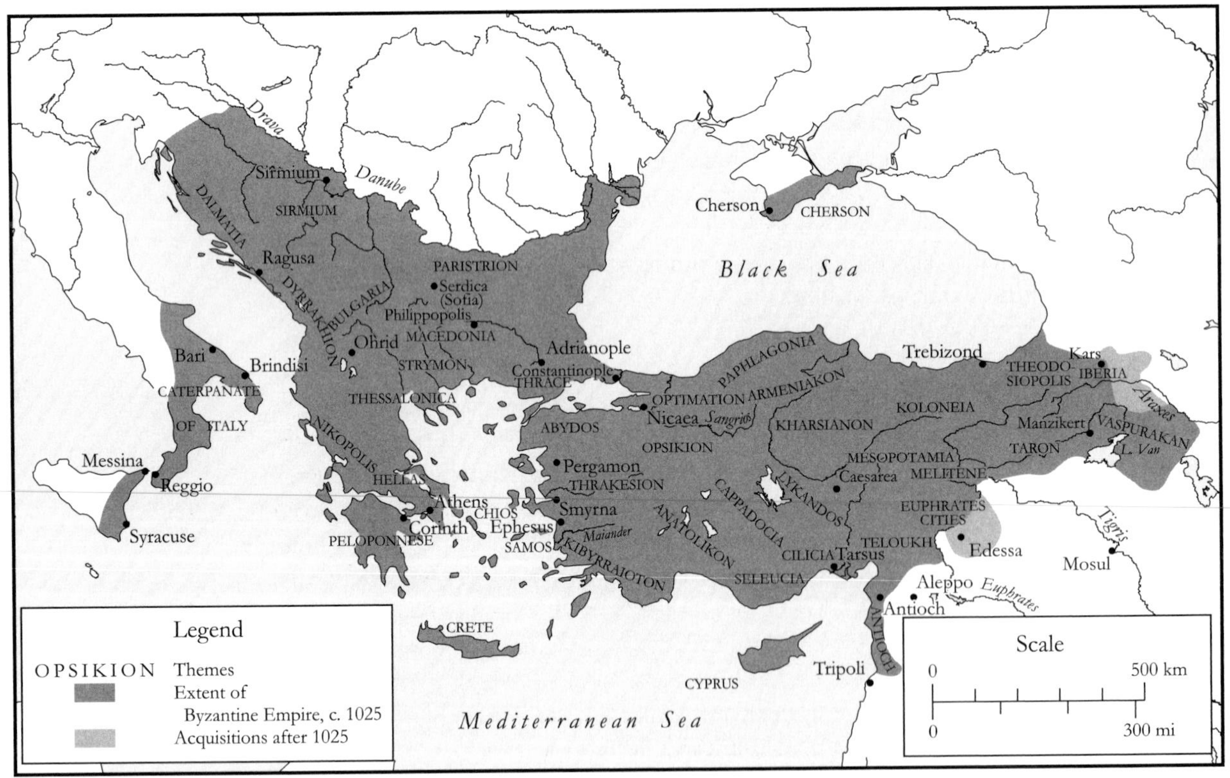

importantly, under Basil II, Bulgaria, a thorn in Byzantium's side since the seventh century, was at last definitively defeated (1018). The entire region was put under Byzantine rule, its territory divided into themes.

Certainly Basil's nickname, the "Bulgar Slayer," was apt. Nevertheless, it hid the fact that the same emperor was also busy setting up protectorates against the Muslims on his eastern front and that at the end of his life he was preparing an expedition to Sicily. By 1025 the Byzantine army was no longer focused on the interior but was rather mobilized at the peripheries of the empire.

This empire was no longer the tight fist centered on Anatolia that it had been in the dark days of the eighth century. On the contrary, it was an open hand: sprawling, multi-ethnic, and multilingual. To the east it embraced Armenians, Syrians, and Arabs; to the north it included Bulgarians and other Slavs as well as Pechenegs, a Turkic group that had served as allies of Bulgaria; to the west, in the Byzantine toe of Italy, it contained Lombards, Italians, and Greeks. There must have been Muslims right in the middle of Constantinople: a mosque was built for them there in 1027. Russian soldiers from the region of Kiev formed the backbone of Basil's "Varangian Guard," his elite troops; by mid-century, Byzantine mercenaries included "Franks" (mainly from Normandy), Arabs, and Bulgarians as well. In spite of ingrained prejudices, Byzantine princesses had occasionally been married to foreigners before the tenth century, but only in Basil's reign did this happen to a sister of the emperor himself.

All this openness went only so far, however. In the tenth century, the emperors expelled Jews from Constantinople, severely curtailing their participation in the silk trade (their traditional profession), and forcing them into the degrading labor of tanners. Some of these restrictions were lifted in the course of the eleventh century, but Jews were never integrated into Byzantine society. Similarly, the annexation of Armenia did not lead to the assimilation of Armenians, who kept their Monophysite beliefs, heretical to many Orthodox Byzantines.

Ethnic diversity was in part responsible for new regional political movements that threatened centralized imperial control. More generally, however, regional revolts were the result of the rise of a new class of wealthy provincial landowners, the *dynatoi* (*sing. dynatos*), "powerful men." Benefitting from a general quickening in the economy and the rise of new urban centers, they took advantage of unaccustomed wealth, buying land from still impoverished peasants as yet untouched by the economic upswing. The *dynatoi* made military men their clients (even if they were not themselves military men) and often held positions in government. The Dalasseni family was fairly typical of this group. The founder of the family was an army leader and governor of Antioch at the end of the tenth century. One of his sons, Theophylact, became governor of "Iberia"—not Spain but rather a theme on the very eastern edge of the empire. Another, Constantine, inherited his father's position at Antioch. With estates scattered throughout Anatolia and a network of connections to other powerful families, the Dalasseni at times could defy the emperor and even coordinate rebellions against him. From the end of the tenth century, imperial control had to contend with the decentralizing forces of provincial *dynatoi* such as these. But the emperors were not dethroned, and a man like Basil II could triumph over the families that challenged his reign to emerge even stronger than before.

The rise of the provincial aristocracy and the prestige of the soldier emperors worked a change in Byzantine culture: from civilian to military ideals. The emperor had long ceased to be "declared" by his troops; but in the eleventh century artists insisted on portraying the emperor hoisted on a shield, symbol of military power. An epic poem, *Digenis Akritas*, begun in the tenth century and probably put into its final form in the eleventh or twelfth, depicts the hero, Digenis, winning battles, wooing beautiful women, and (most important from the aristocratic point of view) giving advice to a respectful emperor. Military saints, such as George, became increasingly popular, while even non-military saints were now sometimes depicted as "knights" on horseback.

Map 4.3 (facing page): Kievan Rus, *c.*1050

The Formation of Kievan Rus

During the eighth and ninth centuries, a fledgling principality had taken shape above the Black Sea, along the Dnieper River. (See Map 4.3.) At first the "Rus" were itinerant raiders and traders from Scandinavia, the eastern counterpart to the Viking invaders of the West. Gradually they imposed their rule over the Slavs inhabiting the broad river valleys connecting the Baltic with the Black Sea, adopting the language of their subjects. At the end of the ninth century, one Dnieper valley chief, Oleg, established control over most of the tribes in southwestern Russia and turned more distant groups into tributaries. The tribal association that he created formed the nucleus of Kievan Rus, named for the city that had become the commercial center of the region and is today the capital of Ukraine.

Rus and Byzantium began their relationship in war, developed it through trade agreements, and sustained it with religion. Around 905, Oleg launched a military expedition to Constantinople, forcing the Byzantines to pay a large indemnity and open their doors to Russian traders in exchange for peace. At the time, only a few Christians lived in Rus, along with Jews and probably some Muslims. The conversion of the Rus to Christianity was spearheaded by Grand Prince Vladimir (*d.*1015). In 988, he adopted the Byzantine form of Christianity, took the name "Basil" in honor of Emperor Basil II, and married Anna, the emperor's sister. Then he reportedly had all of the people of his state baptized in the Dnieper River.

Scale
0
500 km
0
300 mi
Lake Ladoga
Kingdom of Sweden
Kingdom of Denmark
Baltic Sea
Western Dvina
Volga
Vladimir
Suzdal
Kievan Rus
Polatsk
Smolensk
Kolobrzeg
Wolin
Radgošč
Vistula
Poznań
Gniezno
Plock
Oder
Poland
Bautzen
Wroclaw
Chernihiv
Cracow
Czerwien
Volodymyr
Kiev
Pereiaslav
Przemyśl
Halych
Dnieper
Vienna
Nitra
Esztergom
Székesfehérvár
Hungary
Dniester
Zagreb
Kalocsa
Pannonia
Sea of Azov
Croatia
Split
Danube
Doclea
(Serbian Kgdm)
Dubrovnik
Duklja
Adriatic Sea
Serdica
Preslav
Odessos
Black Sea
Bari
Philippopolis
Dyrrhachium
Brindisi
Byzantine Empire

Vladimir's conversion was part of a larger movement of the tenth and eleventh centuries in which most of the remaining non-monotheistic peoples of the western Eurasian land mass adopted one of the four dominant monotheisms: Islam, Roman Catholicism, Byzantine Orthodoxy, or Judaism. Given its geographic location, it was anyone's guess which way Rus would go. On its western flank was Poland, where in 966, Mieszko I (*r.*963-992), leader of the tribe known as the Polanians, accepted baptism into the Roman Catholic faith. Eventually (in 991) he placed his realm under the protection of the pope. The experience of Hungary, just south of Poland, was similar: there Géza (*r. c.* 972-997) converted to Roman Catholicism and, according to a potent legend, his son, Stephen I (*r.*997-1038), accepted a royal crown from the pope in the year 1000 or 1001. Further north the ancestors of the Rus, the Scandinavians, were also turning to Catholic Christianity: the king of the Danes, for example, was baptized around 960. But to the east of Rus were other models: the Khazars were Jewish; the Volga Bulgars converted to Islam in the early tenth century. Why, then, did Vladimir choose the Byzantine form of Christianity? Perhaps because he could drive the hardest bargain with Basil, who badly needed Rus troops for his Varangian Guard.

That momentary decision left lasting consequences. Rus, ancestor of Russia, became the heir of the Byzantine church, customs, art, and political ideology. Adopting Christianity linked Russia to the West, but choosing the Byzantine form meant that Russia would always stand apart from Western Europe.

DIVISION AND DEVELOPMENT IN THE ISLAMIC WORLD

While at Byzantium the forces of decentralization were feeble, they carried the day in the Islamic world. Where once the caliph at Baghdad or Samarra could boast collecting taxes from Kabul (today in Afghanistan) to Benghazi (today in Libya), in the eleventh century a bewildering profusion of regional groups and dynasties divided the Islamic world. Yet this was in general a period of prosperity and intellectual blossoming.

The Emergence of Regional Powers

The Muslim conquest had never eliminated all local powers or regional affiliations. It had simply papered over them. While the Umayyad and Abbasid caliphates remained strong, they imposed their rule through their governors and army. But when the caliphate became weak, as it did in the tenth and eleventh centuries, old and new regional interests came to the fore.

A glance at a map of the Islamic world *c.*1000 (Map 4.4) shows, from east to west, the main new groups that emerged: the Samanids, Buyids, Hamdanids, Fatimids, and Zirids. But the map hides the many territories dominated by petty independent rulers. North of the Fatimid Caliphate, al-Andalus had a parallel history. Its Umayyad ruler took the title of caliph in 929, but in the eleventh century, he too was unable to stave off political fragmentation.

The key cause of the weakness of the Abbasid caliphate was lack of revenue. When landowners, governors, or recalcitrant military leaders in the various regions of the Islamic world refused to pay taxes into the treasury, the caliphs had to rely on the rich farmland of Iraq, long a stable source of income. But in the tenth century, Iraq was attacked by the Qaramita (sometimes called the "Carmathians"), a sect of Shi'ites based in Arabia. In the wake of this war, Iraq's agriculture was both sabotaged and neglected. The result was decisive: the caliphs could not pay their troops. New

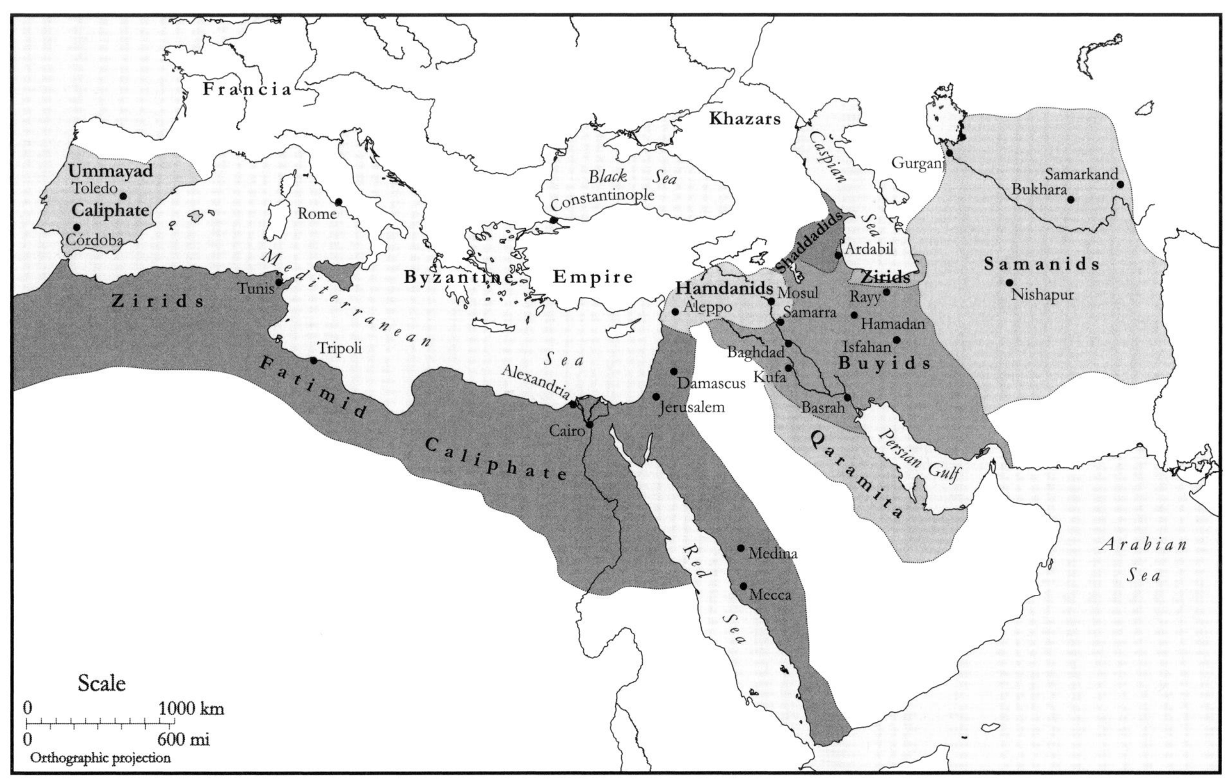

Map 4.4: Fragmentation of the Islamic World

men—military men with their own armies and titles like "commander of commanders"—took the reins of power. They did not wipe out the Abbasid line, but they reduced the caliph's political authority to nothing.

The new leaders represented groups that had awaited their day in the sun. The Buyids, for example, belonged to ancient warrior tribes from the mountains of Iran. Even in the tenth century, most were relatively new converts to Islam. Bolstered by long-festering local discontent, one of them became "commander of commanders" in 945. Thereafter, the Buyids, with the help from their own Turkish mercenaries, dominated the region south of the Caspian Sea, including Baghdad (once again the home of the caliphs) itself. Yet already by the end of the tenth century, their own power was challenged by still more local men, in a political process—the progressive regionalization and fragmentation of power—echoed elsewhere in the Islamic world and in parts of Western Europe as well.

The most important of the new regional rulers were the Fatimids. They, like the Qaramita (and, increasingly in the course of time, the Buyids), were Shi'ites, taking their name from Muhammad's daughter Fatimah, wife of Ali. The Fatimid leader claimed to be not only the true *imam*, descendant of Ali, but also the *mahdi*, the "divinely guided" messiah, come to bring justice on earth. Because of this, the Fatimids were proclaimed "caliphs" by their followers—the true "successors" of the Prophet. Allying with the Berbers in North Africa, the Fatimids established themselves as rulers by 909 in what is today Tunisia and Libya. Within a half-century they had moved eastward (largely abandoning the Maghreb to the Zirids), to rule Egypt, southern Syria, and the western edge of the Arabian Peninsula.

The Fatimids looked east rather than west because the east was rich and because the west was dominated by Sunnis, hostile to Shi'ite rule. The most important of the Sunni rulers were the Umayyads at Córdoba. Abd al-Rahman III (*r.*912–961) took the title caliph in 929 as a counterweight to the Fatimids, although he claimed to rule only all of al-Andalus, not the whole Islamic world. An active military man backed by an army made up mainly of Slavic slaves, al-Rahman defeated his rivals and imposed his rule not only on southern Iberia (as his predecessors had done) but also in northern regions (near the Christian kingdoms) and in the Maghreb. Under al-Rahman and his immediate successors, al-Andalus became a powerful centralized state. But regional Islamic rulers there worked to undermine the authority of the Umayyads, so that between 1009 and 1031 bitter civil war undid the dynasty's power. After 1031, al-Andalus was split into small "kingdoms," called *taifas*, ruled by local strongmen.

Thus in the Islamic world, far more decisively than at Byzantium, newly powerful men came to the fore. They were less tied to private estates than the *dynatoi* of Byzantium, and their dependence on slaves and mercenaries—foreigners without any roots at all in local soil—was also different. At Byzantium the ascendency of the military classes led poets and artists to praise warriors in general. In the Islamic world as well, a few writers proudly portrayed old Persian and Bedouin heroes as model fighting men. In the *Shahnama* (*Book of Kings*) by the poet Firdawsi (*c.*935-*c.*1020), the hero slays demons and saves kings. But on the whole, poets and writers continued to laud "civilian" life and to embroider the old themes of *adab* literature.

Cultural Unity, Religious Polarization

In fact, the emergence of local strongmen meant not the end of Arab court culture but a multiplicity of courts, each attempting to out-do one another in brilliant artistic, scientific, theological, and literary productions. Consider Cairo, for example, which was founded by the Fatimids. Already by 1000 it was a huge urban complex. Imitating the Abbasids, the Fatimid caliphs built mosques and palaces, fostered court ceremonials, and turned Cairo into a center of intellectual life. One of the Fatimid caliphs, al-Hakim, founded the *dar al-ilm*, a sort of theological college plus public library.

Even more impressive was the Umayyad court at Córdoba, the wealthiest and showiest city of the west. It boasted 70 public libraries in addition to the caliphs' private library of perhaps 400,000 books. The Córdoban Great Mosque was a center for scholars from the rest of the Islamic world (the caliph paid their salaries), while nearly 30 free schools were set up throughout the city. A later chronicler boasted, "Córdoba held more books than any other city in al-Andalus, and its inhabitants were the most enthusiastic in caring for their libraries; such collections were regarded as symbols of status and social leadership."[2]

Córdoba was noteworthy not only because of the brilliance of its intellectual life but also because of the role women played in it. Elsewhere in the Islamic world there were certainly a few unusual women associated with cultural and scholarly life. But at Córdoba this was a general phenomenon: women not only were doctors, teachers, and librarians but also worked as copyists for the many books so widely in demand.

Male scholars were, however, everywhere the norm, and they moved easily from court to court. Ibn Sina (980-1037), known to the West as Avicenna, began his career serving the ruler at Bukhara, and then moved to Gurganj, Rayy, and Hamadan before ending up for thirteen years at the court of Isfahan. Sometimes in favor and sometimes decidedly not so (he was even briefly imprisoned), he nevertheless managed to study and practice medicine and write numerous books on the natural sciences and philosophy. His pioneering systematization of Aristotle laid the foundations of future philosophical thought.

Despite its political disunity, then, the Islamic world of the tenth and eleventh centuries remained in many ways an integrated culture. This was partly due to the model of intellectual life fostered by the Abbasids, which even in decline was copied by the new rulers, as we have just seen. It was also due to the common Arabic language, the glue that bound the astronomer at Córdoba to the philosopher at Cairo. Finally, integration was the result of open trade networks. With no national barriers to commerce and few regulations, merchants regularly dealt in far-flung, various, and sometimes exotic goods. From England came tin, while salt and gold were imported from Timbuktu in west-central Africa; from Russia came amber, gold, and copper; slaves were wrested from sub-Saharan Africa, the Eurasian steppes, and Slavic regions.

Although Muslims dominated these trade networks, other groups were involved in commerce as well. We happen to know a good deal about one Jewish community living at Fustat, about two miles south of Cairo. It observed the then-common custom of depositing for eventual ritual burial all writing containing the name of God. For good measure, the Jews in this community privileged everything written in Hebrew: letters, business transactions, shopping lists. By chance, the materials that they left in their *geniza* (depository) at Fustat were preserved rather than burned. These sources reveal a cosmopolitan, middle-class society. Many were traders, for Fustat was the center of a vast and predominately Jewish trade network that stretched from al-Andalus to India. Consider the Tustari brothers, Jewish merchants from southern Iran. By the early eleventh century, the brothers had established a flourishing business in Egypt. Informal family networks offered them many of the same advantages as branch offices: friends and family in Iran shipped the Tustaris fine textiles to sell in Egypt, while they exported Egyptian fabrics back to Iran.

Only Islam, ironically, pulled Islamic culture apart. In the tenth century the split between the Sunnis and Shi'ites widened to a chasm. At Baghdad, al-Mufid (*d.*1022) and others turned Shi'ism into a partisan ideology that insisted on publicly cursing the first two caliphs, turning the tombs of Ali and his family into objects of veneration, and creating an Alid caliph by force. Small wonder that the Abbasid caliphs soon became ardent spokesmen for Sunni Islam, which developed in turn its own public symbols. But many of the new dynasties—the Fatimids and the Qaramita especially—took advantage of the newly polarized faith to bolster their power.

THE WEST: FRAGMENTATION AND RESILIENCE

Fragmentation was the watchword in Western Europe in many parts of the shattered Carolingian Empire. Historians speak of "France," "Germany," and "Italy" in this period as a shorthand for designating broad geographical areas. But there were no national states, only regions with more or less clear borders and rulers with more or less authority. In some places—in parts of "France," for example—regions as small as a few square miles were under the control of different lords who acted, in effect, as independent rulers. Yet this same period saw both England and Scotland become unified kingdoms. And to the east, in Saxony, a powerful royal dynasty, the Ottonians, emerged to rule an empire stretching from the North Sea to Rome.

The Last Invaders of the West

Three groups invaded Western Europe during the ninth and tenth centuries: the Vikings, the Muslims, and the Hungarians. (See Map 4.5.) In the short run, they wreaked havoc on land and people. In the long run, they were absorbed into the European population and became constituents of a newly prosperous and aggressive European civilization.

The Vikings

At the same time as they made their forays into Russia, the Vikings were raiding the coasts of France, England, Scotland, and Ireland. In their longships—often traveling as families with husbands, wives, children, and slaves—they crossed the Atlantic, making themselves at home in Iceland and Greenland and, in about 1000, touching on North America. They settled as well in Ireland, Scotland, England, and Normandy (giving their name to the region: Norman = Northman, or Viking).

In Ireland, where the Vikings settled in the east and south, the newcomers added their own claims to rule an island already fragmented among four or five competing dynasties. In Scotland, however, in the face of Norse settlements in the north and west, the natives drew together under kings who—in a process we have seen elsewhere—allied themselves with churchmen and other powerful local leaders. Cináed mac Ailpín (Kenneth I MacAlpin) (*d.*858) established a hereditary dynasty of kings that ruled over two hitherto separate native peoples. By *c.*900, the separate identities were gone, and most people in *Alba*, the nucleus of the future Scotland, had a common sense of their identity as Scots.

England underwent a similar process of unification. Initially divided into small competing kingdoms, it was weak prey in the face of invasion. By the end of the ninth century, the Vikings were plowing fields in eastern England and living in accordance with their own laws. In Wessex, the southernmost kingdom, King Alfred the Great (*r.*871-899) bought time and peace, paying a tribute with the income from a new tax, later called the Danegeld (it eventually became the basis of a relatively lucrative taxation system in England). Even more importantly, in 878 he mustered an army and, as his biographer, Asser, put it,

> gained the victory through God's will. He destroyed the Vikings with great slaughter, and pursued those who fled as far as the stronghold, hacking them down; he seized everything which he found outside the stronghold—men (whom he killed immediately), horses, and cattle—and boldly made camp in front of the gates of the Viking stronghold with all his army. When he had been there for fourteen days the Vikings, thoroughly terrified by hunger, cold and fear, and in the end by despair, sought peace.[3]

Map 4.5 (facing page): Viking, Muslim, and Hungarian Invasions

Thereafter the pressure of invasion eased as Alfred reorganized his army, set up strongholds of his own (called *burhs*), and created a fleet of ships—a real navy. An uneasy stability was achieved, with the Vikings dominating the east of England and Alfred and his successors gaining control over most of the rest.

On the Continent, too, the invaders came to stay, above all in Normandy. The new inhabitants of the region were integrated into the political system when, in 911, their leader Rollo converted to Christianity and received Normandy as a duchy from the Frankish king Charles the Simple (or Straightforward). Although many of the Normans adopted sedentary ways, some of their descendants in the early eleventh century ventured to the Mediterranean, where they established themselves as rulers of petty principalities in southern Italy; by mid-century they had their eyes on Sicily.

Muslims

Sicily, once Byzantine, was the rich and fertile plum of the conquests achieved by the Muslim invaders of the ninth and tenth centuries. That they took the island attests to the power of a new Muslim navy developed by the dynasty that preceded the Fatimids in Ifriqiya. After 909, Sicily came under Fatimid rule, but by mid-century it was controlled by independent Islamic princes, and Muslim immigrants were swelling the population.

Elsewhere the new Muslim presence in western Europe was more ephemeral. In the first half of the tenth century, Muslim raiders pillaged southern France, northern

Greenland
Reykavik
Iceland
Faroe Is.
Atlantic
Ocean
Shetland Is.
Orkney Is.
North
Sea
Trondheim
Norway
NORSE
Sweden
SWEDES
Birka
Ladoga
Novgorod
Ireland
Dublin
DANES
Trelleborg
Denmark
Baltic Sea
Volga
Hedeby
Saxony
Vistula
SLAVS
Rouen
Normandy
Seine
Paris
Loire
Kiev
Dnieper
Burgundy
Bavaria
HUNGARIANS
al-Andalus
Lisbon
Barcelona
Cremona
Marseilles
Genoa
Rome
Danube
Bulgaria
Black Sea
Seville
Constantinople
Byzantine Empire
Zirids
Sicily
Mediterranean
Sea
Legend
Viking settlements
Viking-raided areas
Disputed area between Hungarians & Croatians
Viking invasions
Hungarian invasions
Muslim invasions
Scale
0
500 km
0
300 mi
Fatimid Caliphate

Italy, and the Alpine passes. But these were quick expeditions, largely attacks on churches and monasteries. Some of these Muslims did establish themselves at la Garde-Freinet, in Provence, becoming landowners in the region and lords of Christian serfs. They even hired themselves out as occasional fighters for the wars that local Christian aristocrats were waging against one another. But they made the mistake of capturing for ransom the holiest man of his era, Abbot Majolus of Cluny. Outraged, the local aristocracy finally came together and ousted the Muslims from their midst.

Hungarians

By contrast, a new kingdom was created by the Hungarians. ("Magyar" was and remains their name for themselves, but the rest of Europe called them "Hungarians," from the Slavonic for "Onogurs," a people already settled in the Danube basin in the eighth and ninth centuries.) The Hungarians who invaded Europe came from the Black Sea region. Living as nomads who raised (and rode) horses, they spoke a language unrelated to any other in Europe (except Finnish). Known as effective warriors, they were employed by Arnulf, king of the East Franks (887-899), during his war against the Moravians and by the Byzantine emperor Leo VI (886-912) during his struggle against the Bulgars. In 894, taking advantage of their position, the Hungarians conquered much of the Danube basin for themselves.

From there, for over fifty years, the Hungarians raided into Germany, Italy, and even southern France. At the same time, however, they worked for various western rulers. Until 937 they spared Bavaria, for example, because they were allies of its duke. Gradually they made the transition from nomads to farmers and coalesced into the Kingdom of Hungary. This is no doubt a major reason for the end of their attacks. At the time, however, the cessation of their raids was widely credited to the German king Otto I (*r.*936-973), who won a major victory over a Hungarian marauding party at the battle of Lechfeld in 955.

Polytheists at the time of their entry into the West, the majority of the Hungarians were peasants, initially specializing in herding but soon busy cultivating vineyards, orchards, and grains. Above them was a warrior class, and above the warriors were the elites, whose richly furnished graves reveal the importance of weapons, jewelry, and horses to this society. Originally organized into tribes led by dukes, the Hungarians coalesced by the mid-tenth century under one ruling house—that of Géza. Determined to put his power on a new footing, Géza accepted baptism, probably by a bishop from Germany, and pledged to convert all his subjects. His son, Stephen I, consolidated the change to Christianity: he built churches and monasteries, and required everyone to attend church on Sundays. Establishing his authority as sole ruler, Stephen had himself crowned "king" in the year 1000 (or possibly 1001).

Public Power and Private Relationships

The invasions left new political configurations as they receded. Unlike the Byzantines and Muslims, Western rulers had no mercenaries and no salaried officials. They commanded others by ensuring personal loyalty. The Carolingian kings had had their *fideles*—their faithful men. Tenth-century rulers were even more dependent on ties of dependency: they needed their "men" (*homines*), their "vassals" (*vassalli*). Whatever the term, all were armed retainers who fought for a lord. Sometimes these subordinates held land from that lord, either as a reward for their military service or as an inheritance for which services were due. The term for such an estate, fief (*feodum*), gave historians the word "feudalism" to describe the social and economic system created by the relationships among lords, vassals, and fiefs. Some recent historians argue that the word "feudalism" has been used in too many different and contradictory ways to mean anything at all: is it a mode of exploiting the land that involves lords and serfs? A state of anarchy and lawlessness? Or a state of ordered gradations of power, from the king on down? All of these definitions have been given. Ordinarily we may dispense with the word feudalism, though it can be very useful as a "fuzzy category" when contrasting, for example, the political, social, and economic organization of Antiquity with that of the Middle Ages.

Lords and Vassals

The key to tenth- and eleventh-century society was personal dependency. This took many forms. Of the three traditional "orders" recognized by writers in the ninth through eleventh centuries—those who pray (the *oratores*), those who fight (the *bellatores*), and those who work (the *laboratores*)—the top two were free. The pray-ers (the monks) and the fighters (the nobles and their lower-class cousins, the knights) participated in prestigious kinds of subordination, whether as vassals, lords, or both. Indeed, they were usually both: a typical warrior was lord of several vassals and the vassal of another lord. Monasteries normally had vassals to fight for them, while their abbots in turn were vassals of a king or other lord. At the low end of the social scale, poor vassals looked to their lords to feed, clothe, house, and arm them. At the upper end, vassals looked to their lords to enrich them with still more fiefs.

Some women were vassals, and some were lords (or, rather, "ladies," the female counterpart). Many upper-class laywomen participated in the society of warriors and monks as wives and mothers of vassals and lords and as landowners in their own right. Others entered convents and became *oratores* themselves. Through its abbess or a man standing in for her, a convent was itself often the "lord" of vassals.

Vassalage was voluntary and public. In some areas, it was marked by a ceremony:

the vassal-to-be knelt and, placing his hands between the hands of his lord, said, "I promise to be your man." This act, known as "homage," was followed by the promise of "fealty"—fidelity, trust, and service—which the vassal swore with his hand on relics or a Bible. Then the vassal and the lord kissed. In an age when many people could not read, a public moment such as this represented a visual and verbal contract, binding the vassal and lord together with mutual obligations to help one another.

Lords and Peasants

At the lowest end of the social scale were those who worked: the peasants. In many regions of Europe, as power fell into the hands of local rulers, the distinction between "free" and "unfree" peasants began to blur; many peasants simply became "serfs," dependents of lords. This was a heavy dependency, without prestige or honor. It was hereditary rather than voluntary: no serf did homage or fealty; no serf kissed his lord as an equal.

Indeed, peasants were barely noticed by the upper classes, except as sources of revenue. In the tenth century, the three-field system became more prevalent; heavy iron-coulter plows which could turn the heavy northern soils came into wider use; and horses (more efficient than oxen) were sometimes used to pull the plows. The result was surplus food and a better standard of living for nearly everyone.

In search of still greater profits, some lords lightened the dues and services of peasants temporarily to allow them to open up new lands by draining marshes and cutting down forests. Other lords converted dues and labor services into money payments, providing themselves with ready cash. Peasants benefitted from these rents as well because their payments were fixed despite inflation. As the prices of agricultural products went up, peasants became small-scale entrepreneurs, selling their chickens and eggs at local markets and reaping a profit.

In the eleventh century, and increasingly so in the twelfth, peasant settlements gained boundaries and focus: they became real villages. (For the example of Toury, see Map 7.5 on p.279 of volume 2) The parish church often formed the center, around which was the cemetery. Then, normally crowded right onto the cemetery itself, were the houses, barns, animals, and tools of the living peasants. Boundary markers—sometimes simple stones, at other times real fortifications—announced not only the physical limit of the village but also its sense of community. This derived from very practical concerns: peasants needed to share oxen or horses to pull their plows; they were all dependent on the village craftsmen to fix their wheels or shoe their horses.

Variety was the hallmark of peasant society for this period of history across the regions of Europe. In Saxony and other parts of Germany free peasants prevailed. In

France and England most were serfs. In Italy peasants ranged from small independent landowners to leaseholders; most were both, owning a parcel in one place and leasing another nearby.

Where the power of kings was weak, peasant obligations became part of a larger system of local rule. As landlords consolidated their power over their manors, they collected not only dues and services but also fees for the use of their flour mills, bake houses, and breweries. In some regions—parts of France, for example—some lords built castles and exercised the power of the "ban": the right to collect taxes, hear court cases, levy fines, and muster men for defense. These lords were "castellans."

Warriors and Bishops

Although the developments described here did not occur everywhere simultaneously (and in some places hardly at all), in the end the social, political, and cultural life of the West came to be dominated by landowners who saw themselves as both military men and regional leaders. These men and their armed retainers shared a common lifestyle, living together, eating in the lord's great hall, listening to bards sing of military exploits, hunting for recreation, competing with one another in military games. They fought in a group as well—as cavalry, riding on horses. In the month of May, when the grasses were high enough for their mounts to forage, the war season began. To be sure, there were powerful vassals who lived on their own fiefs and hardly ever saw their lord—except for perhaps forty days out of the year, when they owed him military duty. But they themselves were lords of knightly vassals who were not married and who lived and ate and hunted with them.

The marriage bed, so important to the medieval aristocracy from the start, now took on new meaning. Long before, in the seventh and eighth centuries, aristocratic families had been large, diffuse, loosely organized kin groups. (Historians often use the German word *Sippe*—clan—to refer to them.) These families were not tied to any particular estate, for they had numerous estates, scattered all about. With wealth enough to go around, the rich practiced partible inheritance, giving land (though not in equal amounts) to all of their sons and daughters. The Carolingians "politicized" these family relations. As some men were elevated to positions of dazzling power, they took the opportunity to pick and choose their "family members," narrowing the family circle. They also became more conscious of their male line, favoring sons over daughters. In the eleventh century, family definitions tightened even further. The claims of one son, often the eldest, overrode all else; to him went the family inheritance. (This is called "primogeniture"; but there were regions in which the youngest son was privileged, and there were also areas in which more equitable inheritance practices continued in place.) The heir in the new system traced his lineage only through the male line, backward through his father and forward through his own eldest son.

What happened to the other sons? Some of them became knights, others monks. Nor should we forget that some became bishops. In many ways the interests of bishops and lay nobles were similar: they were men of property, lords of vassals, and faithful men of patrons, such as kings, who appointed them to their posts. In some cities, bishops wielded the powers of a count or duke. Nevertheless, they were also "pastors," spiritual leaders charged with shepherding their flock. The "flock" included the priests and monks in the diocese, a district that gained clear definition in the eleventh century. And the flock included the laity, among them the very warriors from whose class the bishops came.

As episcopal power expanded and was clarified in the course of the eleventh century, some bishops in the south of France sought to control the behavior of the knightly class through a movement called the "Peace of God," which developed apace from 989 onwards. Their forum was the regional church council, where the bishops galvanized popular opinion, attracting both lords and peasants to their gatherings. There, drawing upon bits and pieces of defunct Carolingian legislation, the bishops declared the Peace: "If anyone takes as booty sheep, oxen, asses, cows, female goats, male goats, or pigs from peasants ... or from other poor people ... let him be anathema [excommunicated]."[4] In the Truce of God, which soon supplemented the Peace, warfare between armed men was prohibited from Lent to Easter, while at other times of the year it was forbidden on Sunday (because that was the Lord's Day), on Saturday (because that was a reminder of Holy Saturday), on Friday (because it symbolized Good Friday), and on Thursday (because it stood for Holy Thursday). Enforcement of the Truce fell to local knights and nobles, who swore over saints' relics to uphold it. The bishops who promulgated the Peace were ambivalent about warriors. There were the bad ones who broke the peace, but there were also others who were righteous upholders of church law. Soon the Peace and Truce were taken up by powerful lay rulers, eager to sanctify their own warfare and control that of others.

The new importance of the fighting man in the West gave rise to a military ethos mirrored in art and literature. It is no accident that the only extant manuscript of *Beowulf* was written *c.*1000:

> Then Halfdan's son presented Beowulf
> with a gold standard as a victory gift,
> an embroidered banner; also breast-mail
> and a helmet; and a sword carried high,
> that was both precious object and token of honour.[5]

The parallels with developments in the Byzantine and Islamic worlds are striking: everywhere a military class, more or less local, rose to power.

Equally important, however, are the differences: in no place but Europe were overlapping lordships the rule. Nowhere else was fealty so important. Nowhere else were rural enclaves the normal centers of power.

Cities and Merchants

Though ruralism was the norm in the West, it was not invariable. In Italy the power structure reflected, if feebly, the political organization of ancient Rome. Whereas in France great landlords built their castles in the countryside, in Italy they often constructed their family seats within the walls of cities. From these perches the nobles, both lay and religious, dominated the *contado*, the rural area around the city.

In Italy, most peasants were renters, paying cash to urban landowners. Peasants depended on city markets to sell their surplus goods; their customers were not only bishops and nobles but also middle-class shopkeepers, artisans, and merchants. At Milan, for example, the merchants were prosperous enough to own houses in both the city center and the *contado*.

Rome, although exceptional in size, was in some ways a typical Italian city. Large and powerful families built their castles within its walls and controlled the churches and monasteries in the vicinity. The population depended on local producers for their food, and merchants brought their wares to sell within its walls. Yet Rome was special apart from its size: it was the "see"—the seat—of the pope, the most important bishop in the West. The papacy did not control the church, but it had great prestige, and powerful families at Rome fought to place one of their sons at its head.

Outside of Italy cities were less prevalent in the West. Yet even so we can see the rise of a new mercantile class. This was true less in the heartland of the old Carolingian empire than on its fringes. In the north, England, northern Germany, Denmark, and the Low Countries bathed in a sea of silver coins; commercial centers such as Haithabu reached their grandest extent in the mid-tenth century. Here merchants bought and sold slaves, honey, furs, wax, and pirates' plunder. Haithabu was a city of wood, but a very rich one indeed.

In the south of Europe, beyond the Pyrenees, Catalonia was equally commercialized, but in a different way. It imitated the Islamic world of al-Andalus (which was, in effect, in its backyard). The counts of Barcelona minted gold coins just like those at Córdoba. The villagers around Barcelona soon got used to selling their wares for money, and some of them became prosperous. They married into the aristocracy, moved to Barcelona to become city leaders, and lent money to ransom prisoners of the many wars waged to their south.

New-style Kingships

In such a world, what did kings do? At the least, they stood for tradition; they served as symbols of legitimacy. At the most, they united kingdoms and maintained a measure of law and order. (See Map 4.6.)

England

Map 4.6 (facing page): Europe, *c.*1050

Alfred was a king of the second sort. In the face of the Viking invasions, he developed new mechanisms of royal government, creating institutions that became the foundation of strong English kingship. We have already seen his military reforms: the system of burhs and the creation of a navy. Alfred was interested in religious and intellectual reforms as well. These were closely linked in his mind: the causes of England's troubles (in his view) were the sins—many due to ignorance—of its people. Alfred intended to educate "all free-born men." He brought scholars to his court and embarked on an ambitious program to translate key religious works from Latin into Anglo-Saxon (or Old English). This was the vernacular, the spoken language of the people. As Alfred wrote in his prose preface to the Anglo-Saxon translation of *The Pastoral Care* of Gregory the Great,

> I recalled how the Law was first composed in the Hebrew language, and thereafter, when the Greeks learned it, they translated it all into their own language, and all other books as well. And so too the Romans, after they had mastered them, translated them all through learned interpreters into their own language.... Therefore it seems better to me ... that we too should turn into the language that we can all understand certain books which are the most necessary for all men to know.[6]

Those "certain books" included writings by the Church Fathers—Gregory the Great, Saint Augustine, Boethius—and the Psalms as well. Soon Anglo-Saxon was used in England not only for literature but for official administrative purposes as well, in royal "writs" that kings and queens directed to their officials. England was not alone in its esteem for the vernacular: in Ireland, too, the vernacular language was also a written one. But the British Isles *were* unusual by the standards of Continental Europe, where Latin alone was the language of scholarship and writing.

As Alfred harried the Danes who were pushing south and westward, he gained recognition as king of all the English not under Viking rule. His law code, issued in the late 880s or early 890s, was the first by an English king since 695. Unlike earlier codes, which had been drawn up for each separate kingdom, Alfred's contained laws

Scale
0
500 km
0
300 mi
Norway
Sweden
North Sea
Scotland
Denmark
Baltic Sea
Haithabu
Ireland
England
Wales
London
Saxony
Magdeburg
Frisia
Hildesheim
Poland
Lower Lotharingia
Cologne
German
Montreuil
Ponthieu
Flanders
Picardy
Vermandois
Beauvais
Franconia
Bohemia
Moravia
Trier
Upper Lotharingia
Worms
Atlantic Ocean
Normandy
Vexin
Dreux
Paris
Troyes
Île-de-France
Kingdom
Brittany
Maine
Blois
Gatinais
Amboise
Anjou
Alsace
Swabia
Bavaria
Hungary
Nevers
Touraine
Bourges
Burgundy
Châteauroux
Carinthia
Aquitaine
Kingdom of Burgundy
Italy
Venice
Venice
Croatia
Gevaudan
Languedoc
Toulouse
Gascony
Patrimony of St. Peter
Adriatic Sea
Byzantine Empire
Doclea
León
Navarre
Aragon
Castile
Barcelona
Marseilles
Pisa
Spoleto
Corsica (Pisan c. 1020)
Rome
South Italian principalities
Barcelona
Islamic
Taifas
Sardinia (Pisan c. 1050)
Córdoba
Mediterranean Sea

from and for all the English kingdoms in common. The king's inspiration was the Mosaic law of the Bible. Alfred believed that God had made a new covenant with the victors over the Vikings; as leader of his people, Alfred, like the Old Testament patriarch Moses, should issue a law for all.

His successors, beneficiaries of that covenant, rolled back the Viking rule in England. (See Genealogy 4.1: Alfred and His Progeny.) "Then the Norsemen departed in their nailed ships, bloodstained survivors of spears," wrote one poet about a battle lost by the Vikings in 937.[7] But, as we have seen, many Vikings remained. Converted to Christianity, their great men joined Anglo-Saxons to attend the English king at court. The whole kingdom was divided into districts called "shires" and "hundreds," and in each shire, the king's reeve—the sheriff—oversaw royal administration.

Alfred's grandson Edgar (*r.c.*959-975) commanded all the possibilities early medieval kingship offered. The sworn lord of all the great men of the kingdom, he

Genealogy 4.1:
Alfred and His Progeny

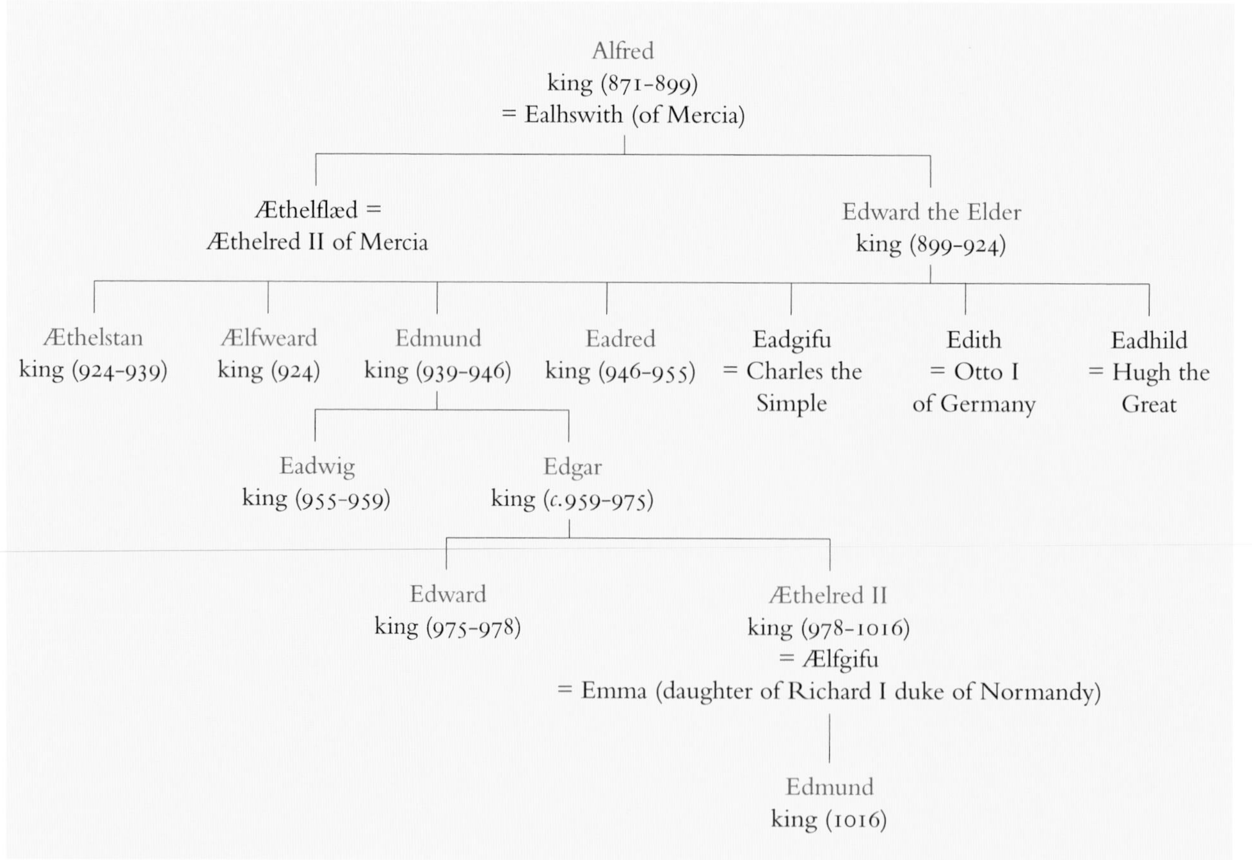

also controlled appointments to the English church and sponsored monastic reform. In 973, following the Continental fashion, he was anointed. Master of burhs and army, Edgar asserted hegemony over many of the non-Anglo-Saxon rulers in Britain. He extended Alfred's legal reforms by proclaiming certain crimes—arson and theft—to be under royal jurisdiction.

From the point of view of control, however, Edgar had nowhere near the power over England that, say, Basil II had over Byzantium at about the same time. The *dynatoi* might sometimes chafe at the emperor's directives and rebel, but the emperor had his Varangian guard to put them down and an experienced, professional civil service to do his bidding. The king of England depended less on force and bureaucracy than on consensus. The great landowners adhered to the king because they found it in their interest to do so. When they did not, the kingdom easily fragmented, becoming prey to civil war. Disunity was exacerbated by new attacks from the Danes. One Danish king, Cnut (or Canute), even became king of England for a time (*r.*1016–

Genealogy 4.2:
The Ottonians

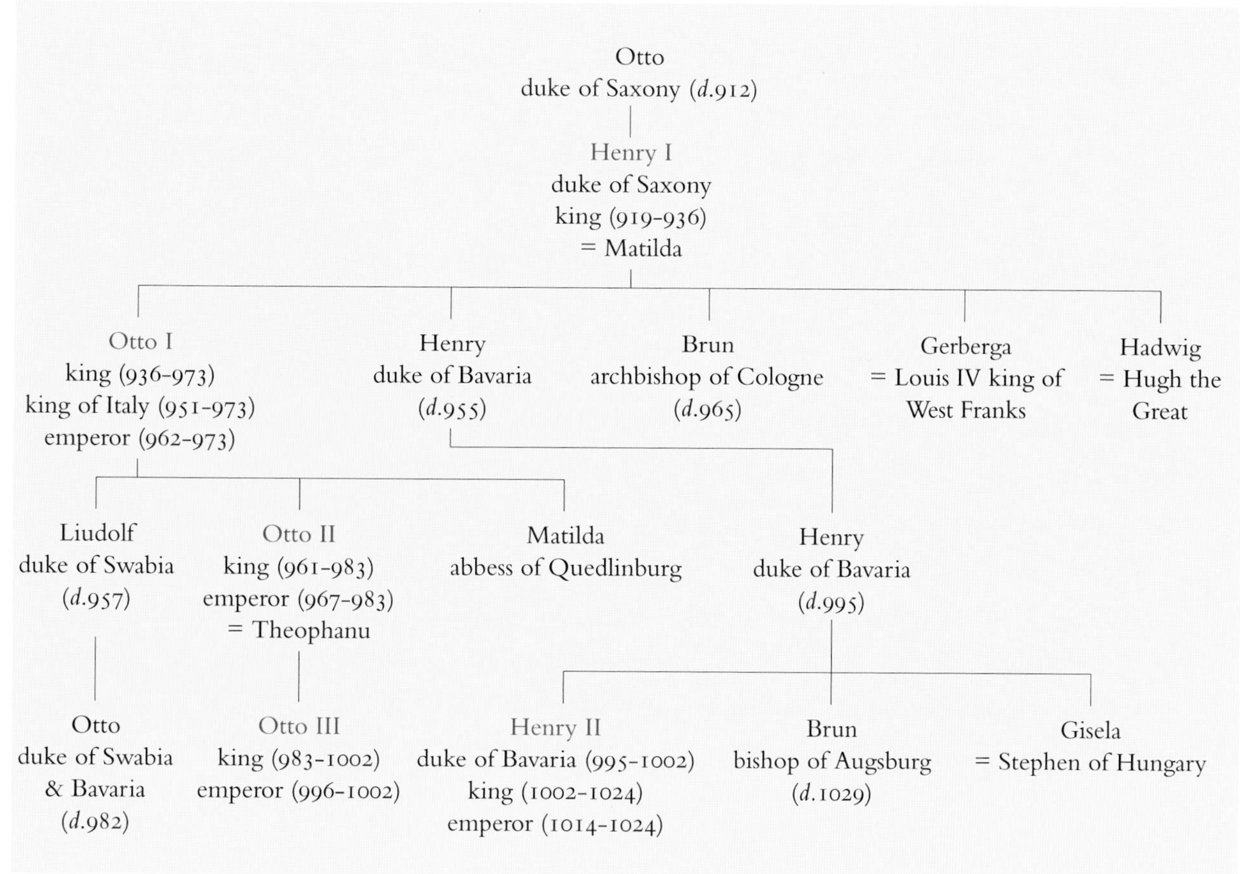

1035). Yet under Cnut, English kingship did not change much. He kept intact much of the administrative, ecclesiastical, and military apparatus already established. By Cnut's time, Scandinavia had been Christianized and its traditions had largely merged with those of the rest of Europe. The Vikings were no longer an alien culture.

Germany

The king of Germany was as effective as the English king—and additionally worked with a much wider palette of territories, institutions, and possibilities. It is true that at first Germany seemed ready to disintegrate into duchies: five emerged in the late Carolingian period, each held by a military leader who exercised quasi-royal powers. But, in the face of their own quarrels and the threats of outside invaders, the dukes needed and wanted a strong king. With the death in 911 of the last Carolingian king in Germany, Louis the Child, they crowned one of themselves. Then, as Magyar attacks increased, the dukes gave the royal title to their most powerful member, the duke of Saxony, Henry I (*r.*919-936), who proceeded to set up fortifications and reorganize his army, crowning his efforts with a major defeat of the Hungarians in 933.

Henry's son Otto I (*r.*936-973) defeated rival family members, rebellious dukes, and Slavic and Hungarian armies soon after coming to the throne. Through astute marriage alliances and appointments, he was eventually able to get his family members to head up all of the duchies. In 951, Otto marched into Italy and took the Lombard crown. He was thus king of Germany and Italy, and soon (in 962) he received the imperial crown that recognized his far-flung power. Both to himself and to contemporaries he recalled the greatness of Charlemagne. Meanwhile, Otto's victory at Lechfeld in 955 (see p.146) ended the Hungarian threat. In the same year, Otto defeated a Slavic incursion, and for about a half-century the Slavs of central and eastern Europe came under German hegemony.

Victories such as these brought tribute, plum positions to disburse, and lands to give away, ensuring Otto a following among the great men of the realm. His successors, Otto II, Otto III—hence the dynastic name "Ottonians"—and Henry II, built on his achievements. (See Genealogy 4.2: The Ottonians.) Granted power by the magnates, they gave back in turn: they gave away lands and appointed their aristocratic supporters to duchies, counties, and bishoprics. Always, however, their decisions were tempered by hereditary claims and plenty of lobbying by influential men at court and at the great assemblies that met with the king to hammer out policies. The role of kings in appointing bishops and archbishops was particularly important because, unlike counties and duchies, these positions could not be inherited. Otto I created a ribbon of new bishoprics in newly converted regions along his eastern border, endowing them with extensive lands and subjecting the local peasantry to episcopal overlordship. Throughout Germany bishops gained the power of the ban, with the right to collect revenues and call men to arms. Once the king chose the bishop (usually with at least the consent of the clergy of the cathedral over which he was to preside), he "invested" the new prelate in his post by participating in the ceremony that installed him into office. Bishop Thietmar of Merseburg, for example, reported on his own experience:

> The archbishop [Tagino of Magdeburg, Thietmar's sponsor] led me to Bishop Bruno's chapel [Bruno was the king's brother], where the king [Henry II] awaited him. After preparing for the celebration of the mass, he commended me into the hands of the king. I was elected by those who were present and the king committed the pastoral office to me with the staff.[8]

With wealth coming in from their eastern tributaries, Italy, and the silver mines of Saxony (discovered in the time of Otto I), the Ottonians presided over a brilliant intellectual and artistic efflorescence. As in the Islamic world, much of this was dispersed; in Germany the centers of culture included the royal court, the great cathe-

Plate 4.1: Christ and the Centurion, Egbert Codex (977-993). Like Ebbo, the patron of the artists of the Utrecht Psalter (**Plate 3.9** on p.127), Egbert was an archbishop with keen interests in the arts. The Egbert Codex contains 51 gospel illustrations, the most extensive cycle up to his day.

Plate 4.2: Christ Asleep, Hitda Gospels (*c.*1000-1020). In this manuscript painting, the moral of the story is right in the picture. As the apostles look anxiously to the mast to save them from the stormy sea, one (in the exact center) turns to rouse the sleeping Christ, the real Savior.

Plate 4.3 (facing page): Saint Luke, Gospel Book of Otto III (998-1001). Compare this author portrait to the Saint Luke of the Lindisfarne Gospels (**Plate 2.4** on p.84). The artist working for Otto created a figure of great complexity, with his feet on earth, his seat on a rainbow, and his hands holding up the "cloud of witnesses" mentioned in the New Testament Epistle to the Hebrews 12:1.

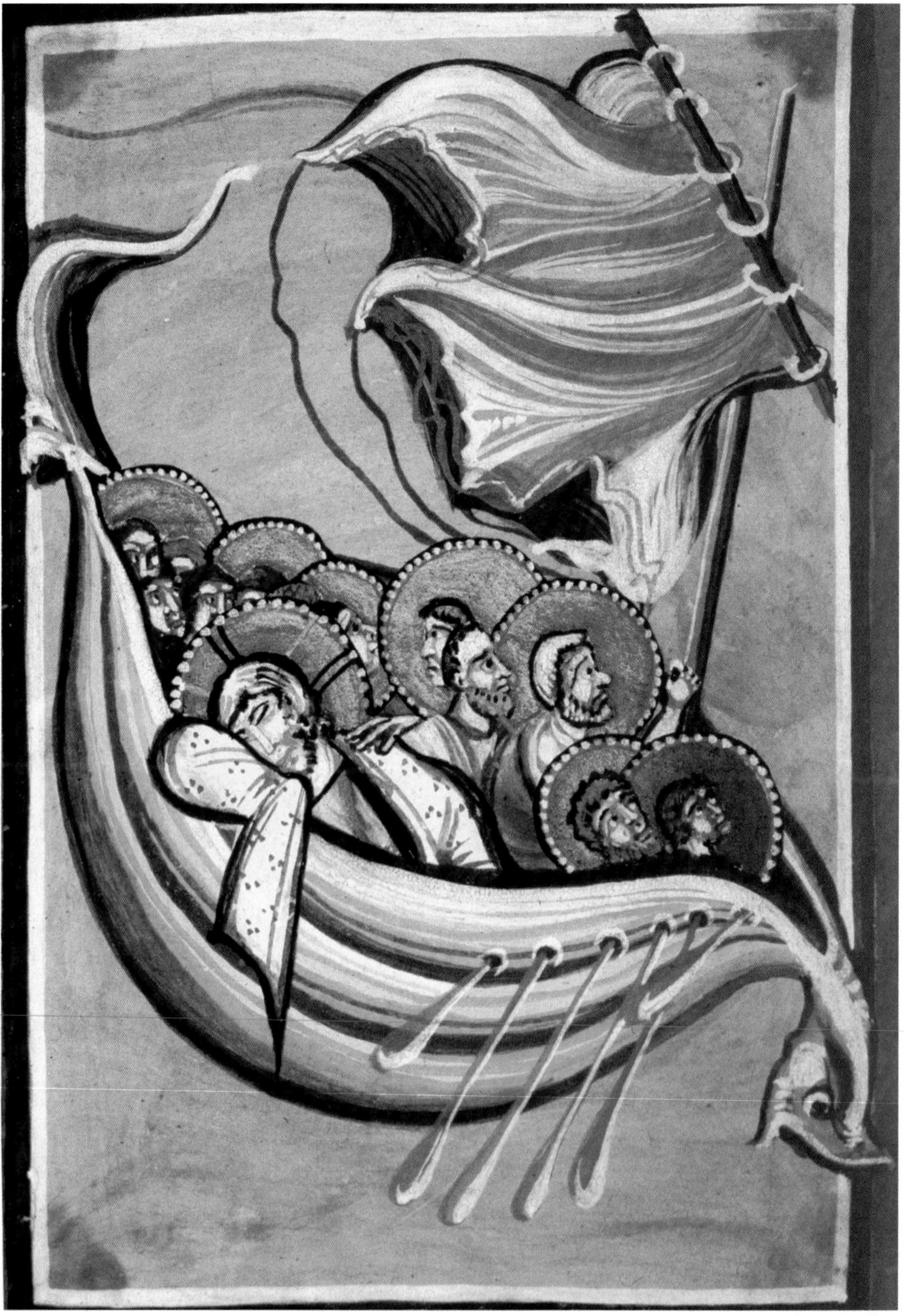

LVC
FONE PATRŨ DUCTAS BOS AGNIS ELICIT UNDAS

dral schools, and women's convents. The most talented young men crowded the schools at episcopal courts such as those at Trier, Cologne, Magdeburg, Worms, and Hildesheim. Honing their Latin, they studied classical authors such as Cicero and Horace as well as Scripture, while their episcopal teachers wrote histories, saints' lives, and works on canon law, such as the *Decretum* (*c.*1020) by Burchard, bishop of Worms, a widely influential work. The men at the cathedral schools were largely in training to become courtiers, administrators, and bishops themselves. But bishops appreciated art as well as scholarship, and some, such as Egbert, archbishop of Trier (*r.*977-993), not only opened schools but also patronized artists and fine craftsworkers. Plate 4.1, an illustration of Christ and the Centurion from the *Egbert Codex* (named, of course, for its patron) is a good example of what is called the "Ottonian style" at the end of the tenth century. Drawing freely on Carolingian work such as that illustrated in Plate 3.6 and Plate 3.7 (see pp.122 and 123), nevertheless, the *Egbert Codex* artist achieves a very different effect. Most importantly, he is utterly unafraid of open space. The figures, while recognizably human, float in a near void of pastel colors. The focus is on their gestures, their hands and fingers exaggerated to convey the amazement of Christ's followers, the centurion's petition, and Christ's gracious consent. (For the story, see Matt. 8:5-13.)

At around the same time, in convents that provided them with comfortable private apartments, noblewomen were writing books and (in the case of Hrotsvitha of Gandersheim) Roman-style plays. Ottonian noblewomen also supported other artists and scholars. Plate 4.2, from a manuscript made at Cologne between *c.*1000 and *c.*1020 for Abbess Hitda of Meschede, shows a more eclectic sensibility than the *Egbert Codex*. The artist draws from Byzantine as well as Carolingian traditions to produce a calm Christ, asleep during a wild storm on the Sea of Galilee that ruffles the sails of the ship and seems to toss it into sheer air. The marriage of Otto II to a Byzantine princess, Theophanu, helps account for the Byzantine influences.

Among the most active patrons of the arts were the Ottonian kings themselves. In a Gospel book made for Otto III, the full achievement of Ottonian culture is made clear in a work both artistically compelling and theologically sophisticated. In Plate 4.3, Saint Luke, in a gesture of ecstacy, holds his glory in his hands. Above him is his symbol, the ox; radiating outwards in fiery orbs are five crowned Old Testament prophets, each holding a scroll, each accompanied by an angel (the one at the top has two), while at the bottom lambs drink from the rivers of Paradise. Artistically, it is an emotional, glowing piece in reds, oranges, and gold. Theologically it is a statement about the unity of the Old Testament (the prophets) and the New (Luke himself).

France

By contrast with the English and German kings, those in France had a harder time coping with invasions. Unlike the English kings, who started small and built slowly, the French kings had half an empire to defend. Unlike the Ottonians, who asserted their military prowess in decisive battles such as the one at Lechfeld, the French kings generally had to let local men both take the brunt of the attacks and reap the prestige and authority that came with military leadership. Nor did the French kings have the advantage of Germany's tributaries, silver mines, or Italian connections. Much like the Abbasid caliphs at Baghdad, the kings of France saw their power wane. During most of the tenth century, Carolingian kings alternated on the throne with kings from a family that would later be called the "Capetians." At the end of that century the most powerful men of the realm, seeking to stave off civil war, elected Hugh Capet (*r.*987-996) as their king. The Carolingians were displaced, and the Capetians continued on the throne until the fourteenth century. (See Genealogy 5.3: The Capetian Kings of France, p.189.)

The Capetians' scattered but substantial estates lay in the north of France, in the region around Paris. Here the kings had their vassals and their castles. This "Ile-de-France" (which was all there was to "France" in the period; see Map 4.6) was indeed an "island," surrounded by independent castellans. In the sense that he, too, had little more military power than a castellan, Hugh and his eleventh-century successors were similar to local strongmen. But the Capetian kings had the prestige of their office. Anointed with holy oil, they represented the idea of unity and God-given rule inherited from Charlemagne. Most of the counts and dukes—at least those in the north of France—swore homage and fealty to the king, a gesture, however weak, of personal support. Unlike the German kings, the French could rely on vassalage to bind the great men of the realm to them.

★ ★ ★ ★

Political fragmentation did not mean chaos. It simply betokened a new order. At Byzantium, in any event, even the most centrifugal forces were focused on the center: the real trouble for Basil II, for example, came from *dynatoi* who wanted to be emperors, not from people who wanted to be independent rulers. In the Islamic world fragmentation largely meant replication, as courts patterned on or competitive with the Abbasid model were set up by Fatimid caliphs and other rulers. In the West, the rise of regional rulers was accompanied by the widespread adoption of forms of personal dependency—vassalage, serfdom—which could be (and were) manipulated even by kings—such as the Capetians—who seemed to have lost the most from the dispersal of power.

The *real* fragmentation was between the former heirs of the Roman Empire. They did not speak the same language, they were increasingly estranged by their religions, and they knew almost nothing about one another. In the next century, Christian Europeans, newly prosperous and self-confident, would go on the offensive. Henceforth, without forgetting about the Byzantine and Islamic worlds, we shall focus on this aggressive and dynamic new society.

Chapter Four Key Events

*c.*790-*c.*950	Invasions into Europe by Vikings, Muslims, and Hungarians
871-899	Reign of King Alfred the Great of England
c. 909	Fatimids (in North Africa) establish themselves as caliphs
929	Abd al-Rahman III (at Córdoba in al-Andalus) takes title of caliph
955	Victory of Otto I over Hungarians at Lechfeld
962	Otto I crowned emperor
980-1037	Ibn Sina (Avicenna)
988	Conversion of Vladimir, Rus Grand Prince, to Byzantine Christianity
989	Beginning of "Peace of God" movement
991	Mieszko I puts Poland under papal protection
1000 (or 1001)	Stephen I crowned king of Hungary
1025	Death of Basil II the Bulgar Slayer
c. 1031	Al-Andalus splits into *taifas*

NOTES

1. Michael Psellus, *Fourteen Byzantine Rulers: The "Chronographia" of Michael Psellus*, trans. E.R.A. Sewter (Harmondsworth, 1966), p.44, spelling slightly altered.
2. Ibn Sa'id, quoted in Robert Hillenbrand, "Medieval Córdoba as a Cultural Centre," in *The Legacy of Muslim Spain*, ed. Salma Khadra Jayyusi (Leiden, 1994), I:120.
3. "Asser's Life of King Alfred," in *Alfred the Great: Asser's "Life of King Alfred" and Other Contemporary Sources*, trans. Simon Keynes and Michael Lapidge (Harmondsworth, 1983), pp.84-85.
4. "The Acts of the Council of Charroux (989)," trans. Thomas Head in *The Peace of God: Social Violence and Religious Response in France around the Year 1000*, ed. Thomas Head and Richard Landes (Ithaca, NY, 1992), p.327.
5. *Beowulf: A New Verse Translation*, ll. 1019-1023, trans. Seamus Heaney (New York, 2000), p.69.
6. "From the Translations of Gregory's Pastoral Care," in *Alfred the Great*, pp.125-26.
7. Quoted in Gwyn Jones, *A History of the Vikings* (rev. ed., Oxford, 1984), p.238.
8. *Ottonian Germany: The Chronicon of Thietmar of Merseburg*, trans. David A. Warner (Manchester, 2001), p.265.

FURTHER READING

Abels, Richard. *Alfred the Great: War, Kingship and Culture in Anglo-Saxon England*. Harlow, Essex, 1998.

Angold, Michael. *The Byzantine Empire, 1025-1204: A Political History*. 2nd ed. London, 1997.

Berkey, Jonathan P. *The Formation of Islam: Religion and Society in the Near East, 600-1800*. Cambridge, 2003.

Engel, Pál. *The Realm of St. Stephen: A History of Medieval Hungary, 895-1526*. Trans. Tamás Pálosfalvi. London, 2001.

Fine, John V.A., Jr. *The Early Medieval Balkans: A Critical Survey from the Sixth to the Late Twelfth Century*. Ann Arbor, 1991.

Franklin, Simon, and Jonathan Shepard. *The Emergence of Rus, 750-1200*. London, 1996.

Frantzen, Allen. *King Alfred*. Boston, 1986.

Garland, Lynda. *Byzantine Empresses: Women and Power in Byzantium, AD 527-1204*. London, 1999.

Goitein, S.D. *A Mediterranean Society: The Jewish Communities of the Arab World as Portrayed in the Documents of the Cairo Geniza*. 6 vols. Berkeley, 1967-1993.

Jayyusi, Salma Khadra, ed. *The Legacy of Muslim Spain*. 2 vols. Leiden, 1994.

Kazhdan, A.P., and Ann Wharton Epstein. *Change in Byzantine Culture in the Eleventh and Twelfth Centuries*. Berkeley, 1985.

Lev, Yaacov. *State and Society in Fatimid Egypt*. Leiden, 1991.

Maguire, Henry, ed. *Byzantine Court Culture from 829 to 1204*. Washington, 1997.

Moore, R.I. *The First European Revolution, c. 970-1215*. Oxford, 2000.

Reuter, Timothy. *Germany in the Early Middle Ages, c.800-1056*. London, 1991.

Reynolds, Susan. *Fiefs and Vassals: The Medieval Evidence Reinterpreted*. Oxford, 1994.

Stafford, Pauline. *Unification and Conquest: A Political and Social History of England in the Tenth and Eleventh Centuries*. London, 1989.

FIVE

THE EXPANSION OF EUROPE (*c*.1050–*c*.1150)

EUROPEANS GAINED MUSCLE in the second half of the eleventh century. They built cities, reorganized the church, created new varieties of religious life, expanded their intellectual horizons, pushed aggressively at their frontiers, and even waged war over 1400 miles away, in what they called the Holy Land. Expanding population and a vigorous new commercial economy lay behind all this. So too did the weakness, disunity, and beckoning wealth of their neighbors, the Byzantines and Muslims.

THE SELJUKS AND THEIR AFTERMATH

In the eleventh century the Seljuk Turks, a new group from outside the Islamic world, entered and took over its eastern half. Eventually penetrating deep into Anatolia, they took a great bite out of Byzantium. Soon, however, the Seljuks themselves split apart, and the Islamic world fragmented anew under the rule of dozens of emirs.

From the Sultans to the Emirs

Pastoralists on horseback, the Turkish peoples called the "Seljuks" (after the name of their most enterprising leader) crossed from the region east of the Caspian Sea into Iran in about the year 1000. Within a little over fifty years, they had allied themselves with the caliphs as upholders of Sunni orthodoxy, defeated the Buyids, taken over the cities, and started collecting taxes. Between 1055 and 1092, a succession of formidable Seljuk leaders—Toghril Beg, Alp Arslan, and Malikshah—proclaimed themselves rulers, "sultans," of a new state. Bands of herdsmen followed in their wake, moving their sheep into the very farmland of Iran (disrupting agriculture there), then continuing westward, into Armenia, which had been recently annexed by Byzantium. Meanwhile, under Alp Arslan (*r.*1063-1072), the Seljuk army (composed precisely of such herdsmen but also, increasingly, of other Turkish tribesmen recruited as slaves or freemen) harried Syria. This was Muslim territory, but it was equally the back door to Byzantium. Thus the Byzantines got involved, and throughout the 1050s and 1060s they fought numerous indecisive battles with the Seljuks. Then in 1071 a huge Byzantine force met an equally large Seljuk army at Manzikert (today Malazgirt, in Turkey). The battle ended with the Byzantines defeated and Anatolia open to a flood of militant sheepherders. (See Map 5.1.)

Map 5.1: The Seljuk World, *c.*1090

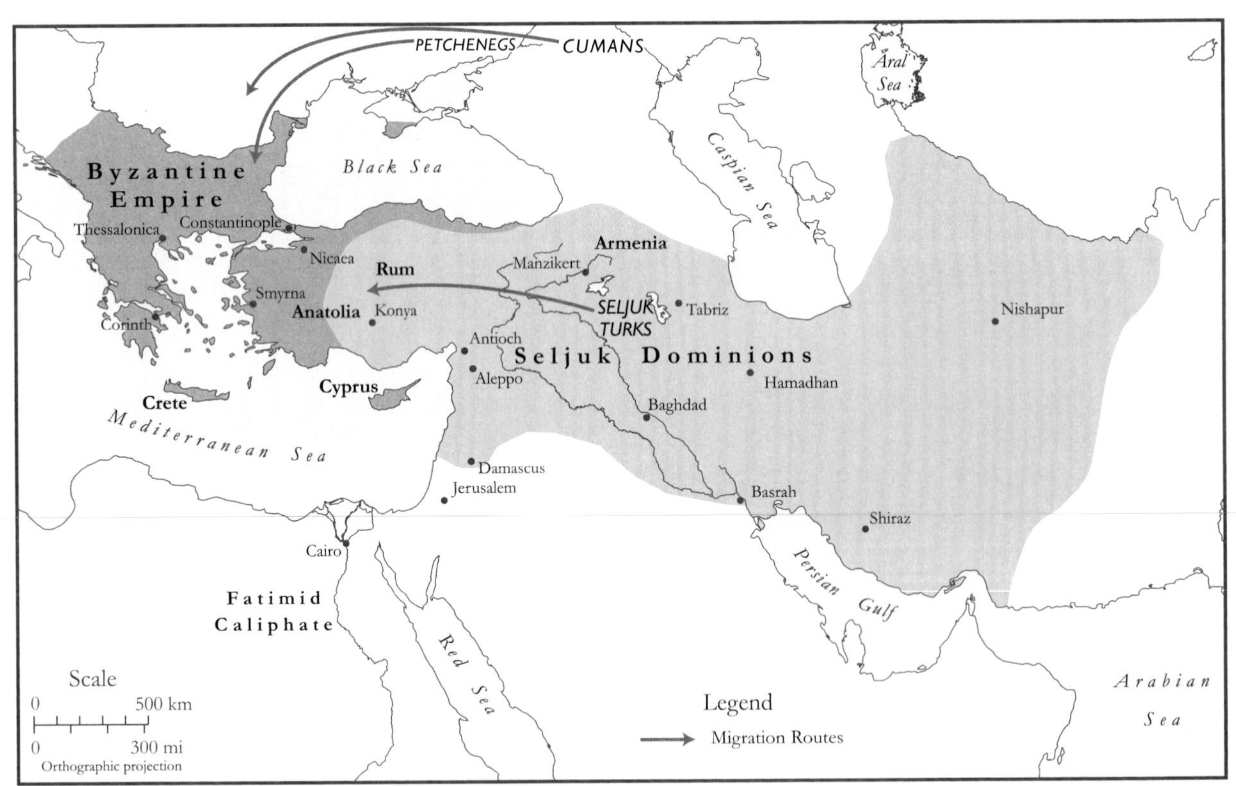

Though "Seljuk" in name, the new inhabitants of Anatolia were effectively independent. They did not so much declare themselves rulers of the region as simply take it over; for them it was Rum, "Rome." Meanwhile, other Seljuks took off on their own, hiring themselves out (as Turks long had done) as military leaders. Atsiz ibn Uwaq is a good example. For a while he worked for Alp Arslan, but in 1070 he was called in by the Fatimid caliph at Egypt to help shore up the crumbling rule of the Fatimids against their own military leaders. Seizing his chance, Atsiz turned the tables to become emir himself of a region that stretched from Jerusalem to Damascus.

Atsiz was the harbinger of a new order. After 1092, the Seljuks could no longer maintain any sort of centralized rule, even though they still were "wanted," if only to confer titles like "emir" on local rulers who craved legitimacy. Nor could the Fatimids prevent their own territories from splintering into tiny emirates, each centered on one or a few cities. Some emirs were from the Seljuk family; others were military men who originally served under them. We shall see that the tiny states set up by the crusaders who conquered the Levant in 1099 were, in size, not so very different from their neighboring Islamic emirates.

In the western part of North Africa, the Maghreb, Berber tribesmen (camel breeders rather than sheep herders) forged a state similar to that of the Seljuks. Fired (as the Seljuks had been) with religious fervor on behalf of Sunni orthodoxy, the Berber Almoravids took over north-west Africa in the 1070s and 1080s. In 1086, invited by the ruler of Seville to help fight Christian armies from the north, they sent troops into al-Andalus. This military "aid" soon turned into conquest. By 1094 all of al-Andalus not yet conquered by the Christians was under Almoravid control. Their hegemony over the western Islamic world ended only in 1147, with the triumph of the Almohads, a rival Berber group.

Together the Seljuks and Almoravids rolled back the Shi'ite wave. They kept it back through a system of schools, the "madrasas." Attached to mosques, these centers of higher learning were where young men came for lessons in religion, law, and literature. Sometimes visiting scholars came to debate in lively public displays of intellectual brilliance. More regularly, teachers and students carried on a quiet regimen of classes on the Qur'an and other texts. Established by the Sunni Seljuks to counter similar colleges in Shi'ite lands, madrasas were soon set up throughout the Islamic world. The fractured Islamic community remained united in the twelfth century by commerce and language, but not by schooling.

Byzantium: Bloodied but Unbowed

What had happened to the triumphant Byzantium of Basil II? It was unable to sustain its successes in the face of Turks on two fronts: in Anatolia, as we have seen, and also in the Balkans, where Pechenegs raided with ease. There was no longer much of a citizen army; many of the themes had lost their defenders; and the emperor's troops—made up largely of Turks, Normans, Franks, and Slavs—were unreliable. When emperor Constantine IX Monomachos (*r.*1042–1055) was unable to prevent the Pechenegs from entering the Balkans, he shifted policy, welcoming them, administering baptism, conferring titles, and settling them in depopulated regions. Much the same process took place in Anatolia, where the emperors at times welcomed the Turks to help them fight rival *dynatoi* and where even some Christians, especially the Monophysites of Armenia and Syria (see p.135), were glad to have new Turkish overlords. The Byzantine grip on its territories loosened and its frontiers became nebulous, but Byzantium still stood.

There were changes at the imperial court as well. The model of the "public" emperor ruling alone for his people gave way to a less costly, more "familial" model of government. To be sure, for a time competing *dynatoi* families swapped the imperial throne. But Alexius I Comnenus (*r.*1081–1118), a Dalassenus on his mother's side, managed to bring most of the major families together through a series of marriage alliances. (The Comneni remained on the throne for about a century; see Genealogy 5.1: The Dynasty of Comnenus.) Until her death *c.*1102, Anna Dalassena, Alexius's mother (rather than a civil servant) held the reins of government while Alexius occupied himself with military matters. At his revamped court, it was his relatives who held the highest positions. Many of them received *pronoiai* (*sing. pronoia*), temporary

Genealogy 5.1: The Dynasty of Comnenus

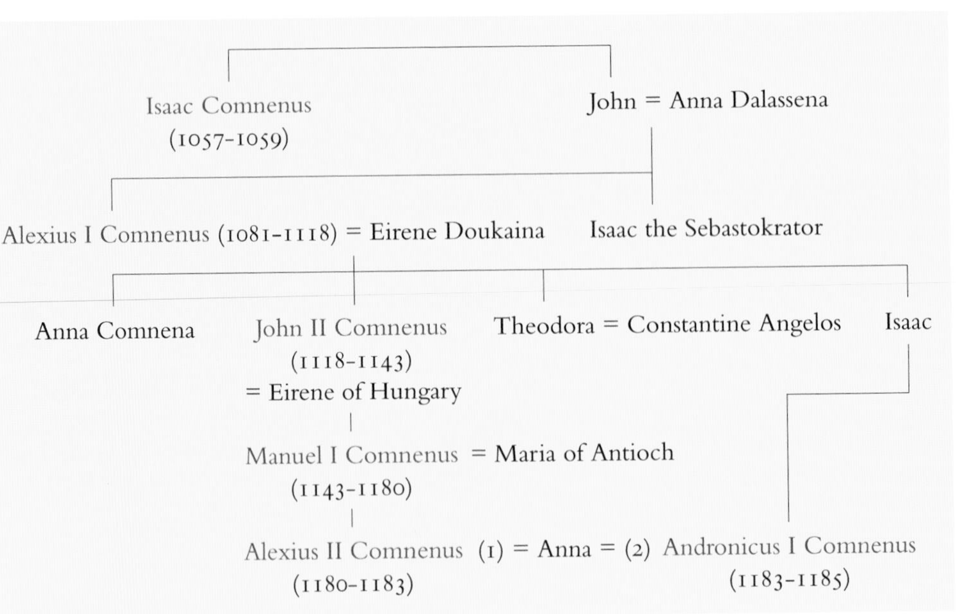

grants of imperial lands that they administered and profited from.

Altogether, Byzantine rulers were becoming more like European ones, holding a relatively small amount of territory, handing some of it out in grants that worked a bit like fiefs, spending most of their time in battle to secure a stronghold here, a city there. Sometimes their hostilities were with westerners themselves. Already before Alexius's time, the Normans—adventurous warriors from Normandy, in France—had taken southern Italy and Sicily; early in his reign he confronted (and defeated) their armies when they tried to conquer Byzantium itself. Clearly Europeans were on the move.

THE TAKE-OFF OF THE EUROPEAN ECONOMY

Behind the new European expansion was a new economy. Draining marshes, felling trees, setting up dikes: this was the backbreaking work that brought new land into cultivation. With their heavy, horse-drawn plows, peasants were able to reap greater harvests; using the three-field system, they raised more varieties of crops. Great landowners, the same "oppressors" against whom the Peace of God fulminated, could also be efficient economic organizers. They set up mills to grind grain, forced their tenants to use them, then charged a fee for the service. It was in their interest that the peasants produced as much grain as possible.

As the countryside became more productive, people became healthier, their fertility increased, and there were more mouths to feed. Even so, surprising surpluses made possible the growth of old and the development of new urban centers. Within a generation or two, city dwellers, intensely conscious of their common goals, elaborated new instruments of commerce, self-regulating organizations, and forms of self-government.

Towns and Cities

Around castles and monasteries in the countryside or at the walls of crumbling ancient towns, merchants came with their wares and artisans set up shop. At Bruges (today in Belgium), it was the local lord's castle that served as a magnet. As one late medieval chronicler put it,

> To satisfy the needs of the people in the castle at Bruges, first merchants with luxury articles began to surge around the gate; then the wine-sellers came; finally the inn-keepers arrived to feed and lodge the people who

had business with the prince.... So many houses were built that soon a great city was created.[1]

Churches and monasteries were the other centers of town growth. Recall Tours as it was in the early seventh century (Map 1.4 on p.42), with its semi-permanent settlements around the church of Saint-Martin, out in the cemetery, and its lonely cathedral nestling against one of the ancient walls. By the twelfth century (Map 5.2), Saint-Martin was a monastery, the hub of a small town dense enough to boast eleven parish churches, merchant and artisan shops, private houses, and two markets. To the east, the episcopal complex was no longer alone: a market had sprung up outside the old western wall, and private houses lined the street leading to the bridge. Smaller than the town around Saint-Martin, the one at the foot of the old city had only two parish churches, but it was big enough to warrant the construction of a new set of walls to protect it.

Early cities developed without prior planning, but some later ones were "chartered," that is, declared, surveyed, and plotted out. A marketplace and merchant settlement were already in place at Freiburg im Breisgau when the duke of Zähringen chartered it, promising each new settler there a house lot of 5000 square feet for a very small yearly rent. The duke had fair hopes that commerce would flourish right at his back door and yield him rich revenues.

Map 5.2: Tours in the Eleventh and Twelfth Centuries

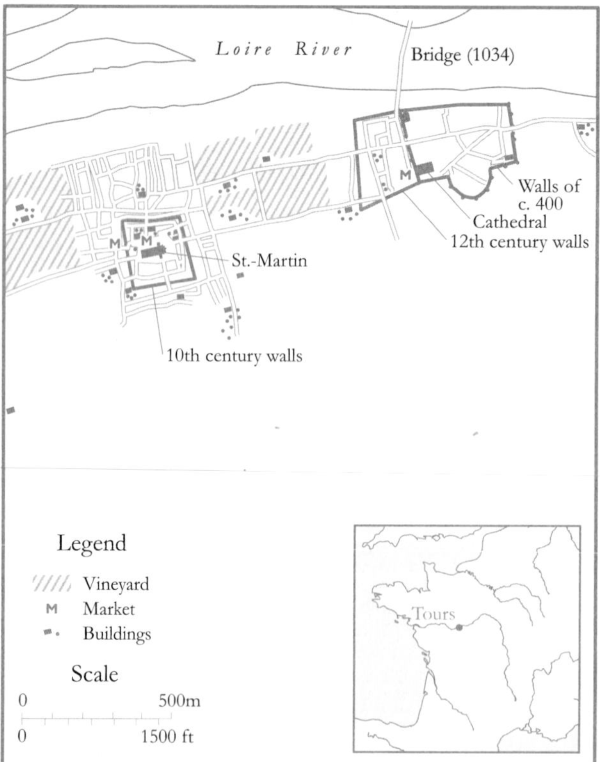

The look and feel of medieval cities varied immensely from place to place. Nearly all included a marketplace, a castle, and several churches. All had rings of walls; by 1100, Speyer had three of them. (See Map 7.4, p.258 of volume 2 for the walls of Bruges.) Within the walls lay a network of streets—narrow, dirty, dark, smelly, and winding—made of packed clay or gravel. Most cities were situated near waterways and had bridges; the one at Tours was built in the 1030s. And most had to adapt to increasingly crowded conditions. At the end of the eleventh century in Winchester, England, city plots were still large enough to accommodate houses parallel to the street; but soon those houses had to be torn down to make way for narrow ones, built at right angles to the street. The houses at Winchester were made of wattle and daub—twigs woven together and covered with clay. If they were like the stone houses built in the late twelfth century (about which we know a good deal), they had two stories: a shop

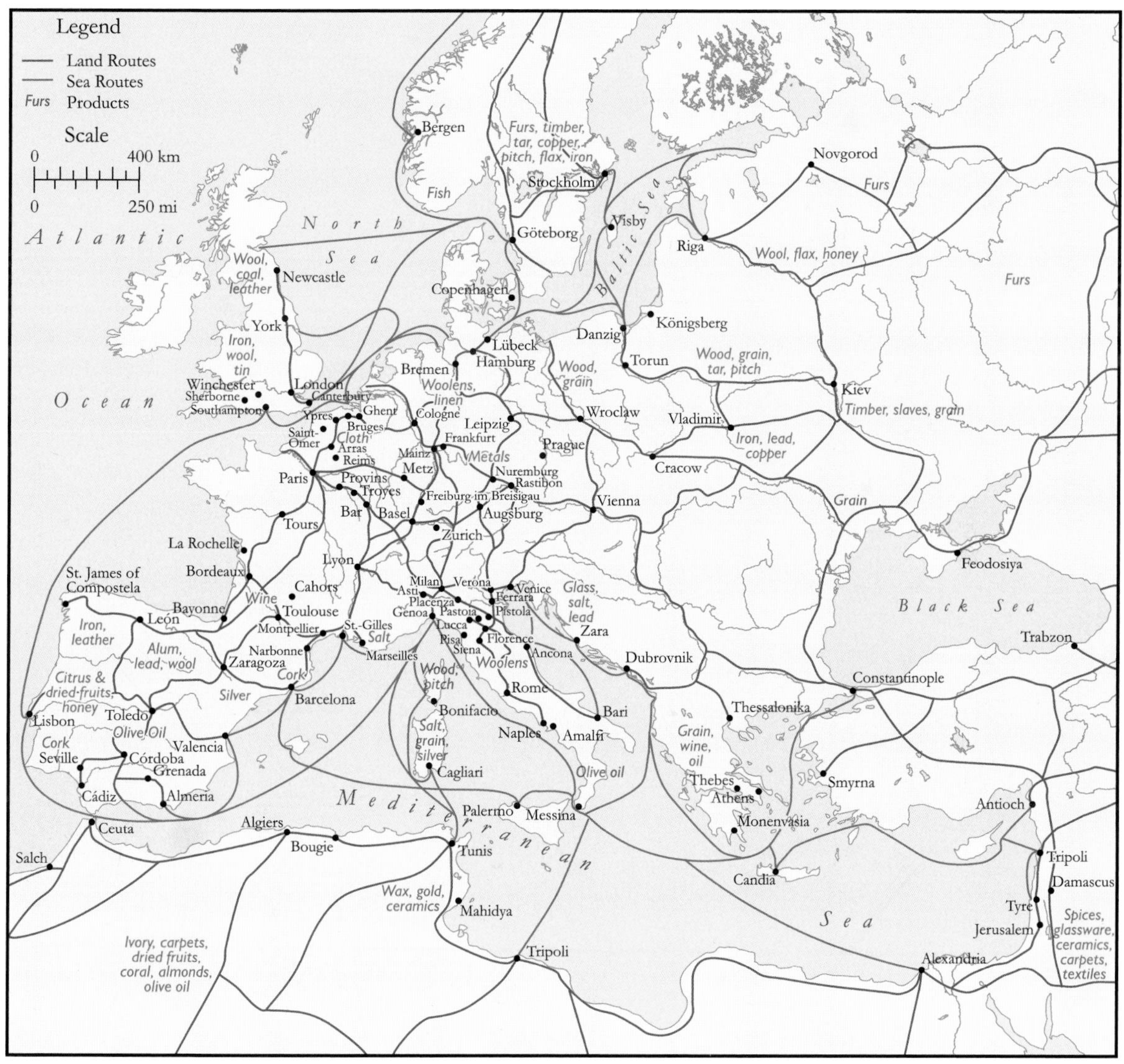

Map 5.3: The Cities and Trade Relations of the West

or warehouse on the lower floor and living quarters above. Behind this main building were the kitchen, enclosures for livestock, and a garden. Even city dwellers clung to rural pursuits, raising much of their food themselves.

Although commercial centers developed throughout western Europe, they grew fastest and most densely in regions along key waterways: the Mediterranean coasts of Italy, France, and Spain; northern Italy along the Po River; the river system of Rhône-Saône-Meuse; the Rhineland; the English Channel; the shores of the Baltic Sea. During the eleventh and twelfth centuries, these waterways became part of a single, interdependent economy. At the same time, new roads through the countryside linked urban centers to rural districts and stimulated the growth of fairs (regular, short-term, often lively markets). (See Map 5.3.)

Business Arrangements

This revival of urban life and expansion of trade, dubbed the "commercial revolution" by historians, was sustained and invigorated by merchants. They were a varied lot. Some were local traders, like one monk who supervised a manor twenty miles south of his monastery and sold its surplus horses and grain at a local market. Others—mainly Jews and Italians—were long-distance traders, much in demand because they supplied fine wines, spices, and fabrics to the aristocracy. Some Jews had long been involved at least part time in long-distance trade as vintners. In the eleventh century, as lords reorganized the countryside, Jewish landowners were driven out and forced into commerce and urban trades full time. Other long-distance traders came from Italy. The key players were from Genoa, Pisa, and Venice; it is no accident that these cities had trading outposts along the Golden Horn at Constantinople. (See Map 4.1 on p.132.) But Italian traders found the Islamic world nearly as lucrative. Establishing bases at ports such as Tunis, they imported Islamic wares—ceramics, textiles, metalwork—into Europe. Near Pisa, for example, the facade of the cathedral of San Miniato (Plate 5.1) was decorated with shiny bowls (Plate 5.2) imported by Pisan traders

Plate 5.1 (facing page): San Miniato (late 12th cent.). The facade of San Miniato was once decorated with *bacini*, bowls that sparkled in the Italian sun. In this picture you can see the small round cavities where they used to be. The *bacino* in **Plate 5.2** was slightly above and just to the left (from the viewer's point of view) of the oculus (the round window). The *bacini* were, in effect, cheap and attractive substitutes for marble or mosaics.

Plate 5.2: Bowl, North Africa (late 12th cent.). This earthenware bowl (*bacino*), imported from North Africa, and decorated with pseudo-Arabic writing, once adorned the facade of San Miniato. Islamic artisans knew how to make a very white tin-based glaze against which the painted colors of the design stood out. (See **Plate 3.3**, p.104, for a far more sophisticated version from the Abbasid period.) The resulting bowls were in great demand by Italians, not only for the façades of their churches but also for their kitchens.

from North African artisans. In turn, merchants from the west exported wood, iron, and woolen cloth to the east.

Merchants invented new forms of collective enterprises to pool their resources and finance large undertakings. The Italian *commenda*, for example, was a partnership established for ventures by sea. A *compagnia* was created by investing family property in trade. Contracts for sales, exchanges, and loans became common, with the interest on loans hidden in the fiction of a penalty for "late payment" in order to avoid the church's ban on usury.

Pooled resources made large-scale productive enterprises possible. A cloth industry began, powered by water mills. New deep-mining technologies provided Europeans with hitherto untapped sources of metals. Forging techniques improved, and iron was for the first time regularly used for agricultural tools and plows, enhancing food production.

Whether driven by machines or handwork, the new economy was sustained by the artisans, financiers, and merchants of the cities. They formed guilds to regulate and protect themselves. In these social, religious, and economic associations, guild members prayed for and buried one another, agreed on quality standards for their products, and regulated their work hours, materials, and prices. Guilds guaranteed their members—mostly male—a place in the market by controlling production within each city. They represented the social and economic counterpart to urban walls, giving their members protection, shared identity, and recognized status.

The political counterpart to the walls was the "commune"—town self-government. City dwellers—keenly aware of their special identity in a world dominated by knights and peasants—recognized their mutual interest in reliable coinage, laws to facilitate commerce, freedom from servile dues and services, and independence to buy and sell as the market dictated. They petitioned the political powers that ruled them—bishops, kings, counts, castellans, dukes—for the right to govern themselves.

Collective movements for urban self-government were especially prevalent in Italy, France, and Germany. Already Italy's political life was city centered; communes there were attempts to substitute the power of one group (the citizens) for another (the nobles and bishops). At Milan in the second half of the eleventh century, for example, popular discontent with the archbishop, who effectively ruled the city, led to numerous armed clashes that ended, in 1097, with the transfer of power from the archbishop to a government of leading men of the city. Outside of Italy movements for city independence—sometimes violent, as at Milan, at other times peaceful—took place within a larger political framework. For example, William Clito, who claimed the county of Flanders, willingly granted the townspeople of Saint-Omer the rights they asked for in 1127 in return for their support of his claims. He recognized them as legally free, with the right to mint coins, make laws, set up courts, and pay fewer taxes.

CHURCH REFORM AND ITS AFTERMATH

Disillusioned citizens at Milan denounced their archbishop not only for his tyranny but also for his impurity; they wanted their pastors to be untainted by sex and by money. In this they were supported by a new-style papacy, keen on reform in the church and society. The "Gregorian Reform," as this movement came to be called, broke up clerical marriages, unleashed civil war in Germany, modified the procedure for episcopal elections, and transformed the papacy into a monarchy. It began as a way to free the church from the world; but in the end the church was deeply involved in the new world it had helped to create.

The Coming of Reform

Freeing the church from the world: what could it mean? In 910 the duke and duchess of Aquitaine founded the monastery of Cluny with some unusual stipulations. They endowed the monastery with property (normal and essential if it were to survive), but then they gave it and its worldly possessions to Saints Peter and Paul. In this way they put control of the monastery into the hands of the two most powerful heavenly saints. They designated the pope, as the successor of Saint Peter, to be the monastery's worldly protector if anyone should bother or threaten it. The whole notion of "freedom" at this point was very vague. But Cluny's prestige was great because of the influence of its founders, the status of Saint Peter, and the fame of its elaborate round of prayers. The Cluniac monks fulfilled the role of "those who pray" in dazzling manner. Through their prayers, they seemed to guarantee the salvation of all Christians. Rulers, bishops, rich landowners, and even serfs (if they could) gave Cluny donations of land, joining their contributions to the land of Saint Peter. Powerful men and women called on the Cluniac abbots to reform new monasteries along the Cluniac model.

The abbots of Cluny came to see themselves as reformers of the world as well as the cloister. They believed in clerical celibacy, preaching against the prevailing norm in which parish priests and even bishops were married. They also thought that the laity could be reformed, become more virtuous, and cease its oppression of the poor. In the eleventh century, the Cluniacs began to link their program to the papacy. When they disputed with bishops or laypeople about lands and rights, they called on the popes to help them out.

The popes were ready to do so. A parallel movement for reform had entered papal circles via a small group of influential monks and clerics. Mining canon (church) law for their ammunition, these churchmen emphasized two abuses: nicolaitism (clerical marriage) and simony (buying church offices). The new patrilineal family taught them the importance of limiting offspring. (In their eyes, celibate priests should have even higher status than first-born sons.) The new profit economy sensitized them to the crass commercial meanings of gifts; in their eyes, churchmen should not give gifts in return for their offices.

Initially, the reformers got imperial backing. In the view of German king and emperor Henry III (*r.*1039-1056), as the anointed of God he was responsible for the well-being of the church in the empire. (For Henry and his dynasty, see Genealogy 5.2: The Salian Kings and Emperors.) Henry denounced simony and personally refused to accept money or gifts when he appointed bishops to their posts. He presided over the Synod of Sutri which, in 1046, deposed three papal rivals and elected another. When that pope died, Henry appointed Leo IX (1049-1054). But Leo

Genealogy 5.2: The Salian Kings and Emperors

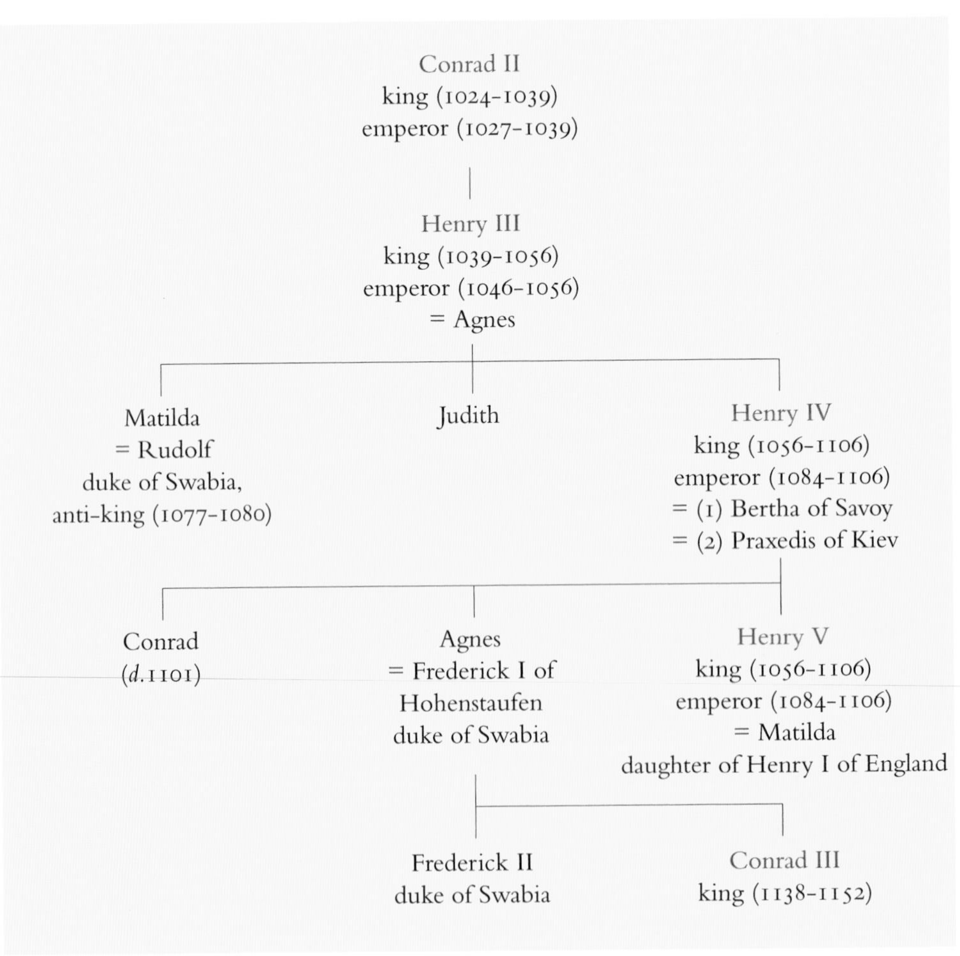

surprised his patron: he set out to reform the church under papal, not imperial, control.

Leo revolutionized the papacy. He had himself elected by the "clergy and people of Rome" to satisfy the demands of canon law. He left Rome (as popes had rarely done before) to preside over church councils and make the pope's influence felt in France and Germany. He sponsored the creation of a canon lawbook—the *Collection in 74 Titles*—that emphasized the pope's power. To the papal curia Leo brought the most zealous church reformers of his day: Peter Damian, Hildebrand (later Gregory VII), and Humbert of Silva Candida.

With Humbert, the newly aggressive papacy was felt at Byzantium. On diplomatic mission at Constantinople in 1054, Humbert argued against the patriarch of Constantinople on behalf of the new, lofty claims of the pope. When the patriarch resisted, Humbert excommunicated him. In retaliation, the patriarch excommunicated Humbert. Clashes between the two churches had occurred before and had been patched up, but this one, called the Great Schism, proved insurmountable (until 1965). After 1054, the Roman Catholic and Greek Orthodox churches largely went their separate ways.

More generally, the papacy began to wield new forms of power. It waged unsuccessful war against the Normans in southern Italy and then made the best of the situation by granting them parts of the region—and Sicily as well—in fief, turning former enemies into vassals. It supported the Christian push into the *taifa* kingdoms of al-Andalus, transforming the "*reconquista*"—the conquest of Islamic Spain—into a holy war: Pope Alexander II (1061-1073) forgave the sins of the Christians on their way to the battle of Barbastro.

The Investiture Conflict and its Effects

The papal reform movement is associated particularly with Pope Gregory VII (1073-1085), hence the term "Gregorian reform." A passionate advocate of papal primacy (the theory that the pope is the head of the church), Gregory was not afraid to clash directly with the king of Germany, Henry IV (*r.*1056-1106), over church leadership. In Gregory's view—an astonishing one at the time, given the religious and spiritual roles associated with rulers—kings and emperors were simple laymen who had no right to meddle in church affairs. Henry, on the other hand, brought up in the traditions of his father, Henry III, considered it part of his duty to appoint bishops and even popes to ensure the well-being of church and empire together.

The pope and the emperor first clashed over the appointment of the archbishop of Milan. Gregory disputed Henry's right to "invest" the archbishop (put him into his office). In the investiture ritual, the emperor or his representative symbolically gave the church and the land that went with it to the bishop or archbishop chosen for the job. This was, for example, the role that Henry II played in Thietmar of Merseburg's episcopal installation (see above, p.157.) In the case of Milan, two rival candidates for archepiscopal office (one supported by the pope, the other by the emperor) had been at loggerheads for several years when, in 1075, Henry invested his own candidate. Gregory immediately called on Henry to "give more respectful attention to the master of the Church," namely Peter and his living representative—Gregory himself.[2] In reply, Henry and the German bishops called on Gregory, that "false monk," to resign. This was the beginning of what historians delicately call the "Investiture Conflict" or "Investiture Controversy." In fact it was war. In February of 1076, Gregory called a synod that both excommunicated Henry and suspended him from office:

> I deprive King Henry [IV], son of the emperor Henry [III], who has rebelled against [God's] Church with unheard-of audacity, of the government over the whole kingdom of Germany and Italy, and I release all Christian men from the allegiance which they have sworn or may swear to him, and I forbid anyone to serve him as king.[3]

The last part of this decree gave it real punch: anyone in Henry's kingdom could rebel against him. The German "princes"—the aristocrats—seized the moment and threatened to elect another king. They were motivated partly by religious sentiments—many had established links with the papacy through their support of reformed monasteries—and partly by political opportunism, as they had chafed under strong German kings who had tried to keep their power in check. Some bishops, too, joined with Gregory's supporters, a major blow to Henry, who needed the troops that they supplied.

Attacked from all sides, Henry traveled in the winter of 1077 to intercept Gregory, barricaded in a fortress at Canossa, high in the Italian alps. It was a refuge provided by the staunchest of papal supporters, Countess Matilda of Tuscany. In an astute and dramatic gesture, the king stood outside the castle (in cold and snow) for three days, barefoot, as a penitent, until Gregory lifted his excommunication and received Henry back into the church. For his part, the pope had the satisfaction of seeing the king humiliate himself before the papal majesty. In any event, the whole episode solved nothing. The princes elected an anti-king, and bloody civil war continued intermittently until 1122.

The Investiture Conflict ended with a compromise. The Concordat of Worms (1122) relied on a conceptual distinction between two parts of investiture—the spiritual (in which the bishop-to-be received the symbols of his office) and the secular (in which he received the symbols of the material goods that would allow him to function). Under the terms of the Concordat, the ring and staff, symbols of church office, would be given by a churchman in the first part of the ceremony. Then the emperor or his representative would touch the bishop with a scepter, signifying the land and other possessions that went with his office. Elections of bishops in Germany would take place "in the presence" of the emperor—that is, under his influence. In Italy, the pope would have a comparable role.

In the end, then, secular rulers continued to influence the appointment of churchmen. But just as the new investiture ceremony broke the ritual into spiritual and secular halves, so too it implied a new notion of kingship separate from the priesthood. The Investiture Conflict did not produce the modern distinction between church and state—that would develop only very slowly—but it set the wheels in motion. At the time, its most important consequence was to shatter the delicate balance among political and ecclesiastical powers in Germany and Italy. In Germany, princes consolidated their lands and powers at the expense of the king. In Italy, the communes came closer to their goals: it was no accident that Milan gained its independence in 1097. And everywhere the papacy took on new authority.

Papal influence was felt at every level. At the abstract level of canon law, papal primacy was enhanced by the publication *c.*1140 of the *Decretum*, written by a teacher of canon law named Gratian. Collecting nearly two thousand passages from the decrees of popes and councils as well as the writings of the Church Fathers, Gratian set out to demonstrate their essential agreement. In fact, the book's original title was *Harmony of Discordant Canons*. If he found any "discord" in his sources, Gratian usually imposed the harmony himself by arguing that the conflicting passages dealt with different situations. A bit later a different legal scholar revised and expanded the *Decretum*, adding Roman law to the mix. At a more local level, papal denunciations of married clergy made inroads on family life. At Verona, for example, "sons of priests" disappeared from the historical record in the twelfth century. At the mundane level of administration, the papal claim to head the church helped turn the curia at Rome into a kind of government, complete with its own bureaucracy, collection agencies, and law courts. It was the teeming port of call for litigious churchmen disputing appointments and for petitioners of every sort.

The First Crusade

On the military level, the papacy's proclamations of holy wars led to bloody slaughter, tragic loss, and tidy profit. We have already seen how Alexander II encouraged the *reconquista* in Spain; it was in the wake of his call that the *taifa* rulers implored the

Almoravids for help. An oddly similar chain of events took place at the other end of the Islamic world. Ostensibly responding to a request from the Byzantine Emperor Alexius for mercenaries to help retake Anatolia from the Seljuks, Pope Urban II (1088-1099) turned the enterprise into something new: a pious pilgrimage to the Holy Land to be undertaken by an armed militia—one commissioned like those of the Peace of God, but thousands of times larger—under the leadership of the papacy. "Enter upon the road to the Holy Sepulcher," Urban exhorted the crowd at Clermont in 1095, "Wrest that land from the wicked race, and subject it to yourselves." On all sides the cry went up: "God wills it!"[4]

The event that historians call the First Crusade (1096-1099) mobilized a force of some 50,000-60,000 combatants, not counting women, children, old men, and hangers-on. The armies were organized not as one military force but rather as separate militias, each authorized by the pope and commanded by a different individual. One band, not authorized by the pope, was made up of commoners. This "Peasants' (or People's) Crusade," which started out before all the others under the leadership of an eloquent but militarily unprepared preacher, Peter the Hermit, took a route through the Rhineland in Germany before going on to Anatolia, where most of its participants were slaughtered.

Peter's indirect route through the Rhineland was no mistake. He was looking for "wicked races" closer to home: the Jews. Under Henry IV many Jews had gained a stable place within the cities of Germany, particularly those along the Rhine. The Jews received protection from the local bishops (imperial appointees, of course) in return for paying a tax. Living in their own neighborhoods—Bishop Rüdiger even built walls around the one at Speyer—the Jews' tightly-knit communities focused on the synagogue, which was a school and community center as well as a place of worship. Nevertheless, Jews also participated in the life of the larger Christian community. Archbishop Anno of Cologne made use of the services of Jewish money-lenders, and other Jews in Cologne were allowed to trade their wares at the fairs there.

Although officials pronounced against the Jews from time to time, and although Jews were at times briefly expelled from some cities (Mainz is one example), they were not persecuted systematically until the First Crusade. Then Peter's peasant crusaders, joined by some local nobles and militias from the region, threatened the Rhineland Jews with forced conversion or death. Some relented when the Jews paid them money; others, however, attacked. The beleaguered Jews occasionally found refuge with bishops or in the houses of Christian friends, but in many cities—Metz, Speyer, Worms, Mainz, and Cologne—they were massacred. Turning from the Rhine to the Moselle, some of the militias forced numerous Jews there to convert. Other armed groups left the Rhineland to seek out the Holy Land via Hungary; at least one stopped off at Prague to massacre more Jews there. Only a small number of these motley armies continued on.

From the point of view of Emperor Alexius at Constantinople, even the "official" crusaders were potentially dangerous. One of the crusade's leaders, the Norman Bohemond, had, a few years before, tried to conquer Byzantium itself. Hastily forcing oaths from Bohemond and the other lords that any previously Byzantine lands conquered would be restored to Byzantium, Alexius shipped the armies off to Nicaea.

The main objective of the First Crusade—to conquer the Holy Land—was accomplished largely because of Muslim disunity. We have already seen how Jerusalem was ruled before the crusaders got there: it had been taken over by Atsiz to the dismay of the Fatimids. As the crusaders made good their conquests (they took Antioch on June 3, 1098, killing every Turk in the city), the Fatimids happily recovered Jerusalem. At that moment, they considered the crusaders potential allies. They were entirely unprepared for the attack which, on July 15, 1099, gave Jerusalem to the Christians.

RULERS WITH CLOUT

While the papacy was turning into a monarchy, other rulers were beginning to turn territories into states. They discovered ideologies to justify their hegemony, hired officials to work for them, found vassals and churchmen to support them. Many of these rulers were women.

The Crusader States

In the Holy Land, the leaders of the crusade set up four tiny states, European colonies in the Levant. Two (Tripoli and Edessa) were counties, Antioch was a principality, Jerusalem a kingdom. (See Map 5.4.) The Europeans held on to them, tenuously, until 1291, though many new crusades had to be called in the interval to shore them up.

Created by conquest, these states were treated as lordships. The new rulers carved out estates to give as fiefs to their vassals, who, in turn, gave portions of their holdings in fief to their own men. The peasants continued to work the land as before, and commerce boomed as the new rulers encouraged lively trade at their coastal ports. Italian merchants—the Genoese, Pisans, and Venetians—were the most active, but others—Byzantines and Muslim traders—participated as well. Enlightened lordship dictated that the mixed population of the states—Muslims, to be sure, but also Jews, Greek Orthodox Christians, Monophysite Christians and others—be tolerated for the sake of production and trade. Most Europeans had gone home after the First

Map 5.4: The Crusader States, *c.*1140

Crusade; those left behind were obliged to preserve the population that remained.

The main concerns of the crusader states' rulers were military, and these could be guaranteed as well by a woman as by a man. Thus Melisende (*r.*1131-1152), oldest daughter of King Baldwin II of Jerusalem, was declared ruler along with her husband, Fulk, formerly count of Anjou, and their infant son. Taking the reins of government into her own hands after Fulk's death, she named a constable to lead her army and made sure that the greatest men in the kingdom sent her their vassals to do military service. Vigorously asserting her position as queen, she found supporters in the church, appointed at least one bishop to his see, and created her own chancery, where her royal acts were drawn up.

But vassals alone, however well commanded, were not sufficient to defend the fragile crusader states, nor were the stone castles and towers that bristled in the countryside. New knights had to be recruited from Europe from time to time, and a new and militant kind of monasticism developed in the Levant: the Knights Templar. Vowed to poverty and chastity, the Templars at the same time devoted themselves to war. They defended the town garrisons of the crusader states and ferried money from Europe to the Holy Land. Even so, they could not prevent a new Seljuk leader, Zengi, from taking Edessa in 1144. The slow but steady shrinking of the crusader states began at that moment. The Second Crusade (1147-1149), called in the wake of Zengi's victory, came to a disastrous end. After only four days of besieging the walls of Damascus, the crusaders, whose leaders could not keep the peace among themselves, gave up and went home.

England under Norman Rule

Anglo-Saxon England was early linked to the Continent by the Vikings, who settled in England's eastern half. In the eleventh century it was further tied to Scandinavia under the rule of Cnut (*r.*1016-1035), king of a state that extended from England to Denmark, Norway, and part of Sweden. But it was with its conquest by William, duke of Normandy, that England was drawn inextricably into the Continental orbit.

William the Conqueror, duke of Normandy, carried a papal banner with him when he left his duchy in 1066 to dispute the crown of the childless King Edward the Confessor. The one-day battle of Hastings was decisive, and William was crowned the first Norman king of England. (See Genealogy 6.1: The Norman and Angevin Kings of England, on p.213 of volume 2.) Treating his conquest like booty (as the crusaders would do a few decades later in their new states), he kept about 20 per cent of the land for himself and divided the rest, distributing it in large but scattered fiefs to a relatively small number of his barons—his elite followers—and family members, lay and ecclesiastical, as well as to some lesser men, such as personal servants and soldiers. In turn, these men maintained their own vassals; they owed the king military service (and the service of a fixed number of their vassals) along with certain dues, such as reliefs (money paid upon inheriting a fief) and aids (payments made on important occasions).

These were noble obligations; William expected their servile counterpart from the peasantry. In 1086, he ordered a survey of the land and landholders of England. Quickly dubbed "Domesday Book" because, like the records of people judged at doomsday, it provided facts that could not be appealed, it was the most extensive inventory of land, livestock, taxes, and people that had ever been compiled anywhere in medieval Europe. According to a chronicler of the time, William

> sent his men over all England into every shire and had them find out how many hundred hides [a measure of land] there were in the shire, or what land and cattle the king himself had in the country, or what dues he ought to receive every year from the shire.... So very narrowly did he have the survey to be made that there was no single hide nor a yard of land, nor indeed ... one ox or one cow or one pig left out.[5]

The surveys were made by the king's men by consulting Anglo-Saxon tax lists and by taking testimony from local jurors, men sworn to answer a series of formal questions truthfully. Summarized in Domesday, the answers gave William what he needed to know about his kingdom and the revenues—including the Danegeld, which was now in effect a royal tax—that could be expected from it.

Communication with the Continent was constant. The Norman barons spoke a brand of French; they talked more easily with the peasants of Normandy (if they bothered) than with those tilling the land in England. They maintained their estates on the Continent and their ties with its politics, institutions, and culture. English wool was sent to Flanders to be turned into cloth. The most brilliant intellect of his day, Saint Anselm of Bec (1033-1109), was born in Italy, became abbot of a Norman monastery, and was then appointed archbishop in England. English adolescent boys were sent to Paris and Chartres for schooling. The kings of England often spent more time on the Continent than they did on the island. When, on the death of William's son, King Henry I (*r.*1100-1135), no male descendent survived to take the throne, two counts from the Continent—Geoffrey of Anjou and Stephen of Blois—disputed it as their right through two rival females of the royal line. (See Genealogy 6.1 again.)

Christian Spain

While initially the product of defeat, Christian Spain in the eleventh and twelfth centuries turned tables and became, in effect, the successful western counterpart of the crusader states. The disintegration of al-Andalus into *taifas* opened immense opportunities to the Spanish princes of the north. Wealth flowed into their coffers not only from plundering raids and the confiscation of lands and cities but also (until the Almoravids put an end to it) from tribute, paid in gold by *taifa* rulers to stave off attacks.

It was not just the rulers who were enriched. When Rodrigo Diaz de Vivar, the Cid (from the Arabic *sidi*, lord), fell out of favor with his lord, King Alfonso VI (*r.*1065-1109) of León-Castile, he and a band of followers found employment with al-Mutamin, ruler of Zaragoza. There the Cid defended the city against Christian and Muslim invaders alike. In 1090, he left employment for good and took his chances at Valencia:

> My Cid knew well   that God was his strength.
> There was great fear   in the city of Valencia
> It grieves those of Valencia.   Know, they are not pleased
> They took counsel   and came to besiege him.[6]

Thus were the two sides depicted in the *Poem of the Cid*, written perhaps a century later: beleaguered inhabitants versus an army of God, even though the Cid had just come from serving a Muslim ruler. In the end, the Cid took Valencia in 1094 and ruled there until his death in 1099. He was a Spaniard, but other opportunistic armies sometimes came from elsewhere. The one that Pope Alexander II authorized to besiege Barbastro in 1064 was made up of Frenchmen.

The French connection was symptomatic of a wider process: the Europeanization of Spain. Initially the Christian kingdoms had been isolated islands of Visigothic culture. But already in the tenth century, pilgrims from France, England, Germany, and Italy were clogging the roads to the shrine of Saint James (Santiago) of Compostela; in the eleventh century, monks from Cluny and other reformed monasteries arrived to colonize Spanish cloisters. Alfonso VI actively reached out beyond the Pyrenees, to Cluny—where he doubled the annual gift of 1000 gold pieces that his father, Fernando I, had given in exchange for prayers for his soul—and to the papacy. He sought recognition from Pope Gregory VII as "king of Spain," and in return he imposed the Roman liturgy throughout his kingdom, stamping out the traditional Visigothic music and texts.

In 1085 Alfonso made good his claim to be more than the king of León-Castille by conquering Toledo. (See Map 5.5.) After his death, his daughter Queen Urraca

Map 5.5: Spain at the Death of Alfonso VI (1109)

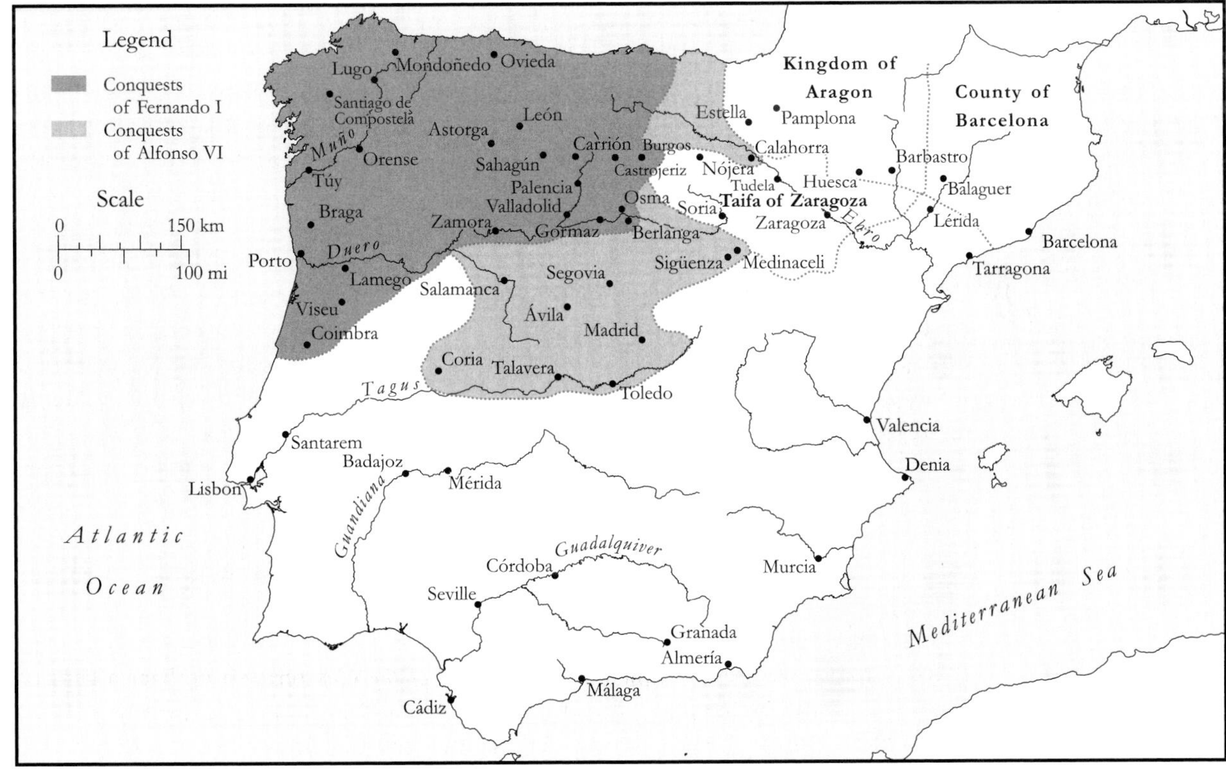

Genealogy 5.3 (facing page): The Capetian Kings of France

(*r.*1109-1126) ruled in her own right a realm larger than England. Her strength came from many of the usual sources: control over land, which, though granted out to counts and others, was at least in theory revocable; church appointments; an army—everyone was liable to be called up once a year, even arms-bearing slaves—and a court of great men to offer advice and give their consent.

Praising the King of France

Not all rulers had opportunities for grand conquest. How did they maintain themselves? The example of the kings of France reveals the possibilities. Reduced to battling a few castles in the vicinity of the Ile-de-France, the Capetian kings nevertheless wielded many of the same instruments of power as their conquering contemporaries: vassals, taxes, commercial revenues, military and religious reputations. Louis VI the Fat (*r.*1108-1137), so heavy that he had to be hoisted onto his horse by a crane, was nevertheless a tireless defender of royal power. (See Genealogy 5.3: The Capetian Kings of France.)

Louis's virtues were amplified and broadcast by his biographer, Suger (1081-1152), the abbot of Saint-Denis, a monastery just outside Paris. A close associate of the king, Suger was his chronicler and propagandist. When Louis set himself the task of consolidating his rule in the Ile-de-France, Suger portrayed the king as a righteous hero. He was more than a lord with rights over the French nobles as his vassals; he was a peacekeeper with the God-given duty to fight unruly strongmen. Careful not to claim that Louis was head of the church, which would have scandalized the papacy and its supporters, Suger nevertheless emphasized Louis's role as protector of the church and the poor and insisted on the sacred importance of the royal dignity. When a pope happened to arrive in France, Louis, not yet king, and his father, Philip I (*r.*1060-1108), bowed low, but (said Suger) "the lord pope lifted them up and made them sit before him like devout sons of the apostles. In the manner of a wise man acting wisely, he conferred with them privately on the present condition of the church."[7] Here the pope was shown needing royal advice. Meanwhile, Suger stressed Louis's piety and active defense of the faith:

> Helped by his powerful band of armed men, or rather by the hand of God, he abruptly seized the castle [of Crécy] and captured its very strong tower as if it were simply the hut of a peasant. Having startled those criminals [Thomas of Marle, a regional castellan, and his retinue], he piously slaughtered the impious, cutting them down without mercy because he found them to be merciless.[8]

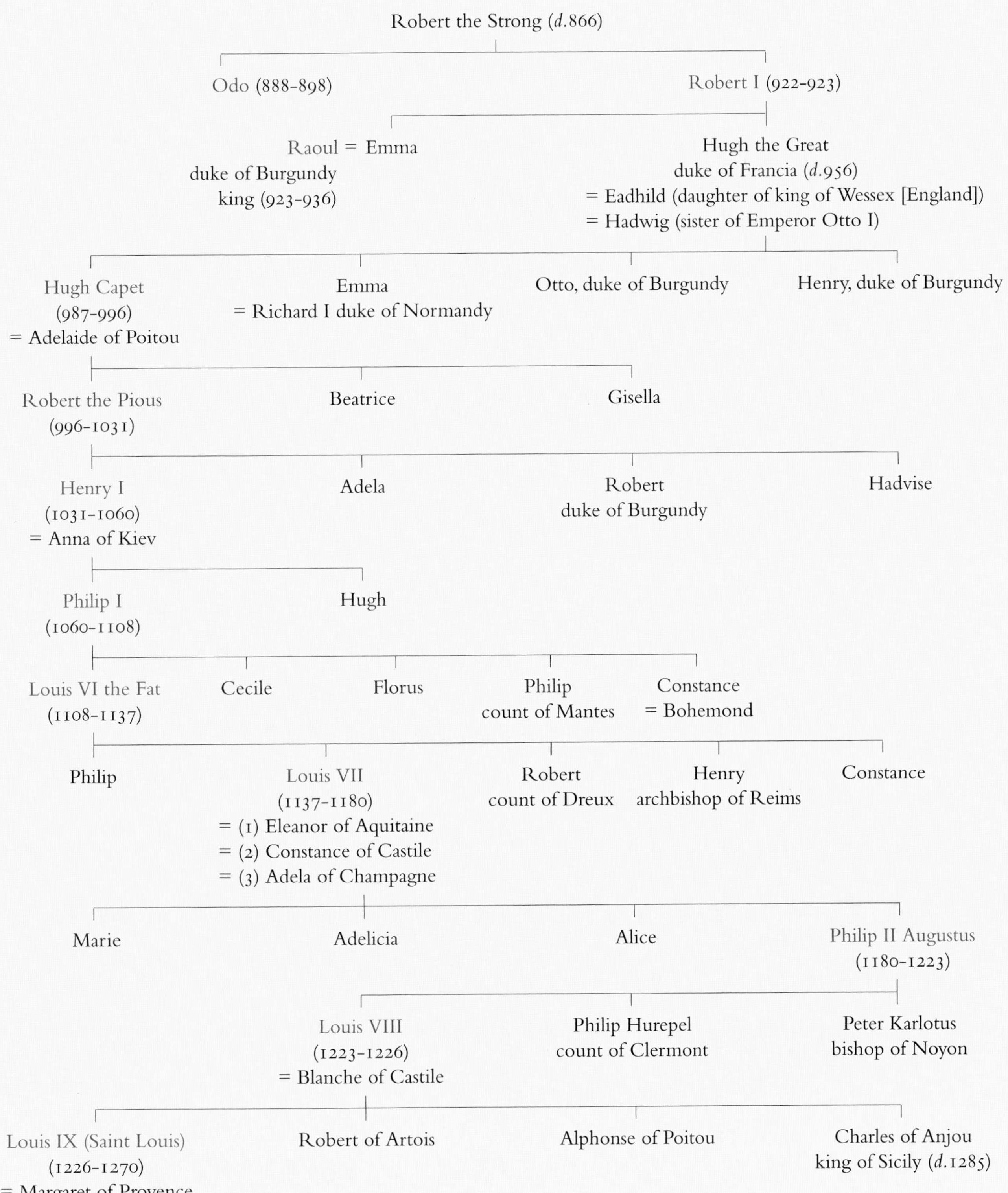

Robert the Strong (*d.*866)
Odo (888-898)
Robert I (922-923)
Raoul = Emma
duke of Burgundy
king (923-936)
Hugh the Great
duke of Francia (*d.*956)
= Eadhild (daughter of king of Wessex [England])
= Hadwig (sister of Emperor Otto I)
Hugh Capet
(987-996)
= Adelaide of Poitou
Emma
= Richard I duke of Normandy
Otto, duke of Burgundy
Henry, duke of Burgundy
Robert the Pious
(996-1031)
Beatrice
Gisella
Henry I
(1031-1060)
= Anna of Kiev
Adela
Robert
duke of Burgundy
Hadvise
Philip I
(1060-1108)
Hugh
Louis VI the Fat
(1108-1137)
Cecile
Florus
Philip
count of Mantes
Constance
= Bohemond
Philip
Louis VII
(1137-1180)
= (1) Eleanor of Aquitaine
= (2) Constance of Castile
= (3) Adela of Champagne
Robert
count of Dreux
Henry
archbishop of Reims
Constance
Marie
Adelicia
Alice
Philip II Augustus
(1180-1223)
Louis VIII
(1223-1226)
= Blanche of Castile
Philip Hurepel
count of Clermont
Peter Karlotus
bishop of Noyon
Louis IX (Saint Louis)
(1226-1270)
= Margaret of Provence
Robert of Artois
Alphonse of Poitou
Charles of Anjou
king of Sicily (*d.*1285)

When Louis VI died in 1137, Suger's notion of the might and right of the king of France reflected reality in an extremely small area. Nevertheless, Louis laid the groundwork for the gradual extension of royal power. As the lord of vassals, the king could call upon his men to aid him in times of war (though the great ones could defy him). As king and landlord, he collected dues and taxes with the help of his officials, called *prévôts*. Revenues came from Paris as well, a thriving commercial and cultural center. With money and land, Louis could employ civil servants while dispensing the favors and giving the gifts that added to his prestige and power.

NEW FORMS OF LEARNING AND RELIGIOUS EXPRESSION

The commercial revolution, the newly reorganized church, close contact with the Islamic world, and the revived polities of the early twelfth century paved the way for the growth of schools and new forms of scholarship. Money, learning, and career opportunities attracted many to the new centers. On the other hand, the cities and the schools repelled others, who retreated from the world to seek poverty and solitude. Yet the new learning and the new money had a way of seeping into the cracks and crannies of even the most resolutely separate institutions.

Schools and the Liberal Arts

Connected to monasteries and cathedrals since the Carolingian period, schools had traditionally trained young men to become monks or priests. Some schools were better endowed than others with books and masters (teachers); a few developed reputations for particular expertise. By the end of the eleventh century, the best schools were those connected to cathedrals in the larger cities: Reims, Paris, Bologna, Montpellier.

Eager students sampled nearly all of them. The young monk Gilbert of Liège was typical: "Instilled with an insatiable thirst for learning, whenever he heard of somebody excelling in the arts, he rushed immediately to that place and drank whatever delightful potion he could draw from the master there."[9] For Gilbert and other students, a good lecture had the excitement of the theater. Teachers at some schools were sometimes forced to find larger halls to accommodate the crush of students. Other teachers simply declared themselves "masters" and set up shop by renting a room. If they could prove their mettle as lecturers, they had no trouble finding paying students.

What the students sought, above all, was knowledge of the seven liberal arts. Grammar, rhetoric, and logic (or dialectic) belonged to the "beginning" arts, the so-called trivium. Logic, involving the technical analysis of texts as well as the application and manipulation of arguments, was a transitional subject leading to the second, higher part of the liberal arts, the quadrivium. This comprised four areas of study that might today be called theoretical math and science: arithmetic (number theory), geometry, music (theory rather than practice), and astronomy. Of these arts, logic had pride of place in the schools, while masters and students who studied the quadrivium generally did so outside of the classroom.

The goal of twelfth-century scholars was to gather, order, systematize, and clarify all knowledge. That God existed, nearly everyone believed. But scholars like Anselm of Bec were not satisfied by belief alone. Anselm's faith, as he put it, "sought understanding." He emptied his mind of all concepts except that of God and then, using the tools of logic, proved God's very existence in his *Monologion*. Gilbert of Poitiers (*c.*1075-1154) systematized Bible commentaries, helping to create the *Glossa Ordinaria*, the standard compendium of all teachings on the Bible. Peter Abelard (1079-1142), who declared that "nothing can be believed unless it is first understood," drew together conflicting authoritative texts on 156 key subjects in his *Sic et Non* (*Yes and No*), including "That God is one and the contrary" and "That it is permitted to kill men and the contrary." Leaving the propositions unresolved, Abelard urged his students to discover the reasons behind the disagreements. Soon Peter Lombard (*c.*1100-1160) adopted Abelard's method of juxtaposing opposing positions, but he supplied his own reasoned resolutions as well. His *Sententiae* was perhaps the most successful textbook of the twelfth century.

One key logical issue for twelfth-century scholars involved the question of "universals": whether a universal—something that can be said of many—is real or simply a linguistic or mental entity. For example, when we look at diverse individuals of one kind, say Fluffy and Mittens, we say of each of them that they are members of the same species: cat. Abelard sneered at one of his teachers, William of Champeaux, who maintained (in Abelard's words) "that ... the whole species was essentially the same in each of its individuals."[10] William was what we call a "realist," for he argued that the species was indeed real. Others, whom we call "nominalists," denied this reality. Abelard was essentially a nominalist, seeing Fluffy and Mittens as radically individual. However, he partly allied himself with the realists by seeking a real basis in individuals for universal terms. This he found in the idea of the status or condition which all individuals of a species share. This was not a "thing," just a mode of being. For Abelard, there was no "thing" common to Fluffy and Mittens; they were not cats by virtue of some extra-linguistic or extra-mental entity. Nevertheless, they *were* really cats by their common status, namely being a cat.

Later in the twelfth century, scholars found precise tools for this and other logical questions in the works of Aristotle. During Abelard's lifetime, very little of Aristotle's work was available in Europe because it had not been translated from Greek into Latin. By the end of the century, however, that lack had been filled by translators who traveled to Islamic or formerly Islamic cities—Toledo in Spain, Palermo in Sicily—where Aristotle had already been translated into Arabic and carefully commented on by Islamic scholars like Ibn Sina (Avicenna) (980-1037) and Ibn Rushd (Averroes) (1126-1198). By the thirteenth century, Aristotle had become the primary philosopher for the scholastics (the scholars of the European medieval universities).

The lofty subjects of the schools had down-to-earth, practical consequences in books for preachers, advice for rulers, manuals for priests, textbooks for students, and guides for living addressed to laypeople. Nor was mastery of the liberal arts the end of everyone's education. Many students went on to study medicine (the great school for that was at Montpellier) or theology (Paris was the center). Others studied law; at Bologna, for example, where Gratian worked on canon law, other jurists—such as the so-called Four Doctors—achieved fame by teaching and writing about Roman law. By the mid-twelfth century, scholars had made real progress towards a systematic understanding of Justinian's law codes (see p. 52). The lawyers who emerged from the school at Bologna went on to serve popes, bishops, kings, princes, or communes. Thus the learning of the schools was preached in the churches, consulted in the law courts, and used on the operating tables. It came to unify European culture.

Figure 5.1 (facing page): Hypothetical Plan of the Monastery of Cluny, 1157

Robert Pullen's life may serve to illustrate the career of a moderately successful schoolman while suggesting some of the practical benefits of the new learning. Born in England, Pullen was sent to school at Laon, in France. Good at his studies, he became a master in turn. Back in England, he was (in the 1130s) the first lecturer in theology at Oxford. But Paris beckoned as the center of theological studies, and as soon as he got a church position in England (and the revenues attached to it), he went off to France. From there, he went to Rome, where his academic training helped him get appointed papal chancellor. He served perfectly capably in this post, meanwhile finding good jobs at the papal curia for some of his students, helping his nephew get a church post (the very one that Pullen had abandoned in England), and obtaining papal privileges for the monastery of yet another of his relatives.

Monastic Splendor and Poverty

That monastery, Sherborne Abbey, was an old-fashioned Benedictine house. There were many others, the most famous of them the monastery of Cluny, which, by the early twelfth century, housed some 400 brothers. Physically, it was a palatial complex of buildings, but the monks, following the *Rule* of Saint Benedict, still slept in a com-

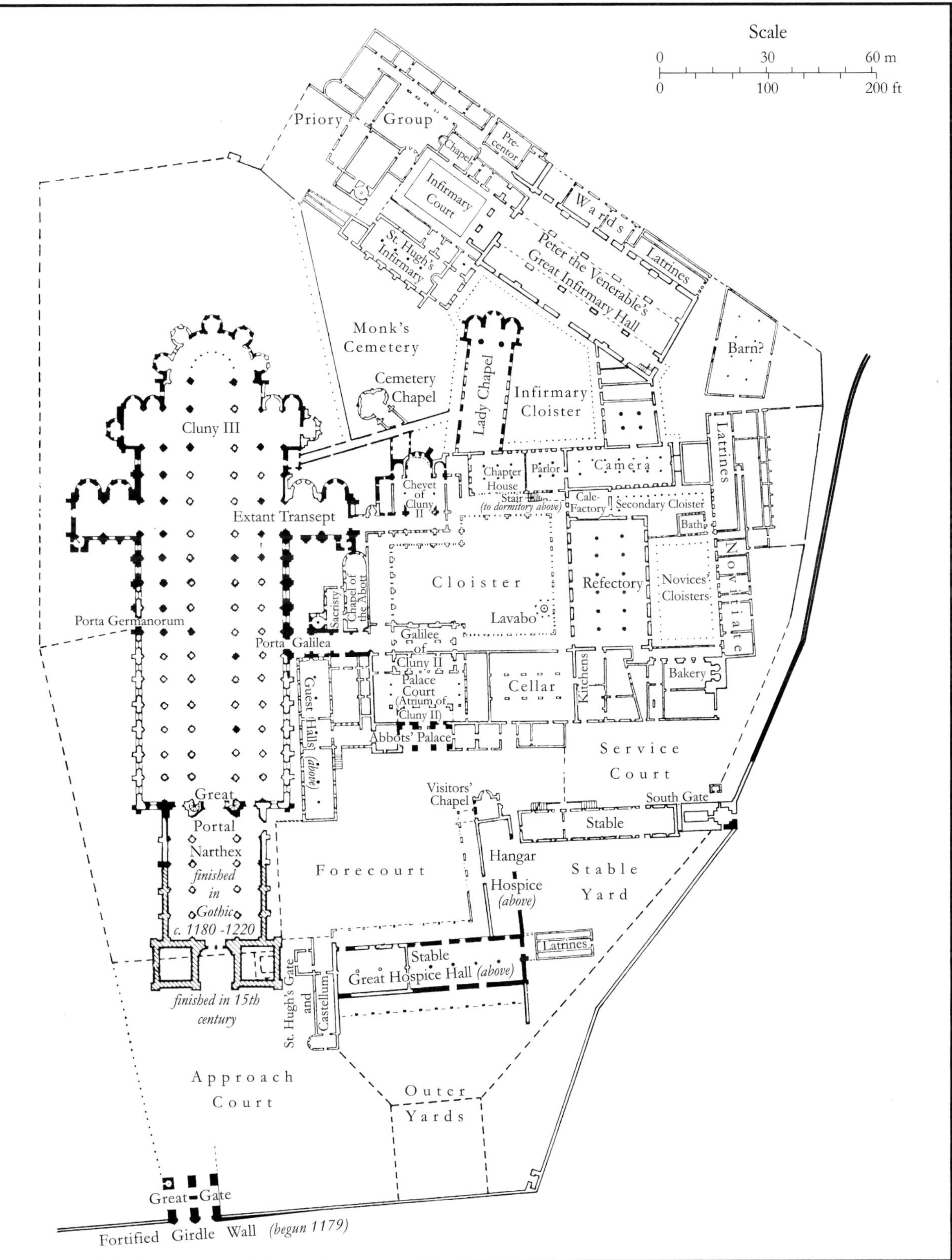
Scale
0
30
60 m
0
100
200 ft
Priory Group
Chapel
Pre-centor
Infirmary Court
Wards
St. Hugh's Infirmary
Peter the Venerable's Great Infirmary Hall
Latrines
Monk's Cemetery
Cemetery Chapel
Lady Chapel
Infirmary Cloister
Barn?
Cluny III
Chevet of Cluny II
Chapter House
Parlor
Camera
Latrines
Stair (to dormitory above)
Cale-Factory
Secondary Cloister
Bath
Extant Transept
Cloister
Refectory
Novices' Cloisters
Noviciate
Sacristy
Chapel of the Abbott
Lavabo
Porta Germanorum
Porta Galilea
Galilee of Cluny II
Palace Court (Atrium of Cluny II)
Cellar
Kitchens
Bakery
Guest Halls (above)
Abbots' Palace
Service Court
Great Portal
Visitors' Chapel
South Gate
Stable
Narthex finished in Gothic c. 1180 -1220
Forecourt
Hangar
Hospice (above)
Stable Yard
Latrines
Stable
Great Hospice Hall (above)
finished in 15th century
St. Hugh's Gate and Castellum
Approach Court
Outer Yards
Great Gate
Fortified Girdle Wall (begun 1179)

mon dormitory and ate in a common dining room. (See Figure 5.1.) They were served—in the kitchen, cellar, and hospital—by men who increasingly lived "off campus" with their wives and children, in a town nestled right outside the monastery doors. By the end of the eleventh century, Pope Urban II, on his way to preach the First Crusade, declared a sacrosanct zone around Cluny, making it a sort of miniature Holy Land in the middle of Burgundy. Within their various circles of power and sanctity, the Cluniacs—and other "black monks" (so-called because of the color of their robes) and also nuns following their example—carried out a life of arduous, nearly continuous prayer. Every detail of their lives was ordered, every object splendid, every space adorned to render due honor to the Lord of heaven.

Since the time of Charlemagne, Gregorian chant had expanded enormously. By the twelfth century, a large repertoire of melodies had grown up, and new methods of musical notation had been elaborated to convey them. Scribes drew staves, sometimes multicolored, to show pitch. In Plate 5.3, a manuscript from the monastery of Saint-Evroult in Normandy, the scribe used a four-line staff (one red, one green, and two others lightly sketched) to indicate the locations of the pitches a-c-e-f. Ever since the Carolingian period, the scalar patterns that these pitches reflected were called "modes." They were so integral to the way that chants were understood and classified that the monks of Cluny personified the modes on some of the columns circling the choir of their church. (See Plate 5.4.)

This sculpture of a chant tone—in high relief yet wedded to the shape and surface of the capital (the top of a column or pier) that it springs from—is in the so-called "Romanesque" style. Another example of this style, this time from the cathedral of Autun (Plate 5.5), is far less tranquil in depicting the suicide of Judas, the apostle who betrayed Christ. Yet even these furious demons and the gagging Judas are contained by the shape of the capital, their cramped postures adding to the emotional frenzy of the composition.

Romanesque, representing the first wave of European monumental architec-

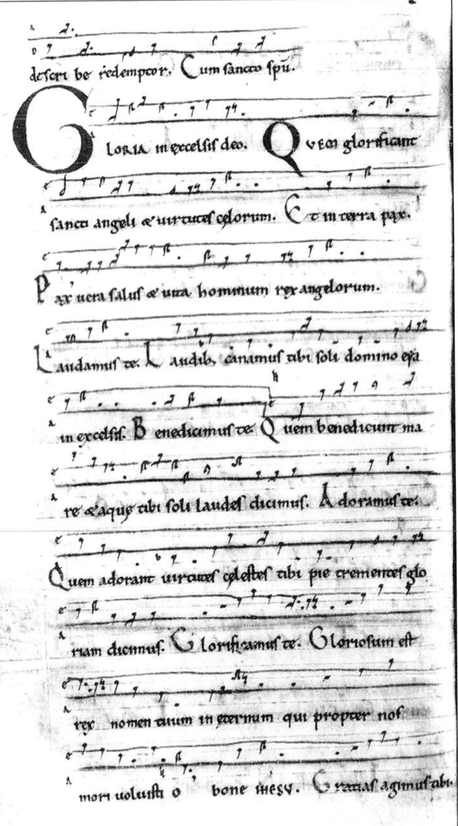

Plate 5.3: Gloria with Musical Notation, Saint-Evroult (12th cent.). The "Gloria," for which this manuscript page gives both text and music, was a chant of the Mass. Here the usual text of the Gloria has additional tropes (new words and music).

Plate 5.4 (facing page): A Mode of the Chant, Cluny (1088-1095). Each of the eight modes of the Gregorian chant was associated with one of four characteristic notes. Four carvings on the capitals of Cluny's choir represented each of these notes; the one on the left here portrays the "third" note, while the one to its right (slightly out of focus) is the fourth tone.

ture, was the style of the building boom—especially of the great Benedictine monasteries—in the early twelfth century. Romanesque churches, built of stone, are massive, weighty, and dignified; but they are enlivened by sculpture, wall paintings, and the texture of patterns. At Durham cathedral (built between 1093 and 1133 in the north of England), the stone itself is a warm yellow/pink color, given added zest by piers incised with diamond or zig-zag patterns. (See Plate 5.6.) At Berzé-la-Ville, a small church near Cluny, wall paintings decorate the interior; Plate 5.7 shows the martyrdom of Saint Vincent, roasting on a grill. At Pisa, the famous leaning tower is in fact a Romanesque bell tower; here (Plate 5.8) the decoration is on the exterior, where the bright Italian sun heightens the play of light and shadow.

Santiago de Compostela (built between 1078 and 1124) may serve as an example of a "typical" Romanesque church, though in fact the most typical aspect of that style is its extreme variety. Most of Santiago's exterior was rebuilt in the Baroque period, but the interior is still much as it must have been when twelfth-century pilgrims entered the shrine of Saint James. (See Plate 5.9.) Striking is the "barrel" or "tunnel" vault whose ribs, springing from thin columns attached to the piers, mark the long church into sections called bays. There are only two levels: the first is for the arches that open onto the side aisles of the church; the second is the gallery. (Many other Romanesque churches have a third story—a clerestory—of windows.) The plan of Santiago (see Figure 5.2) shows its typical basilica shape with a transept crossing and, at the east end, an aisle (called an "ambulatory") that allowed pilgrims to visit the relics housed in the chapels.

Plate 5.5: Suicide of Judas, Autun (1125-1135). According to Matt. 27:3-6, Judas repented betraying Jesus, tried to return the money he had gained for it, and finally "went and hanged himself with a halter." The sculptor of this capital at Autun Cathedral carved the scene, with winged devils pulling the noose.

Plate 5.6 (facing page): Durham Cathedral, Interior (1093-1133). Huge and imposing, Durham Cathedral is also inviting and welcoming, with its lively piers, warm colors, and harmonious spaces. Built by Norman bishops, it housed the relics of the Anglo-Saxon Saint Cuthbert; in just such ways did the Normans appropriate the power and prestige of English saints' cults.

Not all medieval people agreed that such opulence

Plate 5.7: Martyrdom of Saint Vincent, Berzé-la-Ville (late 11th or early 12th cent.). As at many other Romanesque churches, the walls of Berzé-la-Ville are covered with frescoes of religious scenes. Note the contrast between the calm, rounded Saint Vincent (*d.*304) and his frenetic, angular tormentors.

pleased or praised God, however. At the end of the eleventh century, the new commercial economy and the profit motive that fueled it led many to reject wealth and to embrace poverty as a key element of religious life. The Carthusian order, founded by Bruno, one-time bishop of Cologne, was such a group. La Chartreuse, the chief house of the order, was built in an Alpine valley, lonely and inaccessible. Each monk took a vow of silence and lived as a hermit in his own small hut. Only occasionally would the monks join the others for prayer in a common oratory. When not engaged in prayer or meditation, the Carthusians copied manuscripts: for them, scribal work was a way to preach God's word with the hands rather than the mouth. Slowly the Carthusian order grew, but each monastery was limited to only twelve monks, the number of Christ's Apostles.

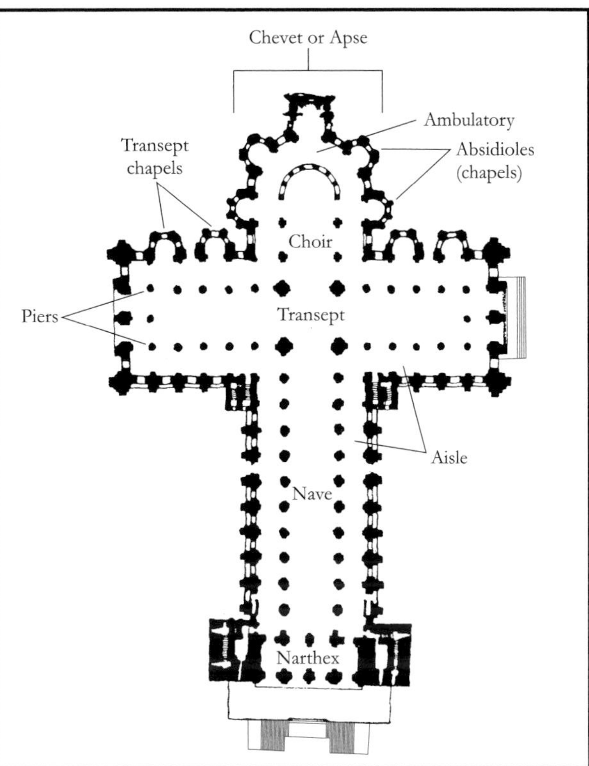

Figure 5.2: A Model Romanesque Church: Santiago de Compostela

By contrast, the Cistercians expanded rapidly, often by reforming and incorporating existing monasteries. The first Cistercian house was Cîteaux (in Latin, *Cistercium*), founded in 1098 by Robert of Molesme (*c.*1027-1110) and a few other monks seeking a more austere way of life. Austerity they found—and also success. With the arrival of Saint Bernard (*c.*1090-1153), who came to Cîteaux in 1112 along with about thirty friends and relatives, the original center sprouted a small congregation of houses in Burgundy. (Bernard became abbot of one of them, Clairvaux.) By the mid-twelfth century there were more than 300 monasteries—many in France, but also in Italy, Germany, England, Austria, and Spain—following what they took to be the customs of Cîteaux. By the end of the twelfth century, the Cistercians were an order: their member houses adhered to the decisions of a General Chapter; their liturgical practices and internal organization were standardized. Many nuns, too, as eager as

Plate 5.8: Leaning Tower (Bell Tower) of Pisa (late 12th cent.). The tower is part of a large cathedral and baptistery complex which, in its layout and design, was meant to imitate—and outshine—the Temple Mount complex at Jerusalem.

Plate 5.9 (facing page): Santiago de Compostela, Interior (1078-1124). Santiago (in the far northwest corner of Spain) was known for its relics of Saint James the Great (*d.*44), apostle and martyr. From the twelfth through fifteenth centuries a major pilgrimage center, the cathedral was built to hold crowds and to usher them, via aisles, from chapel to chapel.

monks to live the life of simplicity and poverty that the Apostles had endured and enjoyed, adopted Cîteaux's customs; some convents later became members of the order.

Although the Cistercians claimed the *Rule* of Saint Benedict as the foundation of their customs, they elaborated a style of life and an aesthetic all their own, largely governed by the goal of simplicity. They even rejected the conceit of dying their robes—hence their nickname, the "white monks." White, too, were their houses. Despite regional variations and considerable latitude in interpreting the meaning of "simplicity," Cistercian buildings had a different feel than the great Benedictine monasteries of black monks. Foursquare and regular, Cistercian churches and other buildings conformed to a fairly standard plan. (See Figure 5.3.) The churches tended to be small, made of smooth-cut, undecorated stone. Wall paintings were eschewed, sculpture modest at best. Indeed, Saint Bernard wrote a scathing attack on Romanesque sculpture in which, ironically, he admitted its sensuous allure:

> What is the point of ridiculous monstrosities in the cloister where there are brethren reading—I mean those extraordinary deformed beauties and beautiful deformities? What are those lascivious apes doing, those fierce lions, monstrous centaurs, half-men and spotted leopards.... It is more diverting to decipher marble than the text before you, and to spend the whole day in gazing at such singularities in preference to meditating upon God's laws.[11]

The Cistercians had few such diversions, but the simplicity of their buildings and of their clothing also had its beauty. Illuminated by the pure white light that came through clear glass windows, Cistercian churches were luminous, cool, and serene. Plate 5.10 shows the nave of Fontenay Abbey, begun in 1139. There are no wall paintings, no sculpture, no incised pillars. Yet the subtle play of thick piers and thin

columns along with the alternation of curved and linear capitals lend the church a sober charm.

True to their emphasis on purity, the communal liturgy of the Cistercians was simplified and shorn of the many additions that had been tacked on in the houses of the black monks. Only the liturgy as prescribed in the *Rule* of Saint Benedict and one daily Mass were allowed. Even the music for the chant was modified: the Cistercians rigorously suppressed the B flat, even though doing so made the melody discordant, because of their insistence on strict simplicity.

On the other hand, Benedict's *Rule* did not prevent the Cistercians from creating a new class of monks—the lay brothers—who were illiterate and unable to participate in the liturgy. These men did the necessary labor—field work, stock raising—to support the community at large. A closer look at Figure 5.3 shows that the Cistercian monastery was in fact a house divided: the eastern half was for the "choir" monks, the western half for the lay brethren. Each half had its own dining room, latrines, and dormitories. The monks were strictly segregated, even in the church, where a screen kept them apart.

Plate 5.10 (facing page): Fontenay Abbey Church, Interior (1139–1147). Compare the bare walls of this Cistercian church with the frescoed walls of Berzé-la-Ville (**Plate 5.7**). How do these different artistic sensibilities reflect religious ones?

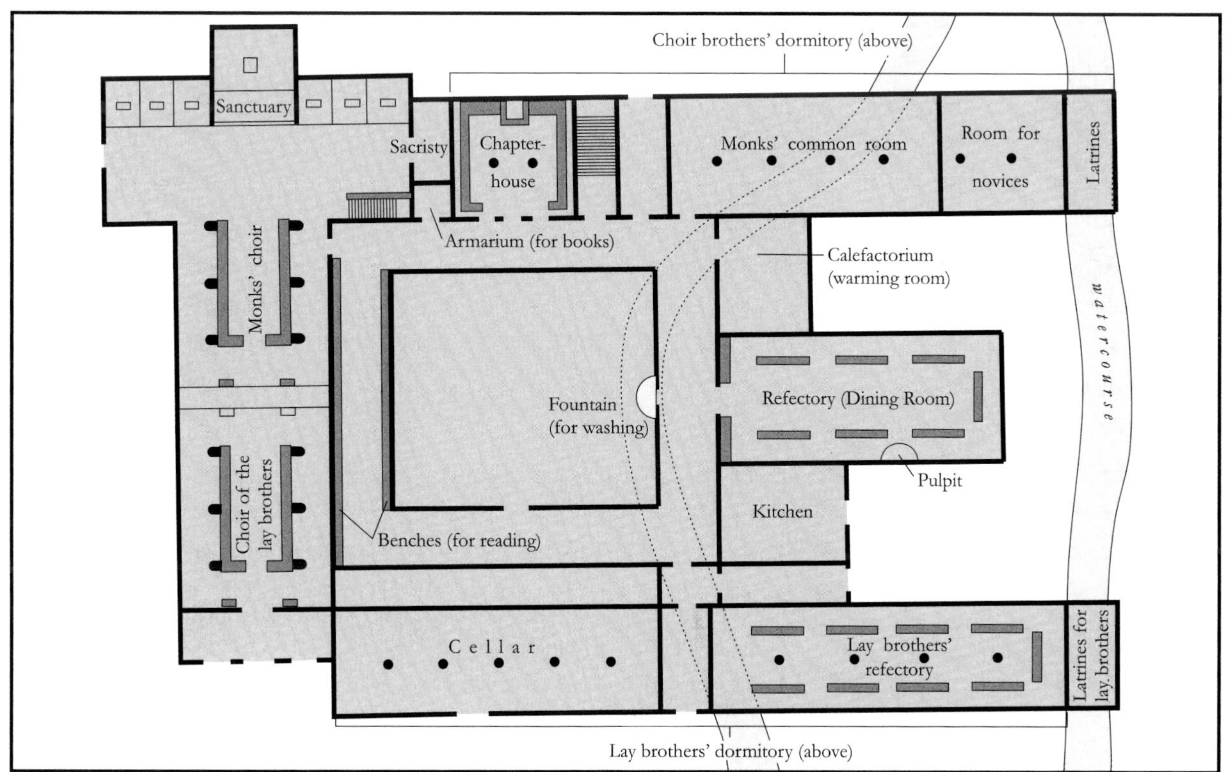

Figure 5.3: Schematic Plan of a Cistercian Monastery

The choir monks dedicated themselves to private prayer and contemplation and to monastic administration. The Cistercian *Charter of Charity* (*c*.1165), in effect a constitution of the order, provided for a closely monitored network of houses, and each year the Cistercian abbots met to hammer out legislation for all of them. All the houses had large and highly organized farms and grazing lands called "granges," and the monks spent much of their time managing their estates and flocks of sheep, both of which yielded handsome profits by the end of the twelfth century. Clearly part of the agricultural and commercial revolutions of the Middle Ages, the Cistercian order made managerial expertise a part of the monastic life.

Yet the Cistercians also elaborated a spirituality of intense personal emotion. As Bernard said,

> Often enough when we approach the altar to pray our hearts are dry and lukewarm. But if we persevere, there comes an unexpected infusion of grace, our breast expands as it were, and our interior is filled with an overflowing love; and if somebody should press upon it then, this milk of sweet fecundity would gush forth in streaming richness.[12]

The Cistercians emphasized not only human feeling but also the humanity of Christ and Mary. While pilgrims continued to stream to the tombs and reliquaries of saints, the Cistercians dedicated all their churches to the Virgin Mary (for whom they had no relics) because for them she signified the model of a loving mother. Indeed, the Cistercians regularly used maternal imagery (as Bernard's metaphor of a flowing breast illustrates) to describe the nurturing care provided to humans by Jesus himself. The Cistercian God was approachable, human, protective, even mothering.

★ ★ ★ ★

In the twelfth century, Europe was coming into its own. Growing population and the profitable organization of the countryside promoted cities, trade, and wealth. Townspeople created new institutions of self-regulation and self-government. Kings and popes found new means to exert their authority and test its limits. Scholars mastered the knowledge of the past and put it to use in classrooms, royal courts, and papal offices. Monks who fled the world ended up in positions of leadership; the great entrepreneurs of the twelfth century were the Cistercians; and Saint Bernard was the most effective preacher of the Second Crusade.

The power of communities was recognized in the twelfth century: the guilds and communes depended on this recognition. So too did the new theology of the time. In his theological treatise, *Why God Became Man*, Saint Anselm put new emphasis on Christ's humanity: Christ's sacrifice was that of one human being for another. The

Cistercians spoke of God's mothering. Historians sometimes speak of the rise of "humanism"—with its emphasis on the dignity of human beings, the splendor of the natural world, and the nobility of reason—in the twelfth century. Yet the new stress on the loving bonds that tied Christians together also led to the persecution of others, like Jews and Muslims, who lived outside the Christian community. In the next century communities would become more ordered, regulated, and incorporated. By the same token, they became even more exclusive.

CHAPTER FIVE KEY EVENTS

1049-1054	Papacy of Leo IX
1066	Norman conquest of England by William of Normandy
1072	Battle of Manzikert
1073-1085	Papacy of Gregory VII
1075-1122	Investiture Conflict
1081-1118	Reign of Alexius I Comnenus
1085	Conquest of Toledo by Alfonso VI
1086	Domesday Book
1094	Al-Andalus under Almoravid (Berber) control
1096-1099	The First Crusade
1097	Establishment of a commune at Milan
1099-1291	Crusader States in the Holy Land
1109	Death of Anselm of Bec, theologian and archbishop of England
1122	Concordat of Worms
*c.*1140	Publication of Gratian's *Decretum*
1142	Death of Peter Abelard
1147-1149	The Second Crusade
1153	Death of St. Bernard

NOTES

1. *Chronique de Saint-Bertin*, quoted in Histoire de la France urbaine, Vol. 2: La ville médiévale (Paris, 1980), p.71, here translated from the French.
2. Gregory, Letter of December 8, 1075, in *The Correspondence of Pope Gregory VII: Selected Letters from the Registrum*, ed. and trans. Ephriam Emerton (New York, 1969), p.87.
3. Roman Lenten Synod (1076), in *The Correspondence of Pope Gregory VII*, p.91.
4. Donald White, ed., *Medieval History. A Source Book* (Homewood, Illinois, 1965), pp.351-52.

5. From the Anglo-Saxon Chronicle "E", a. 1085, quoted in David C. Douglas, *William the Conqueror: The Norman Impact upon England* (Berkeley, 1967), p.348.
6. *Poem of the Cid*, trans. W.S. Merwin (New York, 1959), p.119-20.
7. Suger, *The Deeds of Louis the Fat*, ed. and trans. Richard C. Cusimano and John Moorhead (Washington, 1992), p.48.
8. Suger, p.107.
9. Helene Wieruszowski, *The Medieval University* (Princeton, 1966), pp.123-24.
10. Abelard, "Historia calamitatum," in *The Letters of Abelard and Heloise*, trans. Betty Radice (Harmondsworth, 1974), p.60.
11. Wolfgang Braunfels, *Monasteries of Western Europe: The Architecture of the Orders* (Princeton, 1972), p.242.
12. Bernard of Clairvaux, *On the Song of Songs*, Vol. 1. trans. Kilian Walsh, Cistercian Fathers Series, 4 (Kalamazoo, 1977), p.58.

FURTHER READING

Arnold, Benjamin. *Medieval Germany, 500-1300: A Political Interpretation*. Toronto, 1997.

Benson, Robert L., and Giles Constable, eds. *Renaissance and Renewal in the Twelfth Century*. Cambridge, 1982.

Berman, Constance Hoffman. *The Cistercian Evolution: The Invention of a Religious Order in Twelfth-Century Europe*. Philadelphia, 2000.

Blumenthal, Uta-Renate. *The Investiture Controversy: Church and Monarchy from the Ninth to the Twelfth Century*. Philadelphia, 1988.

Clanchy, Michael T. *Abelard: A Medieval Life*. Oxford, 1997.

Fletcher, Richard. *The Quest for El Cid*. New York, 1989.

Lawson, M.K. *Cnut: The Danes in England in the Early Eleventh Century*. London, 1993.

Little, Lester K. *Religious Poverty and the Profit Economy in Medieval Europe*. Ithaca, NY, 1978.

Miller, Maureen C. *The Formation of a Medieval Church: Ecclesiastical Change in Verona, 950-1150*. Ithaca, NY, 1993.

Phillips, Jonathan. *The Crusades, 1095-1197*. Harlow, 2002.

Reilly, Bernard F. *The Kingdom of León-Castilla under Queen Urraca, 1109-1126*. Princeton, 1982.

Riley-Smith, Jonathan, ed. *The Oxford History of the Crusades*. Oxford, 1999.

Robinson, Ian S. *Henry IV of Germany*. Cambridge, 2000.

Southern, R.W. *Scholastic Humanism and the Unification of Europe*. Vol. 1: *Foundations*. Oxford, 1995.

Weinfurter, Stefan. *The Salian Century: Main Currents in an Age of Transition*. Trans. Barbara M. Bowlus. Philadelphia, 1999.

Winroth, Anders. *The Making of Gratian's* Decretum. Cambridge, 2000.

GLOSSARY

aids In England, this refers to payments made by vassals to their lords on important occasions.

antiking A king elected illegally.

antipope A pope elected illegally.

Book of Hours A book for lay devotion containing readings in honor of the Virgin Mary (see below) based on simplified versions of the Divine Office (see Office below). Often, but not always, lavishly illustrated.

bull An official document issued by the papacy. The word derives from *bulla*, the lead impression of the pope's seal that was affixed to the document to validate it.

canon law The laws of the church. These were at first hammered out as need arose at various regional church councils and in rules issued by great bishops, particularly the pope. Early collections of canon law were incomplete and sometimes contradictory. Beginning in the ninth century, commentators began to organize and systematize them. The most famous of these treatises was the mid-twelfth-century *Decretum* of Gratian, which, although not an official code, became the basis of canon law training in the schools.

cathedral The principal church of a bishop or archbishop.

church To the Roman Catholics of the Middle Ages, this had two related meanings. It signified in the first place the eternal institution created by Christ, composed of the whole body of Christian believers, and served on earth by Christ's ministers—priests, bishops, the pope. Related to the eternal church were individual, local churches (parish churches, cathedrals, collegiate churches, chapels) where the daily liturgy was carried out and the faithful received the sacraments.

cleric A man in church orders.

collegiate church A church for priests living in common according to a rule.

Crucifixion The execution of Jesus by hanging on a cross (*crux* in Latin). The scene, described in some detail in the Gospels, was often depicted in art; and free-standing crucifixes (crosses with the figure of Jesus on them) were often placed upon church altars.

dogma The authoritative truth of the church.

empire Refers in the first instance to the Roman empire. Byzantium thought of itself as a continuation of that empire. In the West, there were several successor empires all ruled by men who took the title "emperor": there was the empire of Charlemagne, which included more or less what later became France, Italy, and Germany; it was followed in the tenth century (from the time of Otto I on) by the empire held (after a crowning at Rome) by the German kings. This could be complicated: a ruler like Henry IV was king of Germany in 1056, at the age of five; he took the real reins of power in 1066; but he was not crowned emperor until 1084. Nevertheless, he *acted* as an emperor long before that. That empire, which lasted until the thirteenth century, included Germany and (at least in theory) Italy. Some historians call all of these successor empires the "Holy Roman Empire," but in fact that term was not used until 1254. The Holy Roman Empire, which had nothing to do with Rome, ended in 1806. By extension, the term empire can refer to other large realms, often gained through conquest, as the Mongol empire or the Ottoman empire.

episcopal — As used for the Middle Ages, this is the equivalent of "bishop's." An "episcopal church" is the bishop's church; an "episcopal appointment" is the appointment of a bishop; "episcopal power" is the power wielded by a bishop.

excommunication — An act or pronouncement that cuts someone off from participation in the sacraments of the church and thus from the means of salvation.

Flagellation — The scene in the Gospels (Matt 27:26, Mk 15:15) where Christ is scourged by his executioners prior to his Crucifixion (see above). The scene was frequently depicted by artists.

fresco — A form of painting using pigments on wet plaster, frequently employed on the walls of churches.

grisaille — Painting in monochrome greys highlighted with color tints.

Guelfs and Ghibellines — Guelf was the Italian for Welf (the dynasty that competed for the German throne against the Staufen), while Ghibelline referred to Waiblingen (the name of an important Staufen castle). In the various conflicts between the popes and the Staufen emperors, the "Guelfs" were the factions within the Italian city-states that supported the papacy, while the "Ghibellines" supported the emperor. More generally, however, the names became epithets for various inter- and intra-city political factions that had little or no connection to papal/imperial issues.

illumination The term used for paintings in medieval manuscripts. These might range from simple decorations of capital letters to full-page compositions. An "illuminated" manuscript is one containing illuminations.

layman/laywoman/laity Men and women not in church orders, not ordained. In the early Middle Ages it was possible to be a monk and a layperson at the same time. But by the Carolingian period, most monks were priests, and, although nuns were not, they were not considered part of the laity because they had taken vows to the church.

Levant The lands that border the eastern shore of the Mediterranean; the Holy Land.

liturgy The formal worship of the church, which included prayers, readings, and significant gestures at fixed times appropriate to the season. While often referring to the Mass (see below), it may equally be used to describe the Offices (see below).

Maghreb A region of northwest Africa embracing the Atlas Mountains and the coastline of Morocco, Algeria, and Tunisia.

Mass The central ceremony of Christian worship; it includes prayers and readings from the Bible and culminates in the consecration of bread and wine as the body and blood of Christ, offered to believers in the sacrament of the "Eucharist," or "Holy Communion."

New Testament This work, a compilation of the second century, contains the four Gospels (accounts of the life of Christ) by Matthew, Mark, Luke, and John; the Acts of the Apostles; various letters, mainly from Saints Paul, Peter, and John to fledgling Christian communities; and the Apocalypse. It is distinguished from the "Old Testament" (see below).

Office In the context of monastic life, the day and night were punctuated by eight periods in which the monks gathered to recite a precise set of prayers. Each set was called an "Office," and the cycle as a whole was called the "Divine Office." Special rites and ceremonies might also be called offices, such as the "Office of the Dead."

Old Testament The writings of the Jewish Bible that were accepted as authentic by Christians, though reinterpreted by them as prefiguring the coming of Christ; they were thus seen as the precursor of the "New Testament" (see above), which fulfilled and perfected them.

referendary A high Merovingian administrative official responsible for overseeing the issuing of royal documents.

relief This has two separate meanings. In connection with medieval English government, the "relief" refers to money paid upon inheriting a fief. In the history of sculpture, however, "relief" refers to figures or other forms that project from a flat background. "Low relief" means that the forms project rather little, while "high relief" refers to forms that may be so three-dimensional as to threaten to break away from the flat surface.

sacraments The rites of the church that (in its view) Jesus instituted to confer sanctifying grace. With the sacraments, one achieved salvation. Cut off from the sacraments (by anathema, excommunication, or interdict), one was damned.

scriptorium (pl. scriptoria) The room of the monastery where parchment was prepared and texts copied, illuminated, and bound.

summa (pl. summae) A compendium or summary. A term favored by scholastics to title their comprehensive syntheses.

The Virgin/ The Virgin Mary/ The Blessed Virgin The Gospels of Matthew (1:18-23) and Luke (1:27-35) assert that Christ was conceived by the Holy Spirit (rather than by a man) and born of Mary, a virgin. Already in the fourth century the Church Fathers stressed the virginity of Mary because it guaranteed the holiness of Christ. In the fifth century, at the Council of Chalcedon (451), Mary's perpetual (eternal) virginity was made a matter of dogma. In the medieval church, Mary was celebrated with four feasts—her Nativity, Purification, the Annunciation (of the birth of Jesus), and her Assumption (into heaven). She was understood as the exact opposite of (and antidote to) Eve. Devotion to her cult increased in the later Middle Ages as her role as intercessor with her son in Heaven was increasingly stressed.

APPENDIX: LISTS

LATE ROMAN EMPERORS

(Usurpers in italics)

Maximinus (235-238)
Gordian I (238)
Gordian II (238)
Balbinus and Pupienus (238)
Gordian III (238-244)
Philip the Arab (244-249)
Decius (249-251)
Trebonianus Gallus (251-253)
Aemilian (253)
Valerian (253-260)
Gallienus (253-268)
Postumus (260-268)
Claudius II Gothicus (268-270)
Quintillus (270)
Aurelian (270-275)
Tacitus (275-276)
Florian (276)
Probus (276-282)
Carus (282-283)
Carinus and Numerian (283-284)

In the West	In the East
Maximian (Augustus) (285-305)	Diocletian (Augustus) (284-305)
Constantius (Caesar) (293-305)	Galerius (Caesar) (293-305)
Constantius (Augustus) (305-306)	Galerius (Augustus) (305-311)
Severus (Caesar) (305-306)	Maximin (Caesar) (305-309)
Severus (Augustus) (306-307)	Galerius (Augustus) (305-311)
Constantine I (Caesar) (306-308)	Maximin (Caesar and Augustus) (305-313)

Maxentius (in Italy) (306-312)

Constantine I (Augustus) (307-337)

Licinius (Augustus) (308-324)

Domitius Alexander (in Africa) (308-311)
Constantine I and Licinius (313-324)
Constantine I (324-337)

Constantine II (337-340)
Constans (340-350)
Magnentius (350-353)
Julian Caesar (355-361)
Julian Augustus (360-363)

Constantius II (337-361)

Gallus Caesar (361-364)

Julian (361-363)
Jovian (363-364)

Valentinian (364-375)
Gratian (375-383)
Valentinian II (375-392)
Maximus (383-388)
Eugenius (392-394)

Valens (364-378)
Theodosius I (379-395)

Theodosius I (394-395)

Honorius (394-423)
(Stilicho regent) (395-408)

Constantius III (421)
John (423-425)
Valentian III (425-455)
Petronius Maximus (455)
Avitus (455-456)
Majorian (457-461)
Libius Severus (461-465)
Anthemius (467-472)
Olybrius (472)
Glycerius (473)

Arcadius (395-408)

Theodosius II (408-450)

Marcian (450-457)

Leo I (457-474)

Julius Nepos (473-475)
Romulus Augustulus (475-476)

Zeno (474-491)
Anastasius I (491-518)
Justin I (518-527)
Justinian I (527-565)
Justin II (565-578)
Tiberius II Constantine (578-582)
Maurice Tiberius (582-602)

BYZANTINE EMPERORS AND EMPRESSES

Justinian I (527-565)
Justin II (565-578)
    Tiberius, Caesar and regent (574-578)
Tiberius II Constantine (578-582)
Maurice Tiberius (582-602)
Phocas the Tyrant (602-610)
Heraclius (610-641)
Constantine III Heraclius (641)
Heraclonas (Heraclius) Constantine (641)
    Martina, regent
Constans II (Constantine) Heraclius the Bearded (641-668)
Constantine IV (668-685)
Justinian II the Slit-Nosed (685-695, 705-711)
Leontius (Leo) (695-698)
Tiberius III Apsimar (698-705)
Philippicus Bardanes (711-713)
Anastasius II Artemius (713-715)
Theodosius III (715-717)
Leo III the Isaurian (717-741)
Constantine V Name of Dung (741-775)
    Artavasdus, rival emperor at Constantinople (741-743)
Leo IV the Khazar (775-780)
Constantine VI the Blinded (780-797)
    Irene the Athenian, regent
Irene the Athenian (797-802)
Nicephorus I the General Logothete (802-811)
Stauracius (811)
Michael I Rhangabe (811-813)

Leo V the Armenian (813-820)
Michael II the Amorian (820-829)
Theophilus (829-842)
Michael III the Drunkard (842-867)
    Theodora, regent (842-856)
Basil I the Macedonian (867-886)
Leo VI the Wise (886-912)
Alexander (912-913)
Constantine VII Porphyrogenitus (913-959)
    Nicholas Mysticus, regent (913-914)
    Zoë Carbonopsina, regent (914-920)
    Romanus I Lecapenus, coemperor (920-944)
Romanus II Porphyrogenitus (959-963)
Basil II the Bulgar-Slayer (963-1025)
    Theophano, regent (963)
    Nicephorus II Phocas, coemperor (963-969)
    John I Tzimisces, coemperor (969-976)
Constantine VIII Porphyrogenitus (1025-1028)
Romanus III Argyrus (1028-1034)
Michael IV the Paphlagonian (1034-1041)
Michael V the Caulker (1041-1042)
Zoë Porphyrogenita (1042)
Constantine IX Monomachus (1042-1055)
Theodora Porphyrogenita (1055-1056)
Michael VI Bringas (1056-1057)
Isaac I Comnenus (1057-1059)
Constantine X Ducas (1059-1067)
Michael VII Ducas (1067-1078)
    Eudocia Macrembolitissa, regent (1067-1068)
    Romanus IV Diogenes, coemperor (1068-1071)
Nicephorus III Botantiates (1078-1081)
Alexius I Comnenus (1081-1118)
John II Comnenus (1118-1143)
Manuel I Comnenus (1143-1180)
Alexius II Comnenus (1180-1183)
    Andronicus Comnenus, regent (1182-1183)
Andronicus I Comnenus (1183-1185)
Isaac II Angelus (1185-1195)
Alexius III Angelus (1195-1203)
Isaac II Angelus (again) (1203-1204)

Alexius IV Angelus, coemperor
Alexius III Angelus, rival emperor
Alexius V Ducas Murtzuphlus (1204)
Alexius III Angelus, rival emperor
Alexius III Angelus (in Thrace) (1204)
Theodore I Lascaris (at Nicaea) (1205-1221)
John III Ducas Vatatzes (at Nicaea) (1221-1254)
Theodore Ducas, emperor at Thessalonica (1224-1230)
John Ducas, emperor at Thessalonica (1237-1242)
Theodore II Lascaris (at Nicaea) (1254-1258)
John IV Lascaris (at Nicaea) (1258-1261)
Michael VIII Palaeologus, coemperor at Nicaea (1259-1261)
Michael VIII Palaeologus (at Constantinople) (1261-1282)
Andronicus II Palaeologus (1282-1328)
Andronicus III Palaeologus, coemperor (1321-1328)
Andronicus III Palaeologus (1328-1341)
John V Palaeologus (1341-1376; 1379-1391)
Anna of Savoy, regent (1341-1347)
John VI Cantacuzenus, coemperor (1347-1354)
Andronicus IV Palaeologus (1376-1379)
Manuel II Palaeologus (1391-1425)
John VIII Palaeologus (1425-1448)
Constantine XI Palaeologus (1449-1453)

POPES AND ANTIPOPES TO 1500* (Antipopes in Italics)

Peter (?-*c.*64)
Linus (*c.*67-76/79)
Anacletus (76-88 or 79-91)
Clement I (88-97 or 92-101)
Evaristus (*c.*97-*c.*107)
Alexander I (105-115 or 109-119)
Sixtus I (*c.*115-*c.*125)
Telesphorus (*c.*125-*c.*136)
Hyginus (*c.*136-*c.*140)
Pius I (*c.*140-155)
Anicetus (*c.*155-*c.*166)
Soter (*c.*166-*c.*175)
Eleutherius (*c.*175-189)
Victor I (*c.*189-199)
Zephyrinus (*c.*199-217)
Calixtus I (Callistus) (217?-222)
Hippolytus (217, 218-235)
Urban I (222-230)
Pontian (230-235)
Anterus (235-236)

* Only since the ninth century has the title of "pope" come to be associated exclusively with the bishop of Rome.

Fabian (236-250)
Cornelius (251-253)
Novatian (251)
Lucius I (253-254)
Stephen I (254-257)
Sixtus II (257-258)
Dionysius (259-268)
Felix I (269-274)
Eutychian (275-283)
Galus (283-296)
Marcellinus (291/296-304)
Marcellus I (308-309)
Eusebius (309/310)
Miltiades (Melchiades) (311–314)
Sylvester I (314-335)
Mark (336)
Julius I (337-352)
Liberius (352-366)
Felix II (355-358)
Damasus I (366-384)
Ursinus (366-367)
Siricius (384-399)
Anastasius I (399-401)
Innocent I (401-417)
Zosimus (417-418)
Boniface I (418-422)
Eulalius (418-419)
Celestine I (422-432)
Sixtus III (432-440)
Leo I (440-461)
Hilary (461-468)
Simplicius (468-483)
Felix III (or II) (483-492)
Gelasius I (492-496)
Anastasius II (496-498)
Symmachus (498-514)
Laurentius (498, 501-c.505/507)
Hormisdas (514-523)
John I (523-526)
Felix IV (or III) (526-530)
Dioscorus (530)
Boniface II (530-532)
John II (533-535)
Agapetus I (535-536)
Silverius (536-537)
Vigilius (537-555)
Pelagius I (556-561)
John III (561-574)
Benedict I (575-579)
Pelagius II (579-590)
Gregory I (590-604)
Sabinian (604-606)
Boniface III (604)
Boniface IV (608-615)
Deusdedit (also called Adeodatus I) (615-618)
Boniface V (619-625)
Honorius I (625-638)
Severinus (640)
John IV (640-642)
Theodore I (642-649)
Martin I (649-655)
Eugenius I (654-657)
Vitalian (657-672)
Adeodatus II (672-676)
Donus (676-678)
Agatho (679-681)
Leo II (682-683)
Benedict II (684-685)
John V (685-686)
Conon (686-687)
Sergius I (687-701)
Theodore (687)
Paschal (687)
John VI (701-705)
John VII (705-707)
Sisinnius (708)
Constantine (708-715)
Gregory II (715-731)
Gregory III (731-741)

Zacharias (Zachary) (741-752)
Stephen II (752-757)
Paul I (757-767)
Constantine (II) (767-768)
Philip (768)
Stephen III (768-772)
Adrian I (772-795)
Leo III (795-816)
Stephen IV (816-817)
Paschal I (817-824)
Eugenius II (824-827)
Valentine (827)
Gregory IV (827-844)
John (844)
Sergius II (844-847)
Leo IV (847-855)
Benedict III (855-858)
Anastasius (Anastasius the Librarian) (855)
Nicholas I (858-867)
Adrian II (867-872)
John VIII (872-882)
Marinus I (882-884)
Adrian III (884-885)
Stephen V (885-891)
Formosus (891-896)
Boniface VI (896)
Stephen VI (896)
Romanus (897)
Theodore II (897)
John IX (898-900)
Benedict IV (900)
Leo V (903)
Christopher (903-904)
Sergius III (904-911)
Anastasius III (911-913)
Lando (913-914)
John X (914-928)
Leo VI (928)
Stephen VII (929-931)
John XI (931-935)
Leo VII (936-939)
Stephen VIII (939-942)
Marinus II (942-946)
Agapetus II (946-955)
John XII (955-964)
Leo VIII (963-965)
Benedict V (964-966?)
John XIII (965-972)
Benedict VI (973-974)
Boniface VII (1st time) (974)
Benedict VII (974-983)
John XIV (983-984)
Boniface VII (2nd time) (984-985)
John XV (or XVI) (985-996)
Gregory V (996-999)
John XVI (or XVII) (997-998)
Sylvester II (999-1003)
John XVII (or XVIII) (1003)
John XVIII (or XIX) (1004-1009)
Sergius IV (1009-1012)
Gregory (VI) (1012)
Benedict VIII (1012-1024)
John XIX (or XX) (1024-1032)
Benedict IX (1st time) (1032-1044)
Sylvester III (1045)
Benedict IX (2nd time) (1045)
Gregory VI (1045-1046)
Clement II (1046-1047)
Benedict IX (3rd time) (1047-1048)
Damasus II (1048)
Leo IX (1049-1054)
Victor II (1055-1057)
Stephen IX (1057-1058)
Benedict (X)(1058-1059)
Nicholas II (1059-1061)
Alexander II (1061-1073)
Honorius (II) (1061-1072)
Gregory VII (1073-1085)

Clement (III) (1080-1100)
Victor III (1086-1087)
Urban II (1088-1099)
Paschal II (1099-1118)
Theodoric (1100-1102)
Albert (also called Aleric) (1102)
Sylvester (IV) (1105-1111)
Gelasius II (1118-1119)
Gregory (VIII) (1118-1121)
Calixtus II (Callistus) (1119-1124)
Honorius II (1124-1130)
Celestine (II) (1124)
Innocent II (1130-1143)
Anacletus (II) (1130-1138)
Victor (IV) (1138)
Celestine II (1143-1144)
Lucius II (1144-1145)
Eugenius III (1145-1153)
Anastasius IV (1153-1154)
Adrian IV (1154-1159)
Alexander III (1159-1181)
Victor (IV) (1159-1164)
Paschal (III) (1164-1168)
Calixtus (III) (1168-1178)
Innocent (III) (1179-1180)
Lucius III (1181-1185)
Urban III (1185-1187)
Gregory VIII (1187)
Clement III (1187-1191)
Celestine III (1191-1198)
Innocent III (1198-1216)
Honorius III (1216-1227)
Gregory IX (1227-1241)
Celestine IV (1241)
Innocent IV (1243-1254)
Alexander IV (1254-1261)
Urban IV (1261-1264)
Clement IV (1265-1268)
Gregory X (1271-1276)
Innocent V (1276)
Adrian V (1276)
John XXI (1276-1277)
Nicholas III (1277-1280)
Martin IV (1281-1285)
Honorius IV (1285-1287)
Nicholas IV (1288-1292)
Celestine V (1294)
Boniface VIII (1294-1303)
Benedict IX (1303-1304)
Clement V (at Avignon, from 1309) (1305-1314)
John XXII (at Avignon) (1316-1334)
Nicholas (V) (at Rome) (1328-1330)
Benedict XII (at Avignon) (1334-1342)
Clement VI (at Avignon) (1342-1352)
Innocent VI (at Avignon) (1352-1362)
Urban V (at Avignon) (1362-1370)
Gregory XI (at Avignon, then Rome from 1377) (1370-1378)
Urban VI (1378-1389)
Clement (VII) (at Avignon) (1378-1394)
Boniface IX (1389-1404)
Benedict (XIII) (at Avignon) (1394-1423)
Innocent VII (1404-1406)
Gregory XII (1406-1415)
Alexander (V) (at Bologna) (1409-1410)
John (XXIII) (at Bologna) (1410-1415)
Martin V (1417-1431)
Clement (VIII) (1423-1429)
Eugenius IV (1431-1447)
Felix (V) (also called Amadeus VIII of Savoy) (1439-1449)
Nicholas V (1447-1455)
Calixtus III (Callistus) (1455-1458)
Pius II (1458-1464)
Paul II (1464-1471)
Sixtus IV (1471-1484)
Innocent VIII (1484-1492)
Alexander VI (1492-1503)

ISLAMIC RULERS

Early Caliphs

Abu-Bakr (632-634)
Umar I (634-644)
Uthman (644-656)
Ali (656-661)

Umayyads

Mu`awiyah I (661-680)
Yazid I (680-683)
Mu`awiyah II (683-684)
Marwan I (684-685)
Abd al-Malik (685-705)
al-Walid I (705-715)
Sulayman (715-717)
Umar II (717-720)
Yazid II (720-724)
Hisham (724-743)
al-Walid II (743-744)
Yazid III (744)
Marwan II (744-750)

Abbasids*

al-Saffah (750-754)
al-Mansur (754-775)
al-Mahdi (775-785)
al-Hadi (785-786)
Harun al-Rashid (786-809)
al-Amin (809-813)
al-Ma`mun (813-833)
al-Mu`tasim (833-842)
al-Wathiq (842-847)
al-Mutawakkil (847-861)
al-Muntasir (861-862)
al-Musta`in (862-866)
al-Mu`tazz (866-869)
al-Muhtadi (869-870)
al-Mu`tamid (870-892)
al-Mu`tadid (892-902)
al-Muqtafi (902-908)
al-Muqtadir (908-932)
al-Qahir (932-934)
al-Radi (934-940)

*Abbasid caliphs continued until 1517.

SOURCES

MAPS

1.4 Tours, *c.*600. Credit: Henri Galinié.

3.1 The Byzantine Empire, *c.*917. Credit: From Mark Whittow, *The Making of Orthodox Byzantium* 600-1025 (University of California Press, 1996), p.166, Copyright © 1996 Mark Whittow. Reprinted by permission of the University of California Press.

4.1 Constantinople before *c.*1100. Credit: From Linda Safran, ed., *Heaven on Earth: Art and the Church in Byzantium* (University Park, PA: The Pennsylvania State University Press, 1998), figs 1.7, 1.9.

5.1 Byzantium and the Islamic World, *c.*1090. Credit: From Christophe Picard, *Le monde musulman du XIe au XVe siècle* © SEDES / HER, 2000. Reprinted by permission of Éditions SEDES, Paris.

PLATES

1.1 Landscape from Pompeii (A.D.*c.*79). Credit: Museo Archaeologico Nazionale di Napoli.

1.2 Theseus the Minotaur Slayer, Pompeii (A.D.*c.*79). Credit: Museo Archaeologico Nazionale di Napoli.

1.3 Trajan's Column, detail (A.D.113). Credit: Scala / Art Resource, NY.

1.4 Head from Palmyra (A.D.1-50). Credit: Studio Zouhabi, Palmira-Syria.

1.5 Decorated Coffer from Jerusalem (1st cent.?). Credit: © Copyright The British Museum.

1.6 Tombstone from near Carthage (2nd cent.?). Credit: © Copyright The British Museum.

1.7 Base of the Hippodrome Obelisk (*c.*390). Credit: Hirmer Fotoarchiv.

1.8 Ivory Pyx (5th cent.). Credit: Hirmer Fotoarchiv.

1.9 Mosaic from San Vitale, Ravenna (c.540-548). Credit: Archivi Alinari Firenze.

1.10 *Icon of the Virgin*. Egypt, Byzantine period, 6th century. Slit and dove tailed-tapestry weave; wool, 178 x 110 cm. Credit: © The Cleveland Museum of Art, 203. Leonard C. Hanna, Jr., Bequest, 1967.144.

2.1 The Embolos, Ephesus. From Clive Foss, *Ephesus After Antiquity* (Cambridge University Press, 1979), p.66, fig. 20. Credit: Reprinted with the permission of Cambridge University Press and Clive Foss.

2.2 The Great Mosque at Damascus (8th cent.). From the Clive Foss Architectural Photographs Collection at Cambridge. Credit: Reprinted with the permission of Clive Foss.

2.3 Belt Buckle from Sutton Hoo (early 7th cent.). Credit: © Copyright The British Museum.

2.4 Saint Luke, Lindisfarne Gospels (late 7th cent.), Cott.Nero.D.IV., fol. 137v. Credit: By permission of the British Library.

2.5 Carpet Page, Lindisfarne Gospels (late 7th cent.), Cott.Nero.D.IV., fol. 138v. Credit: By permission of the British Library.

2.6 First Text Page, Gospel of Saint Luke, Lindisfarne Gospels (late 7th cent.), Cott.Nero.D.IV., fol. 139. Credit: By permission of the British Library.

2.7 Franks Casket (1st half of 8th cent.). Credit: © Copyright The British Museum.

3.1 Byzantine Book Cover (886-912), cod.Marc.Lat I, 101 (2260). Credit: © Biblioteca Nazionale Marciana.

3.2 Ezechiel in the Valley of Dry Bones, Homilies of Gregory Nazianzen (880-886), MS Graeca 510, fol. 438v. Credit: Cliché Bibliothèque nationale de France, Paris.

3.3 Mesopotamian, Samarra, Bowl, 9th Century, Abbasid Period, Earthenware, lustred. H. 2⅜ in. Diam. 9¾ in. Credit: The Metropolitan Museum of Art, H.O. Havemeyer Collection, Gift of Horace Havemeyer, 1941. (41.165.1) Photograph © 1985 The Metropolitan Museum of Art.

3.4 Córdoba, Great Mosque (late 10th cent.). Credit: Alinari / Art Resource, NY.

3.5 Sacramentary of Saint-Germain-des-Prés (early 9th cent.), MS lat. 2291, fol. 14v. Credit: Cliché Bibliothèque nationale de France, Paris.

3.6 Saint Mark, Soissons Gospels (800-810), MS lat. 8850, fol. 81v. Credit: Cliché Bibliothèque nationale de France, Paris.

3.7 First Text Page, Soissons Gospels (800-810), MS lat. 8850, fol. 82r. Credit: Cliché Bibliothèque nationale de France, Paris.

3.8 Saint Mark, Coronation Gospels (*c.*800). Credit: Kröngungsevangeliar Fol. 76v, Kunsthistorisches Museum, Wien oder KHM, Wien.

3.9 Utrecht Psalter (*c.*820-835). Credit: University Library Utrecht, Ms. 32, fol. 4v, Universiteitsbibliotheek Utrecht.

4.1 Christ and the Centurion, Egbert Codex (977-993). Credit: Codex Egberti, Stadtbibliothek Trier MS 24, fol. 22.

4.2 Christ Asleep in the Seastorm, Hitda Gospels (c.1000-1020), MS 1640, fol. 117r. Credit: Hessische Landes- und Hochschulbibliothek Darmstadt.

4.3 Saint Luke, Gospel Book of Otto III (998-1001), Clm 4453, fol. 139v. Credit: Bayerische Staatsbibliothek München.

5.1 View of the Façade, San Miniato Cathedral. Credit: La Scala / Art Resource, NY.

5.2 Bowl, North Africa, late 12th cent. Credit: Musei Nazionali di Pisa.

5.3 Gloria with Musical Notation, Saint-Evroult (12th cent.), Latin 10097, fol. 32v. Credit: Cliché Bibliothèque nationale de France, Paris © BnF.

5.4 A Mode of the Chant, Cluny (1088-1095). Credit: Musée d'art et d'archéologie de Cluny.

5.5 Suicide of Judas, Autun (1125-1135). Credit: Chanoine Denis Grivot, Maître de Chapelle Honoraire de la Cathédrale Conservateur Honoraire des Antiquités et Objets d'Art de Saône-et-Loire, Autun.

5.6 Durham Cathedral (1093-1133), Interior, Nave Looking East. Credit: Anthony Scibilia / Art Resource, NY.

5.7 Martydom of Saint Lawrence. Chapel of the Monks. Early 12th cent. Chapelles des Moines, Berzé-la-Ville, France. Credit: Bridgeman-Giraudon / Art Resource, NY.

5.8 Leaning Tower (Bell Tower) of Pisa (late 12th cent.). Credit: Alinari / Art Resource, NY.

5.9 Santiago de Compostela (1078-1124), Interior. Credit: Instituto Amatller De Arte Hispánico / Institut Amatller D'Art Hispànic.

5.8 Fontenay Abbey Church (1139-1147), Interior, Nave looking East. Credit: Anthony Scibilia / Art Resource, NY.

FIGURES

2.1 The Changing Face of Ephesus. Credit: From Clive Foss, *Ephesus After Antiquity* (Cambridge University Press, 1979), figs. 12 and 35. Reprinted with the permission of Cambridge University Press.

2.2 Black & white line drawing of Yeavering, Northumberland. Credit: From Leslie Webster and Janet Backhouse, *The Making of England: Anglo-Saxon Art and Culture* (British Museum Press, 1991), p. 69, ISBN 0 7141 0555 4, © Trustees of the British Museum.

5.1 Hypothetical Plan of the Monastery of Cluny (1157). Credit: From Kenneth John Conant, *The Pelican History of Art: Carolingian and Romanesque Architecture 800-1200* (New Haven, CT: Yale University Press, 1974), fig. 5-1. Reprinted by permission of Yale University Press.

5.2 A Model Romanesque Church. Plan of the church of Santiago de Compostela. Credit: From John Beckwith, *Early Medieval Art* (New York: Thames & Hudson, 1964), p. 163 ill.155. Reprinted by permission of Thames & Hudson Ltd.

5.3 Schematic Plan of a Cistercian Monastery. *Making of the West*. Lynn Hunt et al. Bedford / St. Martin's, 2001. Adapted from Wolfgang Braunfels *Monasteries of Western Europe*. Princeton, NJ: Princeton University Press, 1972, p. 75. Credit: © Dumont Buchverlag GmbH.

INDEX

Italicized page numbers refer to Plates